Rethinking Adult Career Development

RETHINKING BUSINESS AND MANAGEMENT

The Rethinking Business and Management series is a forum for innovative scholarly writing from across all substantive fields within business and management. The series aims to enrich scholarly inquiry by promoting a cutting-edge approach to management theory and analysis.

Despite the old maxim that nothing is new under the sun, it is nevertheless true that organisations evolve and contexts in which businesses operate change. Business and Management faces new and previously unforeseen challenges, and organisations respond to shifting motivations and are shaped by competing interests and experiences. Academic scrutiny and challenge is an essential component in the development of business theory and practice and the act of re-thinking and re-examining principles and concepts is imperative.

Rethinking Business and Management showcases authored books that address their field from a new angle, expose the weaknesses of existing frameworks, or 're-frame' the topic in some way. This might be through the integration of perspectives from other fields or even other disciplines, through challenging existing paradigms, or simply through a level of analysis that elevates or sharpens our understanding of a subject. While each book takes its own approach, all the titles in the series use an analytical lens to open up new thinking.

For a full list of Edward Elgar published titles, including the titles in this series, visit our website at www.e-elgar.com.

Rethinking Adult Career Development
A Critical Perspective

Laura L. Bierema

*Professor of Adult Learning, Leadership, and Organization
Development, Department of Lifelong Education,
Administration, and Policy, Mary Frances Early College of
Education, University of Georgia, USA*

RETHINKING BUSINESS AND MANAGEMENT

Cheltenham, UK • Northampton, MA, USA

Published by
Edward Elgar Publishing Limited
The Lypiatts
15 Lansdown Road
Cheltenham
Glos GL50 2JA
UK

Edward Elgar Publishing, Inc.
William Pratt House
9 Dewey Court
Northampton
Massachusetts 01060
USA

A catalogue record for this book
is available from the British Library

Library of Congress Control Number: 2024936927

This book is available electronically in the **Elgar**online
Business subject collection
http://dx.doi.org/10.4337/9781035309139

ISBN 978 1 0353 0912 2 (cased)
ISBN 978 1 0353 0913 9 (eBook)

Printed and bound in Great Britain by
TJ Books Limited, Padstow, Cornwall

To the teachers, mentors, and coaches who have helped people choose and sustain fulfilling work and careers.

Contents

Foreword

It is a joy to offer a foreword for this important book. It offers a lifeline for anyone who is in a process of, as Laura describes, exploring, sustaining, or changing careers.

As shared in the introductory chapter, Laura's identity is comprised of many "majoritarian" aspects, such as her status as a full professor at a large research institution. If I may, let me offer some insight into the author that may not be so obvious. Laura has a reflex to use her power in order to reach back or sideways, to offer support for those who may not hold power to have access to it. I have known her for some two decades and have seen this play out in many different ways. Now, with this book (I do not mean that this is the only work Laura has done to equip people with resources to learn and grow but rather as the latest work), Laura puts a one-stop resource in the reader's hands, to deep-dive into career development models and theories. Moreover, the book then provides tools, such as checklists, to provide a tangible guidepost to put into reflection, planning, and implementation.

Laura's work centers the learner within the context of career development; it places the capacity of analysis in the hands of the reader. Put another way, by drawing concepts of adult learning into a career development text, those who might otherwise be relegated to work that is transactional and draining (yet economically necessary), instead can be lifted up above the day-to-day routine of "work" to envision what type of occupation or profession (or job) might actually be enjoyable and meaningful. Conceptually, I think of this book as equipping an earnest reader and student of its content and tools, with the ability to step off the train they are currently on (that might not be going somewhere that is exciting), and instead, identify the next train and create the conditions by which to step on that one.

Work can give meaning and purpose to life. I think we inherently derive joy from contributing from our talents and skills. As one increases their own capacity and self-determination, the greater the possibilities for imagining more promising career prospects. This book helps the reader to broaden their vision, not just to imagine an elusive "someday" in which things might fall into place, or a particular employer or supervisor or other outside entity determine their next steps for them. Certainly, there is nothing wrong with employer provided or directed professional development. I would not advise that it be the primary basis for career development. I mean this neither with sarcasm nor cynicism. Rather, by having the resources to analyze, develop, and execute one's own learning and growth (with respect to career development), there is a sustainable agency, an important portability, which can disrupt inequitable or unfulfilling career outcomes.

This work provides a myriad of ways that the reader can hook into the material and gain tremendous value. I envision a garden that has rich, fragrant, verdant life, and that the garden has a variety of gates and entry ways. A career sustainer might be very interested in how to create the conditions by which they continue to flourish; an explorer may want to figure out how to re-create their career. I see a virtually limitless audience for this work. I think that so much of life might not make sense in the moment, and that the sense-making occurs upon reflection. This book presents a way to shorten the timeframe of how to glean lessons from what might seem like mistakes or even crises, to valuable wisdom-rich incidents or episodes that present with them valuable takeaways that can launch one into higher ground.

I can hear Laura in the book, offering discussion, presentation, analysis, and critique, and then opening up vistas for further exploration. The structure of the book is compelling and fresh, with said presentations that are accompanied by assessments, and then curated toolboxes of resources. Laura's credibility as a researcher, mentor, scholar, change agent, and professor adds a layer of excellence. She *lives* this material. She is committed to respecting foundational works, articulating them, and building upon them.

Laura and I share a fascination with career development. We have other common interests, such as our love of dogs. Sidenote: I am a University of Georgia Bulldog (dawg), like Dr. Bierema, where we graduated from the same program. Because she is a humble person, permit me to take this opportunity to share with you some of Laura's giftedness-in-action, which adds further credence to the significance of a book about adult career development. Laura knows what it means to navigate disruption and to lead through it. It was during Laura's tenure as President of the Academy of Human Resource Development (AHRD), that the pandemic occurred. Under her leadership, the board and others in conference leadership roles navigated through the complex decisions regarding the necessary changes for the annual conference format and venue. It was under President Bierema's leadership that the conference shifted to a virtual format. In measurable as well as intangible ways, this transition was a success within a crisis environment. See Gedro et al. (2020) for a reflection on leadership during crisis, which runs rather parallel. Laura demonstrated the qualities of directing and at the same time, supporting the organization. Keeping the conference, while changing its format, permitted all who had career-related stakes in the conference to achieve their own outcomes. After all, the annual AHRD Conference serves as a career development cornerstone for so many HRD scholars. Before, during, and after the annual conference, significant career development occurs both formally through conference presentations, and non-formally, where networking happens.

In closing, may I offer this: Laura does not see the world in division; she sees it in multiplication through her commitment to learning, growth, and change. *Rethinking Adult Career Development* is the latest demonstration.

Julie A. Gedro

Acknowledgments

I am grateful to the many teachers, scholars, mentors, coaches, and collaborators who have shaped my interpretation and practice of career development. I carry their wisdom in my commitment to helping others in similar ways.

Collaborating with University of Georgia Student and Graduate Research Assistant Eunbi Sim has been a privilege. Eunbi is a thought partner and copy-editor extraordinaire, and passionate about creating equitable organizations. She discovered excellent sources for the book and made brilliant suggestions for improving every chapter.

I am grateful to Edward Elgar Publishing Editor Beatrice McCartney, who urged me to write this book after I delivered a keynote at the 2018 University Forum for Human Resource Development in Newcastle, UK. She is patient and encouraging. I also appreciate all the other Edward Elgar Publishing and production team members who ushered the book to its printed form.

I love Mark for tolerating the writing process and his enduring love, support, and good humor. Kudos to my loyal golden retrievers, Brodie and Skye, who supported the writing by keeping me company at their stations under my desk.

Abbreviations

AE	Adult Education
AL	Adult Learning
CC	Critical Consciousness
CCD	Critical Career Development
CD	Career Development
HRD	Human Resource Development
OD	Organization Development
PWT	Psychology of Work Theory

1. Introducing *Rethinking Adult Career Development*

> ⊔ BOX 1.1 CHAPTER OVERVIEW AND LEARNING OBJECTIVES
>
> The following quote by Chris Guillebeau highlights a vital sentiment to remember about career development (CD) while reading this book and navigating a career:
>
> > It's better to be at the bottom of the ladder you want to climb than the top of one you don't. (Guillebeau, 2016, p. 163)
>
> Toiling away at work that drains the spirit is no way to spend a career or a life. Work will be more fulfilling if you, the reader, find a meaningful, fun, and interesting vocation. What meaning do you draw from Guillebeau's quote?
>
> This chapter aims to introduce *Rethinking Adult Career Development*; provide an overview of the book with advice on how to read it; present key terms and ideas; and introduce work and career concepts and models. Each chapter features boxes, like this one, described in this chapter. The boxes throughout the book include *Chapter Overview and Learning Objectives*, *Adult Career Development by the Numbers*, *Reflective Practice*, and *Tips and Tools for Career Development*.
>
> As a result of reading this chapter and completing the exercise boxes, you, the reader, should be able to:
> 1. Understand the aims of *Rethinking Adult Career Development* and how to read this book.
> 2. Define key adult CD concepts and terms.
> 3. Recognize career models and concepts.

INTRODUCING ADULT CAREER DEVELOPMENT

If you, the reader, have ever searched for books or Googled topics related to work and career decisions, education, challenges, or development, you probably noticed that most of the resources cater to pre- and young adults trying to answer the age-old question, "What do you want to be when you grow up?" Helping pre- and young adults identify their career interests and goals is fundamentally essential and *not* the focus of this textbook. *Rethinking Adult Career Development* is concerned with the challenges, transitions, learning, and change experienced by adults as they navigate careers across their career lifespan or the duration of their career(s) throughout their lifetime. Adults are generally viewed as people with adult-like responsibilities, life and work experience, and the capacity to reflect and think critically. These characteristics separate adults from children. Adulthood is not so much a chronological stage, like finishing high school or a university degree, but rather is defined by having adult responsibilities such as maintaining a household, supporting oneself financially, or caring for dependents. The purpose of this book is to interrogate traditional, unquestioned assumptions about *adult* CD, raise critical questions, and offer strategies for individuals grappling with work and CD. It is also for coaches and mentors providing career guidance, and leaders and policymakers seeking to build inclusive, equitable cultures that engage people in meeting their work and career aspirations. Adult career development is a lifelong learning process where adults build skills, expertise, meaning, and identity around their work through career decisions, transitions, challenges, and accomplishments. This book will refer to adults during their career lifespan as career explorers—adults looking for an ideal vocation; career sustainers—adults maintaining their current vocation; and career changers—adults seeking to shift to a new organization or vocation.

Aims of *Rethinking Adult Career Development*

This book aims to provide a more critical and provocative analysis of adult CD issues and practices than most career education and development textbooks cover. As noted, many CD texts target youth and pre-adults and focus on helping them choose a career. What happens when adults realize they have chosen the wrong career, lose their jobs, experience injustice and discrimination, or are forced to make career shifts they are unprepared to undertake? This book represents a significant departure from the standard CD textbooks available by centering adults and viewing careers as lifelong learning, development, and change processes that are individual learning experiences and engagements within organizational, cultural, and community contexts.

The book covers the basic tenets of adult CD theory and practice. It interrogates the dominant paradigms and practices of CD, teaches readers how to critically assess CD practices and outcomes through an intersectional lens (one that considers race, gender, disability, class, and other identities and positionalities), and provides critical alternatives to practice. This means that, in addition to re-envisioning the way adult CD is described, I, the author, actually name and discuss topics typically omitted from career texts, including sexism, racism, heteronormativity, colonialism, power relations, environmental exploitation, politics, ableism, performativity, and more. I view CD as a contested practice—that is, it is performed in contexts that are often incompatible with individual and community interests—such as maximizing profits while downsizing the workforce, demanding remote workers return to in-person work, or privileging one group (often non-disabled White heterosexual cisgender men) while marginalizing other less powerful groups in the organization. I hope to convey that CD is challenging. When historically excluded and other marginalized individuals succeed, their presence creates a new paradox of joining and advancing the same exclusionary system that previously prevented them from progressing. Their dilemma is to either assimilate into this oppressive system or actively work to change the status quo to make careers more accessible to everyone. How do women, people of color, gender and sexual minorities (GSM—including, but not limited to people identifying as lesbian, gay, bisexual, asexual, transgender, Two-Spirit, queer, and/or intersex), disabled people, and other marginalized groups change the culture once they advance into a masculine, patriarchal culture?

This book is rethinking adult CD by discussing it as a learning and development process throughout the lifespan, with a particular focus on adulthood and intersectionality. Adults have different needs and interests as they progress through their careers and can experience gradual and sudden changes. Gradual changes include developing expertise, aging, experiencing subtle injustice that prevents advancement and equity, and advancing in a given career. Sudden changes may be personal such as health crises, unjust treatment, family crises, or job loss. Changes can also be collective such as a global pandemic, natural disasters, or other unanticipated events that cause adults to pause and evaluate what matters to them. The global COVID-19 pandemic forced workers into remote work and life overnight, proving that drastic change can be swift worldwide (Gambuto, 2020; Korten, 2020). The pandemic also prompted many people to evaluate their work lives, discover the challenges and joys of working from home, and reassess their work and values in ways that affected resignations and job and career changes. Adults also make choices and experience careers differently based on their positionality or the interweaving of their multiple identities and socialization that is known as intersectionality (Crenshaw, 1989).

Introducing the Author

As the author, sharing my identities and positionalities is essential because they shape how I think about work and CD for adults. I am a White cisgender heterosexual woman from Michigan and a United States citizen. Although I live in the Southern US, I am a Midwesterner at heart. I am a first-generation college graduate and a professor at a research-intensive university—an unlikely career given my family's educational history. I began my career in the automotive industry as a front-line labor relations representative on the management side. I worked at a 1,000-employee sparkplug plant in Ohio organized by the United Auto Workers and moved up into executive human resources roles during my corporate career. Early in my career, I began working in learning and development and conversing with people about their career paths. These interests led me to complete a doctorate in adult education and eventually become an academic with research interests in CD, adult learning, women's leadership, leadership development, gender identity and equity, coaching, and critical human resource development. Being a professor is a privilege and joy—what other job invites creativity and helps other people realize their career and life dreams?! This work closely aligns with my values and work style—key factors in matching people with their work environments. I also created the first graduate CD course in my academic program at the University of Georgia and have been creating content for this book for over a decade. Having regular career conversations led me to pursue an executive coaching certificate. I have coached for 15 years, am recognized as a master coach, and founded the University of Georgia Graduate Certificate in Organization Coaching. It is fair to you, the reader, to know that I am a coach and use the pages of this book to coach you as you learn about the theory and practice of CD for adults.

Reflecting on the Intended Audience for *Rethinking Adult Career Development*

Experiencing a satisfying, affirming career should be the norm and a human right. How can individuals attain career aspirations and simultaneously balance life? How can mentors and career coaches counsel career explorers, sustainers, and changers? How can career decisions and developmental practices enhance diversity, equity, inclusion, and belonging? How can those who attain career advancement lift and amplify those coming behind them without replicating oppressive structures? How can leaders and policymakers address systemic issues that affect careers? These questions will be answered in *Rethinking Adult Career Development* with theoretical connections and practical interventions that potentially make CD more equitable and just. This book provides a map for navigating these contested career issues for individuals, leaders, and organizations.

Although this book is written for anyone interested in reflecting on their career, understanding the dynamics of adult CD, or helping another person navigate career issues, it is also written with the helping professionals in mind: those who mentor, coach, teach, counsel, facilitate, and advise others in career choice and development. Human resource development (HRD) professionals are among this mix of helpers, and they will find this book anchored in theory and applied in practice for making CD interventions on individual, group, organization, and system levels. As Gedro (2017) emphasized, "Ultimately, there is a way to argue that all human resource activities are, in some way, related to career development. Understanding and appreciating career development models provides valuable scaffolding for HRD professionals" (p. 11). Whatever your goals, as a career explorer, sustainer, and changer, I welcome you to delve into career development for adults!

You, the reader, are encouraged to use your career as a unit of analysis to examine CD theory and practice for adults. What has been your process of CD? What challenges have you encountered? Who has helped you? To get the most out of this book, take regular pauses to reflect on how these principles and tools can assist your CD and perhaps that of others. Work through the exercises in the boxes and talk with your family, friends, colleagues, mentors, and others who can be helpful during your career journey. Help others navigate their careers and you will also learn and benefit in the process. Box 1.2 provides an opportunity to reflect on job changes to get you into the rhythm of reading this textbook.

ıl BOX 1.2 ADULT CAREER DEVELOPMENT BY THE NUMBERS

Job Changes and Time Adults Spend Working

People tend to change jobs 10 to 15 times, with an average of 12 times (Belli, 2018; Doyle, 2020). That is a lot of change for anyone. As a career explorer, sustainer, or changer:

1. How many times have you changed jobs or careers?
2. How does that compare to your grandparents, parents, peers, or children?
3. What are the implications of so much change for individuals, organizations, and industries?

Overviewing the Book Contents

Rethinking Adult Career Development has nine chapters that build toward the goal of the book to reconsider adult work and CD by discussing it as a lifelong learning and development process characterized by the dilemmas and challenges adults face from an intersectional perspective dedicated to creating more equity. Chapter 1, "Introducing *Rethinking Adult Career Development*," introduces the book's goals, audience, and features and overviews the history and key terms associated with CD. Chapter 2, "Situating Adult Career Development in Social Context," addresses dynamics influencing adults' work and CD atmosphere. Chapter 3, "Understanding Adult Career Development Theory," summarizes key dominant CD theories, noting significant contributions, relevance for adults, and critiques. Chapter 4, "Exploring Critical, Intersectional Adult Career Development," delves into topics often neglected in most CD books and theories, such as critical perspectives and intersectionality.

Chapter 5, "Interpreting Career Development as Adult Learning and Change," examines CD as a process of adult learning, growth, meaning-making, and change. Chapter 6, "Connecting Career Development with Meaning in Life and Work," investigates how adults derive meaning and purpose from their lives and work by discussing theoretical perspectives and presenting practical strategies for connecting work and meaning. Chapter 7, "Appreciating Work and Career Challenges Based on Positionality and Intersectionality," explores identities that often intersect to understand career challenges based on gender, age, race, socioeconomic status, gender identity and sexuality, and disability. Chapter 8, "Considering Work and Career Challenges, and Making Interventions," concerns identifying appropriate interventions for facilitating adult CD at the individual, team, leadership, organization, and community levels. Chapter 9, "Introducing a Critical, Intersectional, Feminist Model of Adult Career Development Theory," concludes the book with a proposal to reframe how work and CD for adults is understood, researched, and implemented.

Presenting the Book Features

Rethinking Adult Career Development features integrated activity boxes to provide chapter overviews, prompts for reflective practice, connections of evidence to practice, and tips and tools for CD (Table 1.1). To make the most of these features, it is recommended you complete them while reading and taking a reflective pause to apply the ideas to your career education and development as a career explorer, sustainer, or changer.

Table 1.1   *Rethinking Adult Career Development features*

📖 **Chapter Overview and Learning Objectives**		🗨 **Reflective Practice**
This box provides a short summary of the chapter and what readers will learn by the end of the chapter.		This box contains reflective activities and offers a chance to pause and consider the implications of a specific idea, theory, or practice as it relates to career development useful for self-exploration and helping other people.
📊 **Adult Career Development by the Numbers**		💡 **Tips and Tools for Career Development**
This box contains summaries of the best evidence available to inform adult career development.		This box features tips and tools and applied activities and ideas to help navigate career development.

HISTORICAL PERSPECTIVES OF ADULT CAREER DEVELOPMENT

Career development (CD) emerged as an applied field to help people make work and learning decisions. CD's history is long, spanning primarily Western countries, traceable to the second half of the 1800s—a time of rapid industrialization, economic development, urbanization, immigration, and rising social inequality (McMahon & Arthur, 2018). These social upheavals facilitated the rise of the first documented attempts to offer career guidance to promote just and equitable employment practices for individuals who may have been disenfranchised by rapid social change. Early career assistance was through placement services (Patton, 2019; Pope, 2000). Vocational guidance followed in industrialized countries, focused on teaching character and identity development, preparing people for skilled work, and enabling the school-to-work transition (McMahon & Arthur, 2018). McMahon and Arthur (2018) noted that the international nature of CD is often overlooked due to the dominance of Frank Parsons (1909), a US figure who wrote one of the earliest theoretical books on vocational guidance, *Choosing a Vocation*. McMahon and Arthur (2018) also observed, "These early social reform efforts to assist people in finding jobs and making occupational decisions paved the way for the development of numerous theories and models that focus on vocational guidance and career development" (p. 4). CD theories began emerging primarily out of vocational psychology, sociology, and organizational psychology, spanning a range of topics, including individual traits, CD stages, career decision-making, career learning, and the influence of context (McMahon & Arthur, 2018).

Career guidance and counseling developed in the 19th and early 20th centuries. Since that time, both processes have become worldwide phenomena. Theories of career behavior and, less so, of career practice have been developed and have gained credibility across national, social, and economic contexts (Savickas & Walsh, 1996). Career development knowledge affirms that individuals differ in how they view the meaning of work and its value or salience in their lives. These differences arise from gender, cultural experience, educational level, economic status, and life-role obligations (Super & Šverko, 1995; Super, 1990). Contextual factors are fundamentally crucial in CD. These include workplace demands and limits on individual choice by socioeconomic class and characteristics of the family unit that constrain decision-making freedom. Regardless of the context, theorists and researchers construe individual career behavior as oriented to meaning-making and constructing one's reality by the decisions one makes or avoids rather than simply being passive receptors of information or knowledge from external sources. Individuals making meaning of their career experiences captures the essence of constructivism (Peavey, 1998; Rosen & Kuehlwein, 1996). Researchers and theorists have demonstrated that virtually all persons experiencing transition points in their lives can benefit from career guidance and counseling and that the career questions and concerns of the child, the adolescent, the young, mid-career, and older adult may have common elements but are developmentally and experientially different and require career guidance and counseling programs that differ in emphases and interventions (Herr & Cramer, 1998).

DEFINING CAREER DEVELOPMENT CONCEPTS AND TERMS

Today, the term career hardly needs explanation as it is a concept people begin learning about as soon as they can hear, as people continuously refer to their work, job, vocation, and calling. Yet the term became common in the mid-20th century (Herr, 2001; McDonald & Hite, 2023; Moore et al., 2007). Sullivan and Baruch (2009) defined career as:

> An individual's work-related and other relevant experiences, both inside and outside of organizations that form a unique pattern over the individual's life span. This definition recognizes both physical movements and psychological transitions, such as between levels, jobs, employers, occupations, and industries, as well as the interpretation of the individual, including his or her perceptions of career events (e.g., viewing job loss as failure vs. as an opportunity for a new beginning), career alternatives (e.g., viewing limited vs. unlimited options), and outcomes (e.g. how one defines career success). (p. 543)

Standard terms in the career development lexicon are defined in Table 1.2. As a career explorer, sustainer, or changer, how have you experienced the common CD activities listed in the table?

Table 1.2   *Common career development terms*

Term	Definition
Career	A course of events constituting a life impacted by the many roles played during the life course. It is also defined as the totality of work done in a lifetime.
Vocation	This concept is more profound than "career" because it involves doing work that makes a difference and has meaning. The Latin word *vocare*, which means "to call," is the root of the word vocation. A vocation is a calling that requires looking and listening. It is not immediately recognizable, and one must be attuned to the message for it to be heard (Webber, 1998). Finding meaningful work, therefore, involves listening for those internal signals that signify "deep interests" and then allowing the interests to lead to work aligned with a "core self."
Career satisfaction	A measure concentrated on correlating external job factors with global satisfaction measures (Henderson, 2000a; Savickas, 2000).
Career happiness	An emergent concept defined by Henderson (2000a, 2000b) and several colleagues (see the Winter 1999–2000 issue of *Career Planning and Adult Development Journal*), career happiness results when individuals find or develop careers that allow them to express their core identities and values that tap into their true essence.
Career development	The lifelong psychological and behavioral processes, as well as contextual influences shaping one's career across the lifespan. It includes career patterns, decision-making styles, integration of life roles, value expression, and self-concept.
Career development interventions	Activities that empower people to cope effectively with CD tasks. This might include developing self and occupational awareness, learning decision-making and job-searching skills, adjusting to occupational choices, and coping with job stress and transition.
Career counseling	A relationship with a professional counselor who assists an individual or a group in coping more effectively with career concerns.
Career education	The systematic attempt to influence the CD of students and adults through providing occupational information, infusing career-related concepts into the curriculum, offering worksite-based experiences (e.g., internships), and offering career planning courses.
Career development programs	Systematically planned, counselor-coordinated information and experiences to help facilitate individual CD.

UNDERSTANDING CAREERS CONCEPTS AND MODELS

Table 1.2 presented standard career development (CD) terms. There are also career concepts and models that have evolved over the decades. Baruch and Sullivan (2022) noted that career research has shifted over the past 40 years from focusing on traditional, linear career models to employing nontraditional, contemporary models to portray the diversity of career patterns displayed by an increasingly diverse workforce. These two generations of career concepts are presented in this section.

First Generation of Contemporary Career Concepts

Baruch and Sullivan's (2022) description of the landscape of career concepts presented a comprehensive view of research on contemporary careers and the theoretical concepts and models used to describe them. They split the discussion into two streams of first and second generation. The first-generation theories and concepts explain a workplace adjusting to rapid technological advancement, globalization, and downsizing of white-collar workers during the 20th century. Their framework will be used to introduce career concepts and models.

Traditional careers

A traditional career involves a long-term employee-employer relationship based on mutual loyalty and trust. It is rather uncommon today for a person to work for their entire career for one organization, but that is the type of career the traditional arrangement represents. The expectation for an employer to bear significant responsibility for one's CD characterizes this career theory. Although uncommon today, a traditional career is commonly desired by many people in their quest for employment security and upward mobility (Hall & Moss, 1998). These hopes are likely built into unspoken expectations where people expect or seek help from their employer to develop a career over time. This type of employment arrangement has eroded recently as there is more volatility and uncertainty in the economy and job markets.

Boundaryless careers

A boundaryless career situates jobs in a fluid job market with permeable borders where workers move between organizations with greater frequency and seamlessness than in a traditional career (Arthur & Rousseau, 1996). A boundaryless career might be a carpenter, real estate agent, consultant, artist, or other occupation where the workers are not limited to one employer, position, or organization. Boundarylessness depends on physical mobility and a boundaryless mindset (Volmer & Spurk, 2011), or physical and psychological career mobility between various career roles (Sullivan & Arthur, 2006). Although this type of career can give people more flexibility and autonomy, it is also more uncertain. Bad jobs or those with little or no security may put the worker into continual and unwelcome boundarylessness, creating precarity for some people. Boundarylessness appeals in a globally competitive, hyper-technologically connected context characterized by shifting employment relationships, psychological contracts, and downsizing, which can create ongoing job or occupational changes. Career activities may happen externally from the employer through networks or information. Workers are independent of the organization in this type of career. Examples might be consultants or contingent workers.

Protean careers
The protean career is the idea that CD and growth need to be driven by the person, not the organization. The term protean is rooted in Greek mythology in the character of Proteus, a sea god who had a gift of prophecy and used metamorphosis to shift shape. Homer called Proteus "Old Man of the Sea" in the *Odyssey*, inferring the liquid and continuing changing nature of water. Protean is synonymous with adaptive, mutable, flexible, and changeable (Hall, 1976, 2002). In this sense, a career is controlled by the person, not the organization. A protean career is a self-directed endeavor where internal values guide a person focused on self-fulfillment and ongoing development (Briscoe & Hall, 2006). A protean career might be one of author, artist, academic, or entrepreneur. Skromme Granrose and Baccili (2006) argued that protean and boundaryless careers mirror ambiguous, uncertain relationships between workers and organizations. This career type views individuals as self-directed and internally driven by their values, including the management of education, training, employment, leisure, and family life. Protean careerists view their careers as transformative, helping them gain a more authentic sense of self and success. The notion of the protean career integrates Super's (1975) and Levinson et al.'s (1974) developmental career stage models and the boundaryless career concept, which are discussed in this chapter. This career approach suggests that multiple, shorter learning cycles occur over a lifespan and that these mini-stages of exploration-trial-mastery-exit transcend work boundaries.

Post-corporate careers
Peiperl and Baruch (1997) suggested the concept of post-corporate careers as a way of integrating protean and boundaryless concepts and the self-directed and responsibility-taking that individuals assume for managing their careers and meeting their needs for job satisfaction and financial rewards. The idea was to juxtapose traditional and contemporary career models with the notion

that individuals working alongside bureaucratic organizations have various career options (Baruch & Sullivan, 2022). Although Peiperl and Baruch's work is now over 25 years old, their advice remains relevant in a workplace changed by the COVID-19 pandemic and other dynamics of a global economy. They predicted that "careers in the twenty-first century really will transcend both organizations and individuals" (Peiperl & Baruch, 1997, p. 20). They explained that these boundaryless careers would "progress in limitless ways through countless jobs, transactions, and connections, involving ever-changing networks of people, places, and businesses" (p. 21). Although they noted that they did not mean to imply that all work would be done via telecommuting, they predicted "more virtual groups and organizations, even among real physical offices" (p. 21). They closed their article by noting, "Those who succeed will be those who cannot only stand on their own but can form and sustain links—links that will take them beyond existing individual and organizational models, to entirely new kinds of careers" (p. 21). Many workers shifted into post-corporate careers during the COVID-19 pandemic, where their work became remote and more self-directed, with workers assuming accountability for completing their work.

Hybrid careers
A hybrid career, like post-structural, melds aspects of traditional, protean, and boundaryless careers, although it is an emergent concept not associated with one scholar (Sullivan & Baruch, 2009). Gander (2021) noted that the term hybrid career emerged in the 1990s when Bailyn (1991) used the term to discuss the need for research and development technical staff to gain varied skills to have career options. Gander (2021) synthesized the literature on the hybrid career as indicating boundary setting and boundary crossing grounded in decisions to make changes—the permeability of boundaries. She suggested that career boundaries were influenced by subjectivity (mental pictures of career possibilities) and objectivity (skill sets leading to employability) as boundaries influencing and shaping CD across the career span. Gander (2021) concluded the hybrid career is under-theorized and underutilized in career scholarship and practice.

Intelligent careers
Intelligent careers are grounded in the idea that three key career competencies of knowing—(a) Why: what motivates a person to choose or remain in a particular career path or lifestyle; (b) How: a person's combination of skills, knowledge, and experiences; and (c) Whom: an individual's networks and relationships—are crucial to choosing careers and making career decisions.

To practice intelligent career planning, a career explorer, sustainer, or changer might ask the following questions:

1. Why am I interested in this career path? What about it is motivating to me?
2. How prepared am I to pursue this career in terms of my skills, knowledge, and experience?
3. Who can help me learn about and develop helpful relationships for pursuing this career path?

The inability to answer these three questions that get at the competencies necessary to pursue a particular career might indicate a mismatch or that more exploration and preparation are needed to pursue a specific career to make the most intelligent career decision.

BOX 1.3 TIPS AND TOOLS FOR CAREER DEVELOPMENT

National and International Resource Repositories

Navigating a career can be daunting. National and international career information repositories make finding information more accessible and provide reputable resources. Some excellent global resources are profiled in this tip. There is helpful information in each of these sites, and they also give a flavor of career education and development globally.

Learn & Work Ecosystem Library (US): https://learnworkecosystemlibrary.com/
The web portal Learn & Work Ecosystem Library is a resource designed to help career explorers, sustainers, and changers make sense of the plethora of resources and information to support careers. The library is a US-based career resource repository intended to support workers and stakeholders. The platform provides physical and digital access to resources, with librarians available to assist and offers customized services.

European Employment Services (EURES): https://ec.europa.eu/social/main.jsp?catId=1400&langId=en
This service supports the free movement of workers in the European Union (EU) by providing information and support to workers and employers and promoting information exchange.

Korean Research Institute for Vocational Education and Training (KRIVET): https://www.krivet.re.kr/eng/eu/index.jsp
This national research institute that collects and analyzes labor market

trends was designated as the National Career Development Center. It takes a lifelong learning approach to career education and development.
South Africa National Skills Fund (NSF): https://nationalgovernment.co .za/units/view/259/national-skills-fund-nsf
NSF focuses on education and training to support workplace-based learning.
Skills Development Scotland—United Kingdom (UK): https://www.skill sdevelopmentscotland.co.uk/
A national body to support the people and businesses of Scotland in developing and applying their skills.

Second Generation of Contemporary Career Concepts

A new generation of career concepts has emerged since the mid-2000s (Baruch & Sullivan, 2022; Sullivan & Baruch, 2009), reflecting the shifts in career context amid more uncertain and complex times. The first generation of career concepts and models focuses more on a person's relationship to their work organization and how they might engage in career education, decisions, and development. The next set of career concepts and models capture labor markets' complexity and uncertainty. The second-generation concepts address how people prepare for and adapt to careers that help them meet the challenges in both work and life that can bolster or derail a career.

Kaleidoscope Career Model
The Kaleidoscope Career Model (KCM) (Sullivan & Mainiero, 2007) employed the metaphor of a kaleidoscope through its focus on three parameters of career decisions, including (a) Authenticity (being true to oneself), (b) Balance between life and work demands, and (c) Challenge (stimulating work and advancement opportunities). Sullivan and Baruch (2009) explained:

> Like a kaleidoscope that produces changing patterns when the tube is rotated and its glass chips fall into new arrangements, the KCM describes how individuals change the pattern of their career by rotating the varied aspects of their lives to arrange their relationships and roles in new ways. These changes may occur in response to internal changes, such as those due to maturation, or environmental changes, such as being laid off. Individuals evaluate the choices and options available to determine the best fit among work demands, constraints, and opportunities as well as relationships and personal values and interests. As one decision is made, it affects the outcome of the kaleidoscope career pattern. (p. 1557)

Importantly, the KCM highlights gender differences in CD, and its authors urged consideration of nontraditional models that examine how career decisions are approached differently based on gender and how life balance factors play out in these decisions.

Career Construction Theory

Career Construction Theory (CCT) is driven by how effectively a person can adapt to their environment as they construct and reconstruct themselves and their careers through their reflections and relationships with others across their lifespan. Career adaptability is "an individual's resources for coping with current and anticipated tasks, transitions, traumas in their occupational roles that, to some degree large or small, alter their social integration" (Savickas & Porfeli, 2012, p. 662). Career adaptability is made up of four resources: (a) Concern—how well people are prepared for anticipated career tasks and challenges; (b) Control—the level of responsibility people take for their CD and influence on their workplace; (c) Curiosity—the extent to which people explore possible future selves, occupations, and work environments; and (d) Confidence—the degree to which people believe they can solve challenges and overcome problems.

Employability

Employability contrasts with traditional career models that focus on securing lifelong employment and instead focuses on how a person can remain viably employed across the lifespan, or essentially how suitable they are to attain and maintain a career and obtain new employment if necessary. Employability refers to a person's characteristics that help them secure work, such as mindsets, education, skills, thoughts, actions, attitudes, and experience within relevant work contexts. Employability of graduates is a key metric most higher education institutions use to measure their performance, and it is not uncommon for universities to boast about the percentage of graduates employed within one year of graduating. For example, my institution, the University of Georgia, reported a 2022 "career outcomes rate" of 96%, which is defined as "the number of students who are employed, continuing their education, or not seeking employment within an average of 6 months after graduation" (University of Georgia Career Center, n.d., para. 2).

Sustainable careers

Sustainable careers are defined as "people's capacity to learn, create, test, and maintain adaptability in managing their own careers" (Baruch & Sullivan, 2022, p. 140). De Vos et al. (2020) suggested three dimensions of career sustainability that speak to career-person fit, including the (a) Person, (b) Context, and (d) Time across measures of health, happiness, and productivity. They proposed indicators of sustainable careers that included mutually beneficial consequences for the person and their surrounding context over a long term, taking a systemic perspective. Health is physical and mental, and how well the fit is with the career and work context. Happiness is a subjective judgment of a person's success or satisfaction with their career. Productivity is how well a person achieves work results and overall employability or career potential.

Chance events and career shocks
A chance event is an unpredictable stroke of luck or misfortune that impacts a person's career, such as receiving a promotion or being fired. Although one might assume positive or negative chance events would lead to parallel positive or negative career outcomes, that is not always the case. For instance, most people would view getting a promotion as a positive chance event that would spur positive events. Instead, the promotion might create stress, change relationships with former peers, and test a person's leadership capacity—all negative aspects of the positive chance event. Similarly, getting fired is an adverse chance event. Yet, many people describe getting fired as yielding positive outcomes because the event caused them to re-evaluate their career path, removed them from a toxic culture, or spurred them to pursue new educational or employment opportunities. A career shock usually follows a chance event, triggering reflection on one's career, which can also be perceived as positive or negative. The COVID-19 pandemic (a chance event) created a career shock for many as they were forced into remote work and life overnight, causing some people to recommit to their career paths and others to abandon their organizations and pursue new careers altogether.

A career ecosystem
A career ecosystem examines a career from a systemic view considering multiple perspectives of interconnected actors as they participate in the labor market, including the individual, organization, community, nations, and societies (Baruch, 2015). Within the career ecosystem, there is boundary crossing as talent flows across the various parts of the system, including organizations, sectors, and nations. Actors in the ecosystem are affected by (a) a continuous flow of human capital, (b) spiral learning processes as the ecosystem adjusts and adapts to new challenges, (c) unceasing change influencing the flow of human capital, and (d) global influences that impact technical, social, legal, and political forces. The career ecosystem is a helpful way of thinking about careers within a more extensive, interconnected system.

☽ BOX 1.4 REFLECTIVE PRACTICE

Identifying my Career Type

This box summarizes the types of career concepts and models defined in Chapter 1. Which definition(s) in Table 1.3 best define you as a career explorer, sustainer, or changer?

Table 1.3 Identifying my career type

Career type	Definition	Check the one(s) you relate to
Traditional	The expectation is for an employer to bear significant responsibility for one's CD as it follows a linear trajectory throughout a career.	
Boundaryless	A person's actual career or the meaning of career transcends the boundary of a single employer.	
Protean	The idea that CD and growth need to be driven by the person, not the organization.	
Post-corporate	Workers transition from organizationally bound career structures to more agile careers offering nontraditional options.	
Hybrid	Like post-corporate, the hybrid career blends ideas from boundaryless and protean careers to expand career options for the individual.	
Intelligent	Knowing why, how, and whom.	
Kaleidoscope	People make career decisions and transitions based on three variables of authenticity, balance, and challenge.	
Career Construction Theory	Focuses on career adaptability according to the resources of concern, control, curiosity, and confidence.	
Employability	The degree to which a person can remain viably employed across the lifespan, or how suitable they are to attain and maintain a career and obtain new employment if necessary.	
Sustainable Careers	A person's capacity to learn, create, test, and maintain adaptability as they navigate a career while balancing life.	

Career type	Definition	Check the one(s) you relate to
Chance Events and Career Shocks	A chance event is an unpredictable stroke of luck or misfortune that impacts a person's career, and may be viewed as positive or negative. A career shock usually follows a chance event, triggering reflection on one's career, which can also be perceived as positive or negative.	
Career Ecosystem	Interconnected actors participate in a system that includes individuals, organizations, communities, and societies with interdependencies and mutual benefits in the labor market.	

Which career type(s) did you check? What was behind your choice(s)? It is recommended you discuss these options with others to help make sense of your career path and learn from another person.

TRANSFORMATIONS IN CAREER DEVELOPMENT MODELS AND CONCEPTS

This chapter has traced the development of first- and second-generation career concepts and models. Baruch (2004) outlined trends in career perspectives on individual, organizational, and societal levels, suggesting that there was a shift from a "linear career system" (p. 58) where people climb toward a career summit in a traditional career sense, perhaps encountering plateaus along the way into a "multidirectional career system" that is full of diverse landscapes as options for career progression (p. 61). Table 1.4 summarizes Baruch's (2004) conclusions about career transitions and transformations from both individual and organizational perspectives.

Table 1.4   *Transitions and transformations in career models and concepts*

Career aspect	Traditional perspective	Transformed perspective
Environment or Context	Stable	Dynamic
Career Decision and Choice	Single decision made at an early age	Multiple decisions, often at different life stages
Responsibility for Career	Organization	Individual
Career Workplace Horizon	One organization	Multiple organizations
Career Time Horizon	Long term	Short term
Scope of Change	Incremental	Transformational

Career aspect	Traditional perspective	Transformed perspective
Work Relationship Expectations	Employers expect loyalty and commitment Employers give job security	Workers give long-term tenure and work long hours Workers invest in their employability
Progress Criteria	Advance based on seniority	Advance according to merit (results and knowledge)
Evidence of Success	Progression up the hierarchy	Intrinsic feelings of accomplishment
Learning and Development	Formalized learning on generalist topics	On-the-job, specific to the organization
Career Trajectory	Linear	Multidirectional

Source: Adapted from Baruch (2004).

CHAPTER SUMMARY

Chapter 1 introduced *Rethinking Adult Career Development* by providing an overview of the book, presenting key terms and ideas, and defining career concepts and models. The chapter began with Guillebeau's (2016) quote, with relevance for you as a career explorer, sustainer, or changer, about it being better to find yourself at the bottom of a ladder you wish to climb instead of at the top of one you do not.

2. Situating adult career development in the social context

⊔ BOX 2.1 CHAPTER OVERVIEW AND LEARNING OBJECTIVES

James Luceno, author of novels and reference books for *Star Wars*, wrote:

> Uncertainty is the first step toward self-determination. Courage comes next. (Luceno, 2012, p. 164)

The context of career development (CD) is uncertain and shifting as social, environmental, economic, and political forces create chaos and ambiguity. At times, it takes courage to persevere in a career.

The purpose of this chapter is to situate work and CD within a social context. The chapter addresses dynamics that influence the adult CD context, covering VUCA, global capitalism, neoliberalism, technology, a multigenerational workforce, the COVID-19 pandemic, workforce equity, diversity, inclusion, and decolonization.

As a result of reading this chapter and completing the exercise boxes, you, the reader, should be able to:
1. Describe the context of adult CD and understand how it affects individual careers, organizations, communities, and nations.
2. Appreciate diversity, inclusion, and decolonization's role in adult CD.

What factors have influenced your career choices and progression as a career explorer, sustainer, or changer? Relationships? Hardship? Challenge? Opportunity, or lack thereof? Economic, social, cultural, or environmental factors? Career development (CD) does not happen in a vacuum. It unfolds in a complex, diverse, changing social system where beings, energies, and intentions converge in ways that influence each other for good or bad. This chapter situates adult CD amid its complexities and vulnerabilities in today's world. Careers unfold in a world shaped by VUCA and dominated by global capitalism fueled by neoliberalism. Technology is constantly changing how people obtain, maintain, and retrain for employment. The workforce is ageing and multigenerational, creating opportunities for conflict and collaboration. The COVID-19 pandemic reshaped many people's relationships with their careers, particularly with new demands for remote work and what for some became the "Great Resignation." Finally, the world is increasingly diverse, and understanding the implications of diverse, equitable, and inclusive careers is imperative for creating socially just and fair workplaces.

VUCA

It is difficult to get through the day without hearing or reading the acronym VUCA, which is shorthand for V-volatile, U-uncertain, C-complex, and A-ambiguous (Van der Steege, 2017; Yoder-Wise, 2021). The United States Army War College coined VUCA to characterize and analyze multifaceted, turbulent, thorny, fluctuating conditions (US Army Heritage and Education Center, 2018; Whiteman, 1998). Current times are aptly VUCA since the global COVID-19 pandemic and career crisis that ensued for many workers and employers; the murder of George Floyd and other Black and Brown people at the hands of US law enforcement; social unrest and race reckoning that followed George Floyd's murder on a global scale; climate change and unstable, violent weather patterns that create crisis and loss of life; and global political instability, among other challenges. These trials present what Rittel and Webber (1973) called "wicked problems"—intractable, unsolvable dilemmas due to their VUCA nature and human capacity to foresee, comprehend, or agree on how to address them.

Canzittu (2022) wrote about career guidance in a VUCA world where workers are expected to respond to complexity by becoming knowledge workers who solve problems and deliver quality solutions appropriate for continuously changing environments and markets. Organizations are expected to build capacity to manage the creation, preservation, and sharing of knowledge to solve wicked problems. Table 2.1 describes VUCA concepts in CD terms using the COVID-19 pandemic as an example of a VUCA situation. Read the table as a career explorer, sustainer, and changer, and assess how well you might handle a future VUCA moment. And if you cannot relate, perhaps you can think of a family member or friend who experienced career challenges during the pandemic. The changes in the past few years are daunting to comprehend yet are expected to continue, making it valuable to build your capacity to respond to crisis and uncertainty.

Table 2.1   *Career development in VUCA terms*

VUCA Term	Definition	Career development examples	Career coping strategies
V Volatility	Unstable change, even in situations that are understandable and identifiable.	The COVID-19 pandemic injected volatility into careers overnight on a global scale. The disruption caused workers who understood their jobs and work contexts to be plunged into sudden job reconfiguration, remote work, new expectations, career changes, technology shifts, digital surveillance, and sometimes job loss.	Find balance and be agile: When the world is unpredictable, find a space, practice, or community that feels safe and centering. Accept change as a constant and develop flexibility to maneuver and change with the fluctuating demands. Create a vision for your next career steps (if leading a team, help them do this as well).
U Uncertainty	The present is unclear, and the future is uncertain. A lack of knowledge about the implications or consequences of a situation prevails, even when its causes and effects are anticipated and recognizable.	The COVID-19 pandemic created a situation that was a health risk and required immediate changes to how work was done as careers were played out remotely, even though it was unclear how long the pandemic would last or what would happen to how and where work was done in the future.	Learn: Seek to understand and build knowledge about the situation. Work on environmental scanning to assess the current reality and anticipate future needs, opportunities, and challenges. Reflect on what you do well and how you can improve. Use the situation to enhance your career learning and knowledge. Keep perspective and attempt to control what is in your sphere of influence. Take care of yourself and your loved ones.

VUCA Term	Definition	Career development examples	Career coping strategies
C Complexity	Multiple factors within a system come into play that create confusion and chaos.	How COVID-19 vaccines were developed and administrated was a global, confusing, and chaotic task. On a more individual level, how teams and organizations decided to organize their work was challenging at first until upheaval and awkwardness of remote work could be tamed.	Communicate: Clearly and often. Whether engaging with peers, supervisees, customers, the boss, or friends and family, transparent exchanges help create alignment on the next steps. Communicating and ensuring people understand expectations also enhances collaboration and results.
A Ambiguity	Little or no clarity exists about the situation.	When the COVID-19 pandemic began, there was little clarity about personal safety measures like masking or social distancing. There was a blurring of personal and professional work for remote workers. Once some organizations began returning to in-person work, many CEOs made, and continue to make, missteps in their policies and communication.	Experiment and foster resilience and flexibility: When the situation is unclear, you may have to try different things. Sometimes that means making an individual decision. It may mean negotiating what is appropriate for the situation and learning new coping skills. Talking about coping with others can also be helpful and therapeutic.

Resisting change is human nature, so when VUCA situations arise, many people feel unmoored and anxious, hurting their ability to focus and remain motivated in life and work. Prolonged malaise, in this sense, can harm career prospects and progress. To avoid becoming a VUCA victim, focus on continuous learning that will be beneficial in the new reality, collaborate with others to make shared meaning, and find ways to be supportive. This advice is not just for work but also for life. Many workers engaged in deep reflection and made career changes during the pandemic. They joined the "Great Resignation" based on a realignment of values, a demand for remote work, a call for higher wages, a desire for learning and development, and the expectation for career pathways (Taylor, 2021). The pandemic surfaced new priorities and behaviors for many people. Such shifts also helped organizations, according to De Smet et al. (2021), who concluded resilient organizations thrived during the COVID-19 pandemic by investing in crafting clear goals and clarifying strategy; empowering small cross-functional teams to make decisions; investing in team building, coaching, and recognition; and learning and adopting new collaboration technologies. VUCA is complicated by global capitalism and fueled by neoliberalism, as discussed in the following sections.

◌ BOX 2.2 REFLECTIVE PRACTICE

Applying VUCA to Life's Challenges

VUCA gives you, as a career explorer, sustainer, or changer, the language to make sense of uncertain, shifting situations. Using Table 2.2, imagine a challenging situation you have faced or are currently facing. Review the definitions, examples, and coping strategies, and imagine how you would cope according to this model and advice. You can add your thoughts in the spaces in the table.

Table 2.2   Applying VUCA to life's challenges

VUCA term	Definition	Coping strategies
V Volatility	Unstable change, even in situations that are understandable and identifiable.	Find balance and be agile by:
U Uncertainty	The present is unclear, and the future is uncertain.	Learn by:
C Complexity	Multiple factors within a system come into play that create confusion and chaos.	Communicate by:
A Ambiguity	Little or no clarity exists about the situation.	Experiment and foster resilience and flexibility by:

GLOBAL CAPITALISM

Globalization is the movement of businesses and other organizations to develop international operations and influence. For example, a McDonald's restaurant can be found in over 100 countries with more than 35,000 locations and 70-million-plus consumers daily (Mulyo, 2023). Despite the food's extensive marketing and worldwide appeal, it is widely considered unhealthy, posing "considerable harm to individual health, collective wellbeing, and environmental sustainability" (Logan et al., 2023, p. 1). Ray Kroc, the founder of McDonald's, said in 1973, when asked about the fortune from his fast-food empire: "I expect money like you walk into a room and turn on a light switch or a faucet, it is not enough" (Anonymous, 1973). Kroc was the epitome of global capitalism and neoliberalism in his insatiable quest to expand and sell more unhealthy fast food. Mulyo (2023) laid out the metanarrative promoted by Kroc and other fast-food purveyors that has encouraged global consumption of ultra-processed foods. While fast food may or may not have anything to do with one's career, it is a powerful example of the reach of global capitalism that convinces the masses to do something that harms them. Similarly, the notion that one should wholeheartedly devote themselves to their work even when real wages have been stagnant or have dipped, the US minimum wage has not been increased since 2009, and inflation is outpacing wage growth (Statista Research Department, 2023) shows how global capitalism causes workers to sometimes act against their self-interest.

A challenging reality is that when people work in organizations, they tend to belong to an enterprise explicitly or implicitly driven by capitalism—economic and political systems controlled by private owners concerned with making a profit. Essentially, it is the mixture of "private property and market exchange ... [that] are legally integrated into a structure of governance" (Centeno & Cohen, 2013, p. 11). Yet, people's work predates capitalism when work means survival and livelihood for one's family and community. Labor journalist Sarah Jaffe (2021), author of *Work Won't Love You Back,* argued that the "love your work" mantra is an artifact of capitalism and allows large corporations to underpay workers and give them fewer benefits by hoodwinking them into believing if they loved their work, it would not be drudgery. What ensued from this metanarrative were unpaid internships, the gender pay gap, and the unspoken expectation that workers should be grateful for the non-monetary rewards of their jobs. Emotion work or emotion management is built into this "love your work" metanarrative—when employees control their emotions and consciously present their emotions to others while at work through suppression, exaggeration, or modulation of their expressions (Callahan & McCollum,

2002) such as putting on a smile or other emotion when one feels like crying, being rude, or quitting.

Global capitalism is how market forces and free trade impact individuals and communities with little influence on their governance (Sklair, 2001), while capitalist enterprises seek the help of political entities for market favor (Wallerstein, 1974). Centeno and Cohen (2013) described capitalism as "a 'deep institution'—a socially constructed, politically contentious and deeply habituated way of understanding and practicing economic life" (p. 4) with global capitalism made up of three intricately linked parts: trade, finance, and consumption; and three challenges: governance, inequality, and the environment. What makes global capitalism so intractable is that in the US, for example, policy and enforcement are the responsibilities of individual states. Yet, the transactions in the global economy occur in spaces overseen by none of them. Global capitalism creates inequalities between nations with its seemingly insatiable, perpetual growth and destruction of the environment.

The earliest indicators of global capitalism date back to the early 17th century (Wallerstein, 1974), distinguished by ownership structure and sheer size encompassing thousands of workers, and included massive territories that were responsible for a large percentage of world trade with global scope (Centeno & Cohen, 2013). The slave trade was one of the earliest forms of global capitalism that has significantly shaped modern management today (Bohonos & James-Gallaway, 2022). As Centeno and Cohen (2013) observed, the origins of global capitalism could be attributed to "the European expansion of power and the imposition of a set of institutional logics designed to produce profit for the elites of that continent" (p. 24).

Global capitalism does not benefit most citizens of the world, especially workers. Cole (2023) offered the Democratic Republic of Congo as an example where death is a daily occurrence in fighting to control the lucrative mineral trade to support global cell-phone, DVD, and computer production. The workforce is primarily women and children who work in cramped, dangerous tunnels with their bare hands or shovels to extract the valued minerals. The mine shafts are dangerous, maiming or killing workers when they collapse. Cole (2023) argued that global capitalism is undemocratic since it is controlled by a tiny group of global elites who command most of the globe's resources and benefit lucratively by creating wealth inequality that benefits them directly. Countries disadvantaged by colonization and imperialism are now suffering under development schemes and the adoption of free trade policies to receive development loans. This money has gone to global corporations operating in these countries that lure people out of rural communities to work in the cities that wind up under-employed and living in crowded, unsafe slums. Global capitalism encourages unsustainable consumerism, depleting the Earth's resources and damaging the environment while simultaneously creating precarious, unstable, part-time, or contract work with low wages that exacerbate poverty, food insecurity, health complications, housing insecurity, and homelessness—not exactly a career dream.

ll BOX 2.3 ADULT CAREER DEVELOPMENT BY THE NUMBERS

The World in Data

Making sense of globalization is a daunting prospect. Visit the website Our World in Data, https://ourworldindata.org/, whose mission is to publish "research and data to make progress against the world's largest problems" (About: para. 4). The site charts multiple global phenomena over time, such as poverty, disease, hunger, climate change, and inequality. These dynamics create the social context where work is accomplished.

Review some of the data on the site and consider how your life and work may be affected by globalization.

NEOLIBERALISM

Neoliberalism, an economic ideology often favored by conservative and right-libertarian organizations and politicians, is a belief in free-market capitalism, minimal governmental interference, and deregulation based on the underlying value that economic freedom leads to economic and social advancement. Neoliberalism eschews governmental oversight and assumes that individuals are responsible for their circumstances. NAFTA (North American Free Trade Agreement) is one example of a neoliberal policy, and such policies promote globalization by lowering trade restrictions and generally resisting unionization. Neoliberalism has adverse effects such as economic inequality, the growth of monopolies (e.g., Amazon or Google), eroding job security due to outsourcing, and indifference to individual needs and hardship that magnify social injustice. Social injustice is "the repression of a person's individual and civil rights [that] could hinder their capacity to achieve full potential to learn and perform (Byrd, 2014)" (Byrd, 2018b, p. 3). Social justice is "a workplace vision of equity, fairness, dignity, and respect across lines of difference" that creates progressive workplace norms to "balance the scale between privilege (decreasing the force exerting power) and marginalization (pushing back to gain power)" (Byrd, 2018b, p. 3). McWhirter and McWha-Hermann (2021) described social justice in vocational and industrial-organizational psychology as "securing basic, non-renounceable human rights over the interests of market, profit, and the maintenance privilege" (p. 2), with decent work being implied as a human right alongside the importance of challenging the influence of neoliberal ideology. Neoliberal economic policy has been good for business, but McWhirter and McWha-Hermann (2021) contended that technological advances and globalization over the past 50 years outpace necessary advances in social justice. Global access to decent work and possibilities for meeting fundamental survival and social needs are impinged by environmental catastrophe, war, and the resulting displacement of people, violence, poverty, inequality, climate change, and the COVID-19 pandemic. They noted these variables "interact with globalization, the increasing precariousness of work, and the ubiquitous influence of neoliberalism" (p. 2).

Neoliberalism affects CD theory and practice by benefiting higher-income settings and relatively privileged workers. McWhirter & McWha-Hermann (2021) identified five marginalizing conditions that perpetuate conditions contributing to social inequalities and restrict progress toward social justice including (a) Group bias, (b) Forced movement of people, (c) Poverty, (d) Unemployment, and (e) Lack of decent work. Good web-based educational tools exist to provide more equitable, free access to education, like the Kahn Academy and Crash Course, which can help more people access quality education. Still, these resources require basic safety and access to technology that is not readily available everywhere.

TECHNOLOGY

Technological innovation is the status quo in a VUCA world where technology has changed how people communicate, shop, date, learn, bank, and work. Smartphone ownership globally is estimated at 6.84 billion with 5% or higher year-over-year increases over the last five years, and China, India, and the US have the most smartphone users in the world, with Germany reporting the most smartphone usage per capita (Howarth, 2023). A total of 5.3 billion people were using the internet at the start of the fourth quarter of 2023, or 65.7% of the global population, with 4.95 billion active social media "identities" as of October 2023 with social media use growing at the rate of 9.6 new users every single second (Datareportal, n.d.). According to Taherdoost (2023), keeping up with new technology is mandatory in a competitive environment where new technologies include cloud computing, the Internet of Things, artificial intelligence, blockchain, big data analytics, virtual and augmented reality, 5g network, and more. Being familiar with these technologies is valuable to any career.

Cloud computing uses a network of remote servers on the internet to store, manage, and access data. The Internet of Things (IoT) consists of objects that have sensors, software, and other technology that connect and share data with other devices and systems in the device cloud, as well as device-to-device, such as a vehicle connecting with a car service network, Alexa or Google home systems, smart watches, remote lighting systems and the like. Artificial intelligence (AI) is a computer system that can perform tasks requiring human intelligence, including speech recognition, decision-making, visual perception, and language translation. Blockchain is a distributed digital ledger that immutably and transparently records transactions across many computers to protect transactions from being altered after they have occurred because it would require consensus across the network. Big data analytics converts raw data into usable information to help improve decision-making, analyze trends, and draw conclusions. It is increasingly used in hiring processes. Virtual reality is a computer technology that simulates experience in a way that makes it seem real, even though it is synthetic or virtual. Augmented reality amplifies surroundings by adding digital elements that can be accessed through a camera or smartphone, such as using Google Translate® to read instructions in a different language while traveling. The 5g network is the fifth-generation mobile network of cellular technology that allows faster upload and download speeds, more consistent connectivity, and improved capacity that can potentially transform how the internet is used and accessed.

Technology trends on the horizon will continue to shape life and work (Universitat Oberta de Catalunya, n.d.). Artificial intelligence has brought innovations like ChatGPT to answer questions on various topics to which the technology will provide a text answer. AI raises cheating concerns in higher education, but creative faculty are devising creative assignments that use the technology (Rasul et al., 2023). ChatGPT is not without its challenges, however, and has been critiqued for being inaccurate, biased, and creating copyright issues.

Technology is relevant to CD in multiple ways, such as providing access to online learning opportunities that can help build credentials desired by employers. Keeping up to date with technological advances in one's field will enhance employability and promotion opportunities. New technologies facilitate hybrid and remote work. Technology is also changing work by providing automation, AI, and routinization of some tasks. Job searches can be enhanced by digital databases that provide relevant information about job descriptions, available positions, and salaries. Employers also use technology to hire workers and provide learning and development to their employees. eMentoring and eCoaching are growing in popularity, and technology will continue to impact, enhance, and evolve career exploring, sustaining, and changing (Bierema, 2022).

AN AGEING AND MULTIGENERATIONAL WORKFORCE

For the first time in history, five generations are working together, including Traditionalists, Baby Boomers, Generation X, Millennials, and Generation Z. See Gerhardt et al.'s (2021) *Gentelligence* for a comprehensive review of the intergenerational workforce and OECD's "Promoting an Age Inclusive Workforce" report (2020) for research on a multigenerational labor force. Multiple generations at work create certain challenges that organizations must address effectively as they create practices and policies that engage every generation (Hastwell, 2023). Different generations may reflect clashing priorities, particularly related to life stage. It is also typical for generations to stereotype and make assumptions about each other, which can lead to misunderstandings, miscommunication, and conflict. Preferred communication modes will also differ by generation, and it is wise for organizations to communicate using multiple methods, including email, text messaging, and virtual and face-to-face meetings. Avoiding "us versus them" attitudes is also important, and these assumptions can be diminished by helping workers develop trust and learn about each other, regardless of age.

The longevity of human life and an ageing population impact the workplace, especially when some workers extend their working lives beyond the traditional retirement age. Some workers' careers span six or more decades (Collinson & Hodin, 2023). Yet, historically, older workers are overlooked by employers—a population that should not be ignored, particularly with the US Bureau of Labor Statistics estimating that nearly one in four workers will be age 55 or older by 2031 and age 65-plus workers are the fastest growing segment of the population (Collinson & Hodin, 2023). A multigenerational workforce brings a diversity of age, experience, and values. It represents an opportunity for individuals and organizations to benefit from the range of skills, perspectives, expertise, and life experience in ways that improve innovation and performance (Collinson & Hodin, 2023; Hastwell, 2023). Yet, not all employers are age-friendly and may have cultures more steeped in ageism than age-friendliness. Ageism is "stereotypes, prejudice and/or age-based discrimination. It is a form of devaluation and non-inclusion of workers, which materializes in a decent work deficit. It affects workers and organizations" (Cebola et al., 2023, p. 1882).

People and organizations embracing age as a form of diversity and prioritizing respect, flexibility, and understanding will avoid multigenerational challenges. Collinson and Hodin (2023) outlined strategies individuals and organizations can enact to make their work lives and workplaces more age-friendly. A key strategy is cultivating lifelong learning, particularly since only 54% of employers emphasize professional learning and development, and less than 30% of organizations that do promote learning and development offer programs to address generational differences and prevent age discrimination (Collinson & Hodin, 2023). Intragenerational programs like reverse mentoring (Chadhuri & Ghosh, 2012), where a younger worker mentors an older worker; internships for workforce reintegration; or multigenerational employee resource groups can be helpful. Flexible work arrangements (Kossek et al., 2021) are approaches to support workers in ways that meet their needs and also help encourage a work-life balance for all workers. Workers engaged in caregiving need flexibility since half of US caregivers work full or part time (Schulz & Eden, 2016), and one in ten workers in Australia, the US, and Europe have unpaid caregiving responsibilities for elderly or disabled family members (Bainbridge & Townsend, 2020). Flexible retirement plans (Scherger, 2021) and drawing a pension while continuing in paid work, usually with reduced hours, can also help retain older workers by offering variable transitions through phased retirement programs. Health and retirement benefits are also perks that enhance workers' longevity within a particular organization.

THE COVID-19 PANDEMIC

The COVID-19 Pandemic is likely one of the most disruptive events of people's lifetimes in the 21st century to date, uprooting life as it was known and replacing it with fear, uncertainty, and opportunity. Hite and McDonald (2020) observed the pandemic was a health and economic crisis, creating ambiguity and unknowns about its impact on careers. Gambuto's (2020) observation perfectly captured the moment and opportunity of the world's temporary closure:

> [The pandemic] is our chance to define a new version of normal, a rare and truly sacred (yes, sacred) opportunity to get rid of the bullshit and to only bring back what works for us, what makes our lives richer, what makes our kids happier, what makes us truly proud. We get to Marie Kondo the shit out of it all. (para. 10)

The pandemic brought remote existence overnight and, in its wake, created resilience, resistance, remote work, resignation, and reinvention (Bierema, 2021). COVID-19 had a particularly profound impact on women, older, and foreign workers (Bierema, 2020a; Bolisani et al., 2020; Ghosh & Chaudhuri, 2023) as they picked up more domestic labor and encountered more instability in the labor market. The COVID-19 pandemic also created global demand for remote work and spurred the trends of the "Great Resignation" and "Quiet Quitting."

Remote Work

Remote work (RW) is the process of people conducting their work from homes or spaces other than their official workplace or "organisational work performed outside the normal organisational confines of space and time" (Olson, 1983, p. 182) and is characterized by a lack of physical workplace, limited opportunities to interact in person with co-workers, and flexibility in work schedule. RW is here to stay, despite some CEOs demanding that people return to work as if it were pre-pandemic times with little or no regard for the transformation in values and priorities many workers experienced during and in the aftermath of the COVID-19 pandemic. RW was introduced as early as the 1960s (Arunprasad et al., 2022; Nilles, 1975) and has been favored by workers and organizations to reduce or eliminate long commutes, facilitate knowledge work, acquire and retain talent, and enhance life balance. According to Daly (2020) and SCORE (2021), RW has grown 91% over the past decade, 73% of teams will have remote workers by 2028, 62% of people work remotely part of the time, 38% work outside the office full time, and flexible work is expected to boost the global economy by US$4.5 trillion. RW enhances worker satisfaction, engagement, and organizational commitment and diminishes work-life conflict through its flexible structure. It also increases worker productivity (Lewis & Cooper, 2005), although increased productivity was found to decrease meaning derived from daily activities (George et al., 2022). Box 2.4 explores data regarding RW.

ꜛꜜ BOX 2.4 ADULT CAREER DEVELOPMENT BY THE NUMBERS

Remote and Hybrid Work Expansion

Remote work (RW) became the norm and new expectation during the COVID-19 pandemic. Here are some data on RW:

*   32% of workers worldwide were expected to be hybrid or fully remote by the end of 2021 (Goasduff, 2021).
*   51% of knowledge workers were predicted to work remotely by the end of 2021 (Goasduff, 2021).
*   A projected 40.7 million Americans will be working remotely by 2026 (Ozimek, 2021).
*   64% of employees are willing to pay for office space themselves. 80% of high-income earners are willing to pay, while only 49% of low-income earners are willing to pay (WeWork, 2021).

- 36% of executives say the biggest challenge of hybrid work environments is the loss of corporate culture (PwC, 2021).
- 30% of employees worked remotely before COVID-19. An estimated 48% would continue to work remotely in some capacity after COVID-19 (Goasduff, 2021).

As a career explorer, sustainer, or changer, how does this information align with your experience or expectations for how you work or will work in the future?

Arunprasad et al. (2022) surmised that the COVID-19 pandemic created a new era of RW and conducted bibliometric analysis and critical review of published research to assess challenges related to RW to develop strategies for managing a remote workforce. They noted many RW reviews focus on individual aspects like life balance, worker performance, employee engagement, technology adoption, and leadership.

The "Great Resignation" and "Quiet Quitting"

The phrases, "Great Resignation," "Big Quit" (Rosenberg, 2022), and "Great Reshuffle" (Fox, 2022), along with the trend of "Quiet Quitting" (Marks, 2023), entered the vernacular during the COVID-19 pandemic. The "Great Resignation" was coined by Anthony Klotz in 2021 at University College London, where he worked as an Associate Professor of Management, signaling a mass departure from jobs in the aftermath of the pandemic, or "the under-pinning premise of the Great Resignation is that the COVID-19 pandemic has led to workers actively choosing to re-think the priorities of their material existence" (Marks, 2023, p. 409). "Quiet Quitting" was termed by economist Mark Boldger in 2008 to describe workforce attitude shifts and gained traction from a TikTok video in July 2022 by @zkchillin (now @zaidleppelin) (Marks, 2023). Some scholars debate the actual merits of these phenomena, questioning whether they are factual events or more aligned with dominant neoliberal ideology, especially since the "Great Resignation" was prediction-based rather than empirically based (Marks, 2023). Despite predictions, more people in the US resigned from positions in 2018–2019 (66,856,000) than in 2020–2021 (63,873,000), and there are mixed indicators for whether the "Great Resignation" existed in the UK (Marks, 2023). Others have suggested the COVID-19 pandemic created the ideal conditions and impetus for workers to resign (Klotz, 2022; Ng & Stanton, 2023). Ng and Stanton (2023) reported other forces contributed to resignations, including the pandemic itself creating the right conditions for labor shifts, economic shifts toward accelerated automation and the adoption of telework and the consequential rise of the digital or remote economy, and an ageing workforce opting to retire or work fewer hours. They urged more research on where and when people work, the work being performed, and the collective agency that causes workers to stay in or leave their positions. Box 2.5 provides data on the "Great Resignation."

Ill BOX 2.5 ADULT CAREER DEVELOPMENT BY THE NUMBERS

The "Great Resignation"

As a career explorer, sustainer, or changer, how have you observed or experienced the phenomenon of the "Great Resignation"? Here are some data on worker expectations and trends in the aftermath of the COVID-19 pandemic:

- In 2021, 52% of US workers considered changing jobs (FastCompany, 2021).
- Almost 30% of job applicants report quitting within 90 days of beginning. 43% reported the role did not match their expectations (Doyle, 2020).
- 18% of hourly workers quit due to a lack of flexibility with their positions (My Work Choice & Workplace Intelligence, 2020).
- 98% of workers want to work remotely at least part of the time (Haan, 2023).
- Top Industry for remote workers in 2023 (Haan, 2023):
  - Computer and IT
  - Marketing
  - Accounting and Finance
  - Project Management
  - Medical and Health
  - Human Resources and Recruiting
  - Customer Service
- Remote work demographics (Haan, 2023):
  - 24–35-year-olds have the highest preference for RW.
  - Advanced degree holders (master's and higher) preferred RW more frequently.
  - A gender gap exists in RW:
    - 38% of men RW full time; 23% part time.
    - 30% of women RW full time; 22% part time.
- Remote workers on average, earn US$19,000 more than in-office workers.

Marks (2023) explored whether a mismatch existed in the popularity of the "Great Resignation" and "Quiet Quitting" in the UK, noting that the concepts "have become popular within common discourse because such ideas resonate with an overworked labour force as well as reinforcing the discourse of individualism, precarity and personal responsibility embedded with a neoliberal employment context (Kalleberg, 2012)" (p. 409). She warned that the notion of the "Great Resignation" may have mass appeal since the idea allows workers to regain control of their work lives through which neoliberalism has encouraged workers to function as self-adjusting entrepreneurs to job markets stoked by social media (e.g., "QuitTock") and fake news.

Gulati (2022) argued the "Great Resignation" would be more aptly called the "Great Rethinking" as workers recognized the neoliberal agenda that created low wages, job insecurity or uncertainty, and deteriorating or poor working conditions. Ng and Stanton (2023) urged that:

> Human resource management practitioners are often at the forefront of worker engagement strategies. It is possible that in a time of acute labor shortages employers might understand the value of formal employee voice mechanisms involving unions to include participation in decision making which can lead to increased employee engagement. Employers might be encouraged to adopt more pluralistic approaches to industrial relations in which human resource management practitioners play a key role. (p. 405)

WORKFORCE EQUITY, DIVERSITY, INCLUSION, AND DECOLONIZATION

Equity, diversity, inclusion, and decolonization (EDID) is also referred to as DEI—diversity, equity, and inclusion, DEIB—diversity, equity, inclusion, and belonging, or other combinations of these values and actions to make cultures more welcoming. EDID focuses on decolonization, recognizing that Western ideologies embody certain values, biases, and practices that influence knowledge production (Bermúdez et al., 2016). Bierema et al. (2024) noted, "As understandings of how power structures exclude participation and silence marginalized individuals and groups progress, new labels for these terms emerge to capture what kinds of practices organizations seek to emphasize" (p. 87). Many organizations focus on diversity, particularly of social identities such as race, gender, age, sexuality, or others, but appreciation for diversity alone is not a strategic approach to creating cultures of inclusivity and equity. Understanding and appreciation for EDID is crucial for individuals navigating careers, leaders working to create equitable workplaces, and organizations to ensure justice and equal access to career opportunities for employees.

Equity

To further define EDID drawing on Bierema et al. (2024), equity promotes fairness and justice in organizations and society by creating a systemic transformation that dismantles barriers to the representation and inclusion of women, gender and sexual minorities, historically excluded racial groups, and other populations who have not been privileged in the culture. Equality is often touted as a strategy, yet it is not necessarily about fairness. For example, women and men may be paid similarly (equality). However, the women will still struggle against implicit gender bias and patriarchal culture that diminish their opportunities for career advancement and make their existence in the culture taxing to their sense of self-efficacy in an environment that is not welcoming.

> Equity occurs when every person and community is resourced with what is required for their survival, development, and thriving. Equity does not imply that every person or group has the exact same needs, but rather unique needs rooted in and contextualized by their history, culture, and experience, as well as negative forces of prejudice and bias, which may function to unravel their ability to succeed. (Bierema et al., 2024, p. 88)

Box 2.6 spotlights equity.

ıl BOX 2.6 ADULT CAREER DEVELOPMENT BY THE NUMBERS

Equity

Preserving and improving workplace equity, inclusion, and justice is an on-going responsibility of leaders and all employees. Recent data shows there is much work to do in this area:

- 86% of workers feel they are not heard fairly or equally (Marcroft, 2021).
- Companies that make employees feel heard are 88% more likely to perform well financially (Marcroft, 2021).
- 14% of Americans were bullied at work. More than half never reported it. (Jobvite, 2018).
- Sull et al. (2022) analyzed over 1.4 million Glassdoor reviews to assess the top predictors of employee turnover during the "Great Resignation" due to:

- Toxic corporate culture, specifically failure to promote diversity, equity, and inclusion; disrespecting workers; and behaving unethically.
- Job insecurity and reorganization that create cultures of layoffs and insecurity.
- High levels of innovation that generally require long hours, fast pace, and stress.
- Failure to recognize employee performance.
- Poor response to COVID-19.

As a career explorer, sustainer, or changer, how have your life and work been affected by equity issues?

Diversity and Inclusion

Diversity is the presence of differences in race, gender identity and expression, ethnicity, sex, social class, (dis)ability, indigeneity, age, religion or spirituality, and other identities and positionalities. Diversity initiatives are often detached from organization strategy, mission, and meaningful change. Corporations and universities have been caught overrepresenting racial diversity in their images on social media. For example, Byrd and Sparkman (2022) called out a diversity strategy that promoted economic and competitive advantages while reproducing social injustice. Inclusion is:

> when differences, and systems of equity which respond to differences, are embraced, nurtured, and encouraged. Inclusion does not mean that everyone assimilates into the same culture or way of being. Inclusion is when an environment has been created such that differences lead to better outcomes. (Bierema et al., 2024, p. 89)

Inclusion should accomplish two things: (a) Validation and similarity to others while simultaneously (b) Valuing uniqueness and individuality. Effective work and social cultures make people feel a sense of welcomeness, belonging-ness, and respectfulness.

Decolonization

Decolonization is understanding the impact of colonialism, which is usually the Western world's imposition of cultural, ideological, and economic systems on less powerful countries (Bierema et al., 2024). Decolonization may occur by country or citizen resistance to outside influence and reinforcement of local culture, customs, and values. Colonial values persist in discourse about careers and in HRD, as noted by Bohonos and James-Gallaway (2022), who wrote:

> To date, no historical writing in HRD has primarily focused on the experiences of racially minoritized peoples in the U.S., leaving the field without an adequate foundation from which to address recent calls for racial inclusivity (AHRD Board of Directors, 2020) that have come in response to high profile acts of racial violence in the U.S. (p. 161)

Colonization is difficult to challenge and change since efforts to decolonize often reinforce colonization and must be done with epistemic and cultural humility (Ewuoso, 2023). Epistemic humility is recognizing the limits of one's knowledge and being willing to identify situations when ignorance can cause potential harm and danger. Additionally, epistemic humility is concerned with how people relate to the truth or rationality of their own beliefs relative to experts' knowledge, recognizing that some situations resist knowability and this non-knowing is an enduring and central condition in decision-making (Parviainen et al., 2021). The absence of epistemic humility was a challenge during the COVID-19 pandemic when widespread ignorance about the disease put people in danger and sometimes influenced policy and health advice. Cultural humility is approaching cultures and situations with an ethic of care and with self-reflexivity (capacity to reflect on oneself), appreciation for the new culture, and openness to learning about it and from the people in the culture. Cultural humility is the opposite of cultural competence or the appreciation of diverse cultures, but not necessarily openness to learning and changing when exposed to other cultures and their members (Lekas et al., 2020). Examples of decolonization are giving voice to those affected by colonialism, making data used for decision-making inclusive of diverse people and places, honoring cultural customs and foods, and, in CD terms, ensuring equity of resources and opportunities for education, employment, and business development.

Decolonizing Career Development

McNicholas and Humphries (2005) emphasized that colonization is a common experience among more than 250 million indigenous peoples in over 70 countries. Pillay (2020) wrote about decolonizing CD in post-apartheid South Africa which had a long history of viewing people of color as manual laborers during apartheid, "coinciding with the racist apartheid policies that favoured specifically the country's white minority" (p. 2). Pillay (2020) emphasized further, "Of course even long before the creation of apartheid, the colonisers of the African continent and other lands treated locals and those whom they shipped from other parts of the colonized world as slave labour" (p. 2). The effects of colonization on CD do not affect just individuals. They have lasting economic impact on families, communities, and nations. Pillay (2020) explained the effects of colonization on careers under colonization:

> The extent to which poorer countries are able to offer its citizens the opportunities for careers may appear to be limited—or is that necessarily so? The priority in middle- and low-income countries is obviously to provide jobs for all to ensure adequate standards of living, nutrition, housing, schooling, and health care, among other necessities. Unfortunately, in many nations, those minimum standards are not met because of broader economic and socio-political factors that militate against the development of sufficient formal employment opportunities. (p. 1)

Concerns about resulting poor career decisions mean long-term disadvantages in the job market for this population, especially people desperate to get out of poverty who have access to education but fail to receive effective guidance about career and job opportunities or market trends, which may result in students abandoning their studies when they are a poor fit and even face mental health challenges. Pillay (2020) advocated for equitable career guidance services available to all to promote more timely and accurate career planning, along with encouragement to pursue a career. McNicholas and Humphries (2005) documented Maori women's call for the transformation of "mono-cultural institutions" in New Zealand that allowed them to maintain their Maori identity while working in a corporate accounting firm, which created pressure to assimilate into the dominant culture.

CHAPTER SUMMARY

Chapter 2 situated career development within the social context, covering dynamics that influence the career development context for adults, including VUCA, global capitalism, neoliberalism, technology, a multigenerational workforce, the COVID-19 pandemic, and workforce equity, diversity, inclusion, and decolonization. These dynamics and current social, environmental, and economic events influence how people move through their careers. Individuals, human resource professionals, organizations, and communities can benefit by being aware of how these forces affect perceptions and sometimes behaviors of the workforce.

3. Understanding adult career development theory

Career development (CD) theories help describe patterns people experience
during the "life cycle" of their careers. Generally, a theory is a set of assumptions or hypotheses that explain the past and predict the future. Theories are
applied to provide explanation and direction and undergo testing to prove their

"truth" or lack thereof. CD theory has a long history, and dozens of theories and models exist. This chapter reviews dominant CD theories and models, especially those most relevant to adults. CD theory is generally classified as structural or developmental. Structural career development theories focus on individual characteristics and occupational tasks and finding an ideal match between the two. For example, if a person were good at working with their hands, they would likely be well-matched in construction or mechanical repair roles. Developmental career development theories focus on human development across the lifespan. For example, as people learn and accrue experiences, their career interests generally grow with them. Someone who did not view themselves as a leader might come to do so as they build a repertoire of leadership skills. Table 3.1 summarizes key theories according to the stream and discussion in this chapter.

Table 3.1   Streams of career development theory

Structural	Developmental
• Parsons' early contributions and Trait and Factor (1909) • Theory of Work Adjustment (TWA) • John Holland (1959, 1997): Vocational Personalities and Environments • Brown (1996, 2002): A Values-based Model of Career Choice	• Gottfredson's (2002) Theory of Circumscription and Compromise • Super's Life-span, Life-space Theory (1957) • Lent et al.'s (1994) Social Cognitive Career Theory • Savickas' (1993) Career Construction Theory and Career Construction Modeling

This chapter aims to provide a scan and critique of significant career theories. For a fuller exploration of career theory, it is worth consulting Brown and Lent's (2021) *Career Development and Counseling: Putting Theory and Research* and Robertson et al.'s (2021) *The Oxford Handbook of Career Development*. Career development is complex, with multiple variables and influences impacting a person's decisions about their vocation. Career choices are influenced by psychological, social, economic, geographical, educational, historical, and physical factors (Gunz, 2009; Yates, 2020). Yates (2020) observed that career theory makes the complex simple, which creates problems, particularly CD theory that may focus on part of the picture, making it challenging to apply systemically. Yates (2020) further observed that early-to-mid-20th-century career theories were shaped by positivist epistemology in their search for a single truth to describe CD objectively.

In contrast, in the 21st century, the theory has been influenced by constructivism, the idea that people create meaning based on their experiences and interpretations of them. Yates (2020) also advocated valuing CD theory based on pragmatism—"what problem do I want to solve" (p. 3), appraising the actions career theories lead to, rather than their philosophical standpoints. She offered a thematic analysis of 40 career theories noting that they tend to focus on *identity* or a person's search to discover who they are and who they might become, the *environment,* which is constantly changing and socially constructed, *career learning* focused on building self- and contextual knowledge and understanding how they influence each other, and *psychological career resources* or the variables that facilitate the effective navigation of a career and the choices needed.

STRUCTURAL THEORIES OF CAREER DEVELOPMENT

As noted, the structural theories of career development (CD) seek to strike the perfect match between a person and their work environment. Yates' (2020) observation was that earlier career theories were positivist—seeking one correct solution to CD. This section reviews Parson's contributions and his trait and factor theory, the theory of work adjustment, Holland's vocational personalities and environments, and the values-based model of career choice.

Frank Parsons

Frank Parsons founded the vocational guidance or career counseling movement in the early 20th century. His theoretical work and practical applications continue to influence CD. However, in a changing work context, a perfect person-job fit today may rapidly become irrelevant as markets shift, technology advances, and the economy becomes unstable.

Parsons' early contributions
Frank Parsons (1909) is one of CD's earliest theorists who shaped career assessment and counseling as it is known today. He was concerned with providing career assistance to the poor and disadvantaged and advocated a tripartite model, which remains foundational to CD that values:

1. A clear understanding of oneself, aptitudes, abilities, interests, resources, limitations, and other qualities
2. Knowledge of the requirements and conditions of career success, advantages and disadvantages, compensation, opportunities, and prospects in different lines of work
3. True reasoning on the relations of these two groups of facts (Parsons, 1909, p. 5).

Parsons advocated matching self-knowledge with work knowledge to arrive at a career decision, which became the basis of the trait and factor and person-environment fit theories of CD.

McMahon and Arthur (2018) emphasized how Parsons' (1909) theoretical work informed career theory's philosophical positions: logical positivism and constructivism. Logical positivism—reliance on scientific, objective, observable knowledge—would suggest that career decisions should be derived through appropriate matching (assessment) and objective knowledge to allow the discovery of the ideal person-job fit. The approach is disconnected from context, a primary critique, which also has implications for whether a person is privileged or marginalized in a particular organization or community. Constructivism—the belief people actively build knowledge and meaning of their reality—would suggest that people actively construct meaning from their experiences and environment and use those. Constructivist career theories came later in the history of CD, although in Parsons' work, finding the ideal person-job fit required meaning-making of the individual.

Parsons' trait and factor theory
Parsons (1909) evolved his early career theorizing into a process whereby a choice of a vocation depended upon (a) An accurate knowledge of oneself to include aptitudes, abilities, interests, ambitions, resources, and limitations; plus (b) A thorough knowledge of job specifications to include requirements and conditions of success, advantages and disadvantages, compensation, opportunities, and prospects in different lines of work. The key to this approach is having the ability to make a proper match between self-knowledge and job knowledge. Two significant assumptions of trait and factor theory are that: (a) Individuals and job traits can be matched, and (b) Close matches positively correlate with job success and satisfaction. Parsons believed there was one vocational choice at one point in time, and his ideas are still part of career counseling approaches today. Box 3.2 provides some questions typical of career advising in this approach.

☙ BOX 3.2 TIPS AND TOOLS FOR CAREER DEVELOPMENT

Following Parsons' Seven Stages for Career Counseling

Parsons (1909) outlined steps for career counselors to work through with clients in his book *Choosing a Vocation.* These have been modified for you, as a career explorer, sustainer, or changer, to work through by yourself or

with a trusted advisor.
1. Make a list of facts about yourself that offer insight into your career exploration, challenge, or desires.
2. Engage in self-analysis of the career facts you have noted in step 1. What are the patterns or themes you notice?
3. Although you may have listed several things in steps 1 and 2, what resonates with you most from these reflections and lists?
4. Test your analysis with people who know you well to see if it aligns with their knowledge of you.
5. Conduct some research on your most favored careers. O*Net, as described in Box 3.3, can be a helpful tool for this step.
6. Seek insights and advice by talking with people in this career. Conduct an informational interview with people in this career. Find out strategies for succeeding at the particular career path.
7. Develop a plan to prepare yourself for this career or career shift.

Theory of Work Adjustment

Theory of Work Adjustment (TWA) was initially developed by René V. Dawis, George England, and Lloyd H. Lofquist in 1964 at the University of Minnesota. The theory conceptualizes work as an interaction between an individual and a work environment. TWA is one of the typical PEC (person-environment congruence) theories. The work environment (E) requires tasks or roles to be performed, and persons (P) bring skills to perform the tasks or roles. In response to the demands of the workplace, the individuals expect to satisfy work values, such as achievement, autonomy, status, altruism, comfort, and safety (C). Table 3.2 summarizes the explanations of the TWA work values.

Table 3.2   TWA work values and definitions

TWA work values	Definition
Achievement:	Results-oriented work is where employees use their strongest abilities, giving them a feeling of accomplishment.
Autonomy (independence):	Employees are trusted to work on their own and make decisions.
Status (recognition):	The role offers advancement, and potential for leadership, and is often considered prestigious.
Altruism (relationships):	Employees provide service to others and work with co-workers in a friendly non-competitive environment.

TWA work values	Definition
Comfort (support):	The work environment is characterized by supportive management that stands behind employees.
Safety (working conditions):	Employees enjoy job security and good working conditions.

TWA is most applicable when there is a good correspondence or match between the person and the environment—a fit between the person, work, and organization. Yet environments are not static and may change over time, potentially creating job instability, such as during a recession or a global pandemic. Sometimes people make poor career choices, and organizations make poor hires, which means the correspondence is deficient or a discorrespondence—a clash between the person and the environment. For example, a person might take a sales position and discover they dislike trying to sell a product or service. The work environment's flexibility can mitigate the lack of correspondence. For example, if the worker did not like the pace of the environment once they adjusted to their job, securing flexibility in work hours might compensate for the lack of correspondence, which might have been flexible hours or working with preferred clients. When the correspondence is high and flexibility is low (the person loves sales but dislikes the long hours), people tend to actively adjust their work environment by shifting the job to be better aligned with their abilities. This might mean the person shifts from sales to product or service support. If this change is not possible, people may seek different working conditions or more variation in the work. In this case, perhaps the salesperson is good at sales, but they dislike the lifestyle and shift to training the sales force. Training can also be an option when correspondence is lacking, where the salesperson learns how to teach other salespeople. Reactive adjustment is the other approach that might result in the person changing their behaviors to better align with the environment or by changing personal priorities or work values. Persistence is the degree to which people or environments adjust before giving up, which usually means the person quits or is fired. Discorrespondence or disconnection can occur for either the person or the environment: people may be unhappy with their work or career choices, or organizations may be dissatisfied with the person.

Swanson and Schneider (2021) concluded that TWA is well-constructed and applicable across the lifespan. TWA is also useful for forecasting occupations that will lead to satisfaction and helping individuals identify work-related needs, values, and abilities. Critiques of TWA include that more research is needed on using this model with diverse populations. A few studies have indicated support of TWA with culturally stigmatized groups, including lesbian, gay, and bisexual individuals, African American workers, Latinx immigrant workers, women of color, late-career workers, and individuals with intellectual disabilities (Swanson & Schneider, 2021). The theory also has relevance for adults since work adjustment and correspondence dynamics are common experiences for many people during their work lives. Box 3.3 introduces O*Net OnLine as a tool to help identify correspondence in career choices according to TWA, among many other resources and services.

⩔ BOX 3.3 TIPS AND TOOLS FOR CAREER DEVELOPMENT

Using O*Net OnLine

An essential aspect of making career decisions is having excellent information. O*Net OnLine is a US Department of Labor tool designed to help "new job seekers, students, and other career explorers investigate over 900 occupations" (O*Net OnLine, n.d., para. 4). The platform provides an interactive web-based tool to help job seekers conduct searches on worker characteristics, worker requirements, experience requirements, occupational requirements, workforce characteristics, occupation-specific information, and more. O*Net has multiple tools, including an interest profiler, veteran support, assessment tools, and search engines that facilitate searching for job titles and locations to learn about salaries and related occupations. Check it out to enhance job searching and occupational knowledge by:

Visiting O*Net:
https://www.onetonline.org/

Seeing the O*NET Overview:
https://www.dol.gov/agencies/eta/onet#:~:text=O*NET%20OnLine%20is %20a,detail%20on%20a%20specific%20subject

Searching O*Net by the TWA work values:
https://www.onetonline.org/find/descriptor/browse/1.B.2/

This section of the O*Net resource provides occupations that reinforce each work value. The work environment and individuals continuously interact to meet each other's requirements. "Correspondence" is the degree to which the requirements of both are met, and "work adjustment" refers to the process of maintaining and achieving correspondence (University of Minnesota, n.d.).

John Holland: Vocational Personalities and Environments

Like TWA, Holland's (1959, 1997) vocational-personality typology is a model of person-environment vocational fit or match (Swanson & Schneider, 2021). Disequilibrium occurs when there is disharmony between the person and the environment. Holland's typology theory was developed to (a) Organize the voluminous data about people in different jobs and the data about different work environments and (b) Suggest how people make career choices and explain how job satisfaction and vocational achievement occur. Holland's approach was based on the belief that people function, grow, and find satisfaction in work environments that reflect their personalities. He inferred that by late adolescence, most people can be distinguished by how closely they resemble six basic personality types of *realistic, investigative, artistic, social, enterprising,* and *conventional* (often referred to by the acronym RIASEC) and likely a result of people's cultural and personal environment incorporating peers, biological heredity, family, social class, culture, and surroundings (Nauta, 2021).

Holland (1959, 1997) emphasized that all six types are present in each person, although most people have a dominant type which is usually evidenced most strongly in career choices. People may even resemble up to three types (Holland, 1997). A brief overview of the six personality types, work-related activities, and sample occupations is presented in Table 3.3.

Table 3.3   *Holland's RIASEC typology*

Type	General job activities	Typical occupations
Realistic	Working with animals, tools, and machines and valuing practical, tangible things that can be created or improved.	Farmer Carpenter Mechanical engineer Athletes
Investigative	Working with information, abstract ideas, and theories to solve problems. Prefers not to lead.	Chemist Physician Computer analyst
Artistic	Creating things like art, drama, crafts, music, writing, or dance that provide variety and independence.	Painter Writer Musician
Social	Helping people through teaching, nursing, information sharing, problem-solving, and serving.	Social worker Counselor Teacher

Type	General job activities	Typical occupations
Enterprising	Persuading and leading others. Sociable.	Entrepreneur Sales representative Manager
Conventional	Organizing data in an orderly fashion and creating solid plans.	Administrative assistant Editor Accountant

Holland (1985) developed assessments of the RIASEC types, including the Vocational Preference Inventory (VPI) and the Self-Directed Search (SDS) (Holland & Messer, 2013).

It is worth noting "Holland's theory emphasizes the accuracy of self-knowledge and career information necessary for career decision making" (Zunker, 1994, p. 49). Although the theory appears to apply to both women and men workers, Holland's theory has been criticized for underlying gender, race, and class bias. For instance, women frequently score predominately in three personality types: artistic, social, and conventional. Holland suggested that sexism inclines women to display a greater interest in feminine-type occupations. Given these shortcomings, people other than White men may want to regard their RIASEC results cautiously and seek different types of assessment before making career decisions.

Values-based Model of Career Choice

Brown's (1996) model of CD is based on the importance of values in career decision-making—cultural, life, and work values. Values are shaped by genetics and environment, and people use them to guide and explain their behavior. The values-based model of career choice is based on seven propositions:

1. Values with high priorities are the most critical determinants of choices made. For example, if service were highly important, a person may work in a non-profit or a helping profession.
2. The values included in the values system are acquired from society. What people learn from family, friends, peers, and their communities shapes what they care about in life.
3. Culture, gender, race, and socioeconomic status influence opportunities and social interaction and thus create considerable variation in values. A person growing up in poverty may value stability, whereas a more privileged person might value upward mobility.
4. Making choices that coincide with values is essential to satisfaction. If relationships are valuable, a career fostering healthy relationships might be important.

5. The result of role interaction is life satisfaction. Life and work roles are satisfying when people can fulfill what is important to them (caretaker, leader, problem solver, and so forth).
6. High-functioning people have well-developed and prioritized values.
7. Success in any role depends on the abilities and aptitudes required to perform the functions of that role.

Box 3.4 provides a chance to examine values related to careers.

⌣ BOX 3.4 REFLECTIVE PRACTICE

Assessing Values and Applying Them to Career Choice

Brown's (1996) Values-based Model of Career Choice put values into three categories with subcategories. In Table 3.4, the categories are elaborated for reflection. An interesting side note is that Kurt Lewin, often called the "Father of Organization Development," is credited with foundational thinking for the Time Perspective Theory that plays a role in cultural values (Stolarski et al., 2015).

Consider the values as a career explorer, sustainer, or changer and how your key values in each area influence your engagement with life and work. Reflect on the questions and complete the activities in each section of Table 3.4.

Table 3.4   Assessing values and applying them to career choice

Cultural values	Life values	Work values
Social relations:	Life roles and choices:	The values I fulfill through work:
• What do I value in my relationships with others? • What do others value in me? • How trustworthy am I?	• What are my primary roles in life? • What choices have I made to fulfill those roles? • Which roles have I neglected?	• What values are most important to me in my work? • Steps to identifying work values: • Make a list of your key work values. • Rank each from 1–10 with 1 = low, 10 = high. • Use the values ranked at 5+ to guide your career.

Cultural values	Life values	Work values
Time: Time perspective is how people focus on the past, present, or future. What is your perspective? • Past: Focus can be positive or negative. Past-positive is a nostalgic, warm, and sentimental view of the past. Past-negative can feel haunting and unpleasant. • Present: Focus can be hedonistic or fatalistic. Present hedonists live in the moment, seek pleasure, and enjoy high-intensity activities. Present fatalistics might feel helpless, hopeless, or that external forces control their lives. • Future: Goal-oriented, sometimes at the expense of the present.	Relationships with significant others: • Relational competence (RC) is forming, developing, and maintaining satisfying relationships (Afifi & Coveleski, 2015). How would you rate your own RC? • Relational cultural theory (RCT) (Singh & Moss, 2016) combines RCs and integrates them with multiculturalism, intersectionality, resilience, and strengths-based foci (Singh & Moss, 2016). How culturally relational are you (e.g., comfortable with people different from you)?	Identify core values: • If you are still unsure after completing your ranking of values, consider these questions: • What work culture would allow you to thrive? • What is your ideal work environment? • What kind of work relationships are ideal? • How do you hope to learn and grow in your work? • What support do you need (e.g., mentoring, coaching)? • Ask your family, friends, and co-workers about their work values.
Relationship to nature: • To what degree do I feel connected to nature? • How do I connect with nature? • What do I do to help preserve nature?	Citizenship: • How informed are you about issues affecting your community? • How do you participate in the democratic process in your community, state, or nation? • How do you serve your community?	Alignment between your values and your work: • How aligned are my key values with my work? • Where are the areas of misalignment?
Activity: • How do I recharge my sense of well-being? • What is my source of exercise? • How do I manage stress?	Work: • How connected is my work to my life's purpose? • What identity does my work hold in terms of how I see myself?	Seek work aligned with your values: • O*NET OnLine allows people to browse by work values of achievement, independence, recognition, relationships, support, and working conditions. • What is important to you among O*NET's list?

Cultural values	Life values	Work values
Self-control:		
• How tuned-in am I to my emotions and desires? • How do I handle disappointment or difficulty? • I would describe my willpower as …		

DEVELOPMENTAL THEORIES OF CAREER DEVELOPMENT

The emergence of developmental theories represented a shift away from the notion that identifying the ideal person-environment fit was crucial to helping people find their best career paths. Developmental theories take account of learning and growth across the lifespan, how they influence career decisions and experiences, and how they affect people's capacity to make meaning about their careers. This section will discuss the theory of circumscription and compromise; life-span, life-space theory; social cognitive career theory; and career construction theory and career construction modeling. Developmental theories tend to draw on constructivist learning theory—people build their own meaning from experience.

Gottfredson's Theory of Circumscription and Compromise

Gottfredson's (2002) theory demonstrates how career aspirations develop based on circumscription—ruling out unacceptable career options based on the person's perceived fit with the developing self-perception, and compromise—people sacrifice roles that may be more compatible with their self-concept for those that appear to be more accessible; of course, these compromises depend on the amount of career information, social networks, and education available. The theory is based on four assumptions:

> (1) The career development (CD) process begins in childhood; (2) career aspirations are attempts to implement one's self-concept; (3) career satisfaction depends on the degree of which the career is congruent with self-perceptions; and (4) people develop occupational stereotypes that guide them in the selection process. (Brown, 2016, p. 80)

Gottfredson (2002, pp. 96–100) suggested four developmental stages. Box 3.5 summarizes the stages and provides reflective questions.

⊙ BOX 3.5 REFLECTIVE PRACTICE

Applying Gottfredson's Four Developmental Stages

Gottfredson's theory of circumscription and compromise was developed to illuminate how children and adolescents may compromise their careers based on their circumstances. However, it has also been applied to women's CD given the competing demands and roles women face at home, work, and in society. Review the stages in Table 3.5 and reflect on how your circumstances as a career explorer, sustainer, or changer impacted your career decision-making or how you compromised your career.

Table 3.5   Applying Gottfredson's four developmental stages

Stage	Age	Developmental process
Orientation to gender roles	6–8	Children at this stage begin to understand the concept of gender roles but focus primarily on their most visible cues, such as overt activities and clothing. Vocational aspiration at this stage reflects a concern with doing what is appropriate for one's gender, and gender stereotypes begin emerging.
Orientation to social valuation	9–13	At this stage, youngsters become very sensitive to social evaluation, whether by peers or the larger society and thus the status conveyed by certain careers. They start to recognize the more concrete symbols of social class (e.g., clothing). Also, they begin to sense a ceiling and a floor for their career aspirations based on their families and communities. Such perceptions lead children to set a "tolerable-effort boundary," above which they are not apt to look again unless their self-conceptions of ability and competitiveness change.
Orientation to the internal, unique self	14+	Adolescents become better able to apprehend and integrate highly abstract, complex information. Occupational exploration is confined to the zone of acceptable alternatives circumscribed at earlier stages. Although the first three stages involve rejecting unacceptable alternatives, this stage is devoted to identifying which acceptable choices are the most preferred and most attainable.

According to Gottfredson, when people are compelled to compromise career choices, they tend to compromise first on the field of work, next on a social level, and finally on gender type, although the research on these choices is mixed (Blanchard & Lichtenbert, 2003; Hesketh et al., 1990). This model is helpful for people of all ages and can be useful in challenging gender stereotypes in career roles. The theory's principles apply to all ages and are important because they capture some of women's challenges and others' caretaking responsibilities. As with any of the theories, engaging in self-assessment and consulting with others can be helpful in decision-making, as will being aware of how history or stereotyping might prevent people from seeking certain roles or careers.

Super's Life-span, Life-space Theory

Donald Super (1957) and other CD theorists recognized the changes people experience as they mature. They suggested that career patterns are determined by (a) Socioeconomic factors, (b) Mental and physical abilities, (c) Personal characteristics, and (d) Exposure to opportunities. Career maturity, a central concept in Super's theory, is manifested in accomplishing age and stage developmental tasks across the lifespan. Super and Thompson (1979) identified six factors in career maturity: (a) Awareness of the need to plan, (b) Decision-making skills, (c) Knowledge and use of information resources, (d) General career information, (e) General world of work information, and (f) Detailed information about occupations of preference.

Super viewed career choice and development in three ways: (a) Movement through discrete developmental stages with corresponding developmental tasks across the lifespan—the course of a person's life; (b) Arrangement of worker and life roles that create the psychosocial life space—roles of child, student, citizen, leisure, worker, friend, and family member—where people design their lives; and (c) The implementation of self-concept—the whole person in terms of physical, emotional, social, and spiritual aspects—in work roles (Hartung, 2021). According to Hartung (2021), people develop a sense of self in contexts of time and space across their lifespan within life space, with vocational behavior that is dynamic, continuous, and fluid. The theory has also proven helpful for creating interventions to assist people with CD across their lifespan. It is one of the most influential and empirically supported CD theories (Hartung, 2021), making it applicable to adult CD.

People seek career satisfaction through work roles in which they can express themselves and implement and develop their self-concepts. Vocational self-concept is an underlying factor in Super's model that develops through physical and mental growth, observations of work, identification with working adults, engagement in the work environment, and general experiences. Super's contribution was formalizing stages and developmental tasks over the lifespan. Table 3.6 in Box 3.6 lists the features of the theory with a column for self-reflection on your experience at each stage as a career explorer, sustainer, and changer.

☺ BOX 3.6 REFLECTIVE PRACTICE

Applying Super's Life Stages, Ages, and Characteristics

Super's CD and choice stages are listed in Table 3.6 with space for you to reflect on your experience with each stage to date as a career explorer, sustainer, or changer. Considerations as you answer each stage might be:

- What were pivotal experiences or turning points in career choices?
- How have your values, interests, and skills evolved influenced your career goals?
- What role has education played in your career?
- How have your relationships impacted your CD?

Table 3.6   Applying Super's life stages, ages, and characteristics

Stage	Age	Characteristics	My reflections on each stage:
Growth	Birth to 14/15	• Shape self-concept • Build capacity • Form attitudes • Consider future • Cultivate interests and work habits • Identify needs • Formulate a general concept of work • Assume responsibility for life	
Exploratory	15–24	• "Try out" potential careers through: • Classes • Work experience • Hobbies • Make career choices • Complete appropriate training • Collect relevant information • Engage in skill development related to choices • Build healthy relationships	
Establishment	25–44	• Enter a career path • Build skills and knowledge • Perform work effectively • Stabilize in a career • Accrue experience • Hone attitude and productive work habits	

Stage	Age	Characteristics	My reflections on each stage:
Maintenance	45–64	• Make continual adjustments • Seek advancement • Continue learning	
Decline	65+	• Reduce output • Prepare for retirement • Disengage from work activities • Transition to retirement	

Although Super originally presented the stages and tasks in a sequential manner, he later refined his position to account for recycling through the developmental tasks over the lifespan. Adults adapt to personal and workplace changes throughout their lives as they, their work, or the environment change. Table 3.7 summarizes vocational development tasks, when they typically occur, and their characteristics.

Table 3.7   *Super's vocational developmental tasks, ages, and characteristics*

Vocational developmental task	Ages	General characteristics
Crystallization	14–18	Developing and planning a tentative vocational goal
Specification	18–21	Firming the vocational goal
Implementation	21–24	Training for and obtaining employment
Stabilization	24–35	Working and confirming career choice
Consolidation	35+	Advancement in career

Lent, Brown, & Hackett's Social Cognitive Career Theory

Lent et al.'s (2002) social cognitive career theory (SCCT) builds upon the assumption that cognitive factors are essential in CD and decision-making. People's career possibilities and developmental paths are influenced by personal attributes (e.g., interests, abilities, values), socialization and learning experiences, access to resources and opportunities, and encounters with barriers (Lent, 2021). Lent (2021) explained that none of these factors determines a CD trajectory but rather the complex ways they interact.

SCCT is closely linked to Krumboltz's theory and based on Bandura's (1977) social cognitive theory and seeks to unify understanding of how people develop career interests, make career decisions, attain career success and stability, experience a satisfying work environment, and manage predictable work events (decisions, multiple roles, or transitions) (Lent, 2021). The theory concerns how people, behaviors, and environments influence each other. SCCT underscores the complex, dynamic ways people see themselves, strive for future goals, and behave within their work contexts with varying degrees of social support and financial stability. This theory also recognizes that people or environments can change in ways that bring about change. The COVID-19 pandemic served as an environmental change that affected levels of support and financial stability and caused some people to reassess their self-concept, future career goals, or work behaviors. Other environmental factors such as globalization, downsizing, or technological change can also shift people's career trajectories. SCCT highlights the following three concepts that influence each other and enable agency in CD (Lent, 2021): self-efficacy beliefs, outcome expectations, and personal goals.

Self-efficacy beliefs
Self-efficacy beliefs are the judgments people make about their capabilities. Bandura (1986) identified these beliefs as key determinants of thought and action. Self-efficacy is not synonymous with self-esteem, or sense of self-worth. It is beliefs about performing activities in specific contexts. For example, a person may have strong self-efficacy in their ability to analyze data but less confidence about describing the data analysis in public. Lent (2021) explained how beliefs about personal capabilities can change based on future experiences and the social context. For instance, the data analyst might have an unsupportive manager who is impatient with their technical explanations, and they might do better when discussing their work in a safer environment or through writing up their results. Beliefs about capabilities are acquired and modified according to four sources of information (Lent, 2021), including (a) Personal performance accomplishments, (b) Vicarious learning (e.g., observing others), (c) Social persuasion, and (d) Psychological and affective states. Returning to the data analyst example, they might challenge themselves to perform better when presenting analysis (personal performance), learn from watching colleagues skilled at presenting (vicarious learning), receive encouragement and support from colleagues, or feel peer pressure to do better (social persuasion), or perform differently based on how confident or safe they are feeling with the context (psychological and affective states).

Outcome expectations
Outcome expectations are beliefs about the outcomes or consequences of behavior. "Whereas self-efficacy beliefs are concerned with one's capabilities (e.g., 'Can I do this?'), outcome expectations involve imagined consequences of particular courses of action (e.g., 'If I do this, what will happen?')" (Lent,

2021, p. 133). These dynamics play a role in the careers people seek and avoid. Self-efficacy may influence a person to take on expensive training or a difficult challenge, such as becoming a medical doctor, and the outcome expectations could be either focused on the prestige or helping ethic of physicians. However, another outcome expectation might be a belief the person would not have good bedside manner or excel at science. Lent also explained that sometimes, a person's self-efficacy is high, but they still have low outcome expectations, like a woman who is excellent at math but does not want to take math courses or pursue an engineering career because of adverse social reactions or discrimination. A woman friend of mine reacted differently. She studied engineering for her graduate degree (high self-efficacy). Still, she was continually being graded harder than the men, so she changed her name to a gender-neutral one, and her experience shifted because she was able to influence outcome expectations ("If I change my name, will I be graded more fairly?"). Of course, it is inexcusable that she was forced to take that course of action, but in the end, it allowed her to excel at her chosen career. Most people prefer to work with people and organizations where their work is valued and outcomes are positive, which would influence people's levels of engagement, effort, persistence, and results, according to this theory.

Personal goals
Personal goals are a person's determination to engage in certain activities or seek particular outcomes. SSCT distinguishes *choice-content goals*—the activity or career one wants to pursue—from *performance goals*, the level of performance sought for a particular activity. SCCT is less concerned with ages and stages of life and more focused on factors that help or hurt career behaviors across developmental tasks over time (Lent, 2021). Wang et al. (2022) identified the advantages and disadvantages of SCCT. SCCT is beneficial as it provides a systemic approach to CD that responds to a person's development in interaction with social context across their career. It also focuses on special needs in making career decisions, including people with mental health disorders, institutionalized youth, immigrant high schoolers, rural students, and secondary school students with mild special education needs. They also outlined challenges with this theory, such as a lack of qualitative research methods to validate the SCCT framework, a lack of qualitative assessment tools, and a lack of intervention approaches.

SCCT was created to understand the CD processes of diverse people with consideration for gender, race, ethnicity, gender identity and expression, social class, age, (dis)ability, culture, and other identities (Lent, 2021). The theory has been applied to understanding women's CD in particular. However, Lent (2021) observed that additional research is needed on how social cognitive variables interact with various identities and positionalities.

Rethinking adult career development

Career Construction Theory and Career Construction Modeling

Career construction theory (CCT) and career construction modeling (CCM) take a holistic approach to consider people's interpretive and interpersonal processes that influence how they organize personal characteristics and take vocational actions (Savickas, 2021). Considered a theory applicable to multicultural societies in a global context, career construction theory studies how people build careers by making meaning of vocational behavior. This theory fills a void in constructivist CD theories and practices where people create career meaning, particularly in a rapidly shifting job market where people may be preparing for jobs that currently do not exist (Grier-Reed & Conkel-Ziebell, 2009). CCT also applies to adult learning and constructivist education theory that views learners as active creators of knowledge, not passive recipients of what they are told to think or how to act. Career construction modeling composes activities associated with CCT, often with the support of a career counselor, to help people use their life stories, interests, talents, and goals to develop a career plan. Grier-Reed and Conkel-Ziebell (2009) shared their CD course that drew on Super's self-concept (1990) and meaning-making (Savickas, 1993; Schultheiss, 2007) with emphasis on three significant perspectives of CD of a career as (a) Self-realization, (b) Growing experiences, and (c) Context conceptualization using the tools of narrative (career storytelling), action (experimenting and building insight about culture, values, and beliefs), construction (creating identity within a context), and interpretation (informing career choices with personal identity and meaning).

Understanding the self-constructing processes of organizing, regulating, and conceiving characterize CCT, where people develop as social actors— intellectual abilities and personal characteristics that build a person's reputation, motivated agents—developers of educational and career goals with plans to achieve them, and autobiographical author-composers of career story narratives (Savickas, 2021). Box 3.7 provides the opportunity to apply aspects of CCT to career experiences.

⸱ BOX 3.7 TIPS AND TOOLS FOR CAREER DEVELOPMENT

Constructivist Career Questions for Reflection

Grier-Reed and Conkel-Ziebell (2009) described activities to help learners reflect on the self, experiences, and context to make meaning about their career. Glavin and Savickas (2010) have created a website, Vocopher, with

CD tools. Answer the questions and complete the activities as a career explorer, sustainer, and/or changer.

1. Career as self-realization: Consider identities and positionalities that most define how you see yourself, such as race, gender, sexuality, gender identity and expression, class, spirituality, religion, work, education level, family, ability, neighborhood or community, or other important identities. Once you have pinpointed salient aspects for yourself, answer the following questions:
   a. I think about this aspect of my identity the most:
   b. I think about this aspect of my identity the least:
   c. The aspect of my identity most emphasized in my family was/is:
   d. The aspect of my identity least stressed in my family was/is:
   e. I feel most discomfort about this part of my identity:
   f. The part of my identity that most affects how people treat me is:
   g. The most painful experience I had as a result of this discomfort:
   h. The most rewarding experience I had as a result of this discomfort:
2. Career growing experiences:
   a. What is one example of when my career was stalled and not developing? What did I or can I learn from this experience?
   b. What is one example of a time when my career grew and developed? What did I or can I learn from this experience?
3. Career context conceptualization using tools: Visit www.Vocopher .com and complete the CCT exercises or activities that appeal to you as a career explorer, sustainer, or changer. To use the restricted areas, use code 7375.

CAREERS AS METAPHORS

Theory can be challenging to digest, although it is helpful to see something through the vocational choices, challenges, and changes adults make during their career lifespan. This section takes an alternative approach to understanding adult CD and reviews its metaphors. A metaphor is a way of comparing a phenomenon to something that lacks literal truth, or to things that are not related. For example, someone might describe a demanding workday as "a nightmare," or "a trainwreck," or a good day as "a dream" or "triumph." None of these descriptors is literally true, but they provide a visualization of the experience. Inkson (2004) offered a metaphorical framework to understand careers, observing,

> For most of us, careers are figural. We watch our own careers avidly; narrate, compose, and analyze them in our minds; and try as best we can to make sense of the past, decisions for the present, and plans for the future. (p. 96)

Metaphors provide a symbolic way of understanding and applying career theory to real life. Inkson called them "lenses" or "images," and some career metaphors become a part of regular discourse as people often talk about work. Familiar career metaphors often heard might refer to "being in a rut," "hitting a plateau," "climbing the ladder," "working in a dead-end job," "developing a career path," "hitting the glass or concrete ceiling," or "being on the fast track," to mention several. Inkson's ten metaphors are briefly introduced in this section with definitions, examples, and theoretical bases drawing on Inkson (2004) and Yates (2022). They are included as alternative ways to make meaning of theory and translate it to adult life experience. Metaphors are also helpful in seeing the flaws of CD theories and practice.

Legacy Metaphor: Career as Inheritance

Career choice is socialized and passed from generation to generation, influenced by positionalities of social class, gender, ethnicity, and other factors that shape career values and aspirations. These choices are known as career inheritance (Goodale & Hall, 1976). For example, a medical doctor might come from generations of physicians, or women might be socialized into gendered occupations such as teaching, service, or nursing. Similarly, the cycle of poverty can be replicated in this metaphor, where family socioeconomic and occupational status are repeated in the next generation. Inkson (2004) emphasized "Individuals consciousness of their career inheritance may empower them to decide whether they will seek to reject the inheritance and pursue their careers autonomously. Everyone who takes careers seriously needs to consider the extent and power of the inherited aspect" (p. 101). Legacy career theory can be understood through Roberts' (2009) opportunity structures (how available opportunities temper aspirations), Law's (1981) theory on community interaction's influence on career perceptions, and Gottfredson's (2002) theory of conscription and compromise that considers how family context influences career choice.

Craft Metaphor: Career as Construction

This metaphor centers the individual as the primary actor in forging a career with the agency to self-author a career identity that helps develop a sense of self and balances functionality and creativity as the person crafts a career. Inkson (2004) explained that the creative process seeks to unify self and work, help learning through work, and integrate the career process and product in the person's life space. He noted, "The product (the career) simultaneously enables the individual to solve life-problems (such as earning a living) in a practical way, and to implement his or her personal sense of self" (p. 101). Likely influenced by constructivism, this approach is about people making meaning about their work and selves as they blur the lines between work and life, akin to Savickas et al.'s (2009) description of career processes as "Life Design." Theoretical ties are also Super and Šverko's (1995) life-span, life-space model and Lent et al.'s (2002) socio-cognitive career choice theory. This approach also ties in with Gedro's (2017) identity and CD work.

Seasons Metaphor: Career as Cycle

Perhaps the best-known theories regarding the human life cycle are Levinson's (1978) *The Seasons of a Man's Life* and Sheehy's (1995) *New Passages: Mapping your life across time.* These developmental approaches recognize sequential age-related career phases (e.g., Levinson's 1978 exploration, direction, mid-life transition, maintenance, or classifying career stages as early, mid, and late) and how different life stages bring new career challenges and foci. For example, the priorities and worries of a single adult starting a career will be different from one with a family dependent on their income who makes a mid-life career change. Theoretical bases of career cycles include Super's (1957) developmental theory, Mainiero and Sullivan's (2005) kaleidoscope model that incorporates the influence of gender on career motivators, or Boyatzis et al.'s (2000) description of career processes as spiraling.

Matching Metaphor: Career as "Fit"

The saying, "You can't fit a square peg in a round hole," captures the essence of a career as "fit." Parsons (1909) was the first to write about matching people to their work environments and has been highly influential on the development of career theory and practice, or the quest to pair the person with the work environment, for example, putting a highly sociable person in a service-oriented role. Inkson (2004) described the "fit" metaphor as a mental model of career development practice. This metaphor influenced Holland's (1997) vocational personality theory and corresponding assessment. Inkson lamented,

> The metaphor of matching raises conceptual and practical issues. What characteristics of people and situations really matter, and how are they best conceptualized? How measurable are individuals and environmental opportunities and characteristics, and how accurate are assessments? Is fit achieved by matching people to positions or positions to people? Most crucially, does the fit metaphor induce static thinking about dynamic processes? The imagery of pegs and holes has a stolid character, and socializing institutions such as families, schools, trade, unions, and professional associations often emphasize permanence of fit. (p. 103)

The notion of the protean career (Hall, 1996) is the polar opposite of "fit," where adults adjust their career fit to suit their current circumstances.

Path Metaphor: Career as Journey

Inkson (2004) described the journey metaphor as "conceptualiz[ing] the career as *movement*, which may take place geographically, between jobs, between occupations, or between organizations. The journey metaphor is attractive because of its ability to incorporate two key underlying facets of career: *movement between places*, and *time*" (p. 103, italics in original). He noted that the notion of journey was problematic because journeys can take multiple forms with or without a destination, route, or direction. Career theorists gravitating to the journey concept refer to the movement as linear and spiral (Driver, 1985).

Network Metaphor: Career as Encounters and Relationships

Inkson (2002, 2004) described the network as the most common career metaphor that threads through people's talk about their work lives. An informal network is "the set of job-related contacts that a manager relies on for access to task-related, career, and social support" (Ibarra, 1995, p. 674).

"Networking is connecting, communicating, and interacting with peers within a community" (Bierema et al., 2024, p. 242), and one of the key developmental relationships that are important to career progression, in addition to mentoring, sponsoring, and coaching. Developmental relationships are "the people and connections that ... promote interdependent generative connections that result in growth and learning among individuals" (Hutchins & Ghosh, 2022, p. 1).

Networks serve social and political purposes—social in cultivating long-term relationships that support career progression and political in relying on these relationships to secure career advancement and advantage. "Through encounters and the development of relationships we integrate ourselves into wider systems and structures, which often shape and are shaped by the career itself" (Inkson, 2004, p. 104). The adage, "It's not what you know, it's who you know," captures the importance of networks in accessing career opportunities. The network approach is less of a theory and more of a career strategy, or as Inkson (2004) phrased it,

> Networking becomes a way of life, a key skill. Moreover, as forces of power and domination of institutions are reflected into personal career environments, the micro-skills of self-promotion, organizational politics, impression management, reputation-building, and contact-hunting may be critical—they have certainly become a focus of the career self-help movement (e.g., Bolles, 2002; Keys & Case, 1990; Moses, 1998)—creating an additional image of the career as a political campaign. (p. 104)

Theater Metaphor: Career as Role

Adults form a sense of identity throughout their lives and a career provides a long-term stage to hone and modify social roles at work. Inkson (2004) equated career-as-role as enacting a performance and career self-management as a performing art drawing on theatrical devices such as theme, plot, costume, props, oratory, and symbolism as the work role is enacted and re-enacted in response to work role expectations.

Economic Metaphor: Career as Resource

Viewing the career as a resource might ring familiar to human resource development (HRD) professionals as the performative discourse of this metaphor is dominant in HRD. Per Inkson (2004), "Is your career a resource? If so, whose?" (p. 105). This metaphor focuses on the potential of a career to create wealth for organizations and the corresponding view of labor as a cost that often gets restructured or downsized. Inkson cautioned:

> Metaphor may steal your career from you! The notion of "human resource management" potentially expropriates and transforms careers for organizational purposes, reduces people to malleable inputs to productive processes, and entrusts career development to the superior knowledge of the company. Practices such as corporate career workshops, assessment centers, training, development and mentorship programs, and performance appraisal assist companies to manage their employees' careers. They also provide opportunities for individual employees to use such activities proactively for their career development. But they leave open the question of career ownership as between individual and organization. Alternative models stress career self-management, individuals' ownership of their own careers, and the personal cultivation of one's own resource or "career capital" (Inkson & Arthur, 2001). Awareness of the human resource metaphor and its implications is of benefit to career protagonists and managers alike. (p. 105)

The counternarrative to workers as "resources" is "labor as a valuable asset" to the organization. Inkson and Arthur's (2001) notion of "career capital" offered a perspective of a career as individual property with the following precepts: careers are key energizers and organizers of economic life; worker's careers are personal property that organizations should provide supportive contexts for developing; people are more energized by career self-interest than organization's interests in survival and growth; individuals serve their interests through the accumulation of capital; individual capital is tradable knowledge that is valued in a knowledge economy; and career capitalists follow the principles of knowing why they work, knowing how to do their career, and knowing who can be helpful to career advancement.

Narrative Metaphor: Career as Story

Adults create stories to make meaning out of their lives; this metaphor focuses on the discourse of careers. Stories, or narratives, are not necessarily factual accounts of careers as they may be embellished, described linearly when they are not, and be incomplete, shifting, and contradictory accounts that capture the complexity of careers (Inkson, 2004). Career stories may be akin to the hero's journey (Campbell, 2003) or the heroine's journey (Murdock, 2020). Inkson also wrote about archetypical career stories in the narratives about "boundaryless" and "protean" careers and the urging for people to create individual "brands."

Serendipity Metaphor: Career as a Series of Chance Events

Yates (2022) added a tenth serendipity metaphor to Inkson's (2004) list. This metaphor is about how luck and chance impact career planning and progression. Yates underscored how the theory of planned happenstance (Mitchell et al., 1999) capitalized on chance through the idea that people need to watch for and take advantage of opportunities that cross their paths. Box 3.8 provides an opportunity to identify career metaphors that resonate with various career paths.

◌ BOX 3.8 REFLECTIVE PRACTICE

What is your Career Metaphor?

Inkson (2004) offered a framework to understand careers by creating career metaphors. As a career explorer, sustainer, or changer, see if you can identify in Table 3.8 one or more metaphors that help you make meaning of your career path.

Table 3.8   Career metaphors and definitions

Career metaphors and definitions: which fits you?	
Legacy metaphor: Career as inheritance	Craft metaphor: Career as construction
Seasons metaphor: Career as cycle	Matching metaphor: Career as "fit"
Path metaphor: Career as journey	Network metaphor: Career as encounters and relationships
Theater metaphor: Career as a role	Economic metaphor: Career as resource
Narrative metaphor: Career as story	Serendipity metaphor: Career as a series of chance events

CRITICALLY ASSESSING CAREER DEVELOPMENT THEORY'S EFFICACY FOR ADULTS

Herr (2001) identified several voids in career theory and practice that hold true today. One of the problems is that many of the hypotheses and existing principles of career development originated from samples of White Western men. Much of the research related to the application of career development theory has been validated by samples of convenience (e.g., university undergraduates), rather than samples representative of populations across age and socioeconomic spectrums, with the ensuing results questionable in their generalizability. The field has lacked a systematic approach to understanding career development for people of color, women across socioeconomic classes, gender and sexual minorities (GSM), the rural and urban poor, and other marginalized groups in society.

This chapter has reviewed several career development theories, and often they have been viewed as competing or alternative explanations of the same population or behavior rather than complementary ways of knowing and understanding complex phenomena. As career development theories and career interventions grow in the comprehensiveness with which they are applied to populations across the lifespan and in different settings, there will need to be increased and systematic collaboration between theorists, researchers, and practitioners as joint members of research teams. Although perhaps frustrating, it is unlikely that any one career development theory will be adequate to explain career behavior across the lifespan with the diversity in gender, physical ability, race, ethnicity, education, socioeconomic level, and other indices. Instead, it will likely be necessary to focus on segmented theories that explain more fully the specific career contextual factors, obstacles, barriers, received messages, and related variables common across groups and those factors that differentiate these groups. This means it is necessary to develop a more comprehensive understanding of persons characterized by intersectionality, which will be further explained in Chapter 4. Such concerns will need to look at the cost-benefit ratios for different career interventions (e.g., individual or group counseling, planned programs of career guidance or career education, organization-focused interventions, computer-assisted career guidance systems, the internet) as well as under what conditions and for whom career counseling and personal counseling should be treated as separate interventions or fused.

GENERAL CRITIQUES OF PREVAILING CAREER THEORIES

Existing career development theory is valuable in multiple ways as it helps match people to fulfilling careers and make meaning of their career experiences during their lifetimes. Theories, however, have limitations since they are the best guess about a phenomenon based on the best evidence available, or as Lewis (1947) observed, to see something through career development. Gedro (2017) advised:

> Traditional career models are insufficient to explain the current context of career development. People are living longer, the workforce is now more diverse than ever (although there is a persistent tendency for white males to achieve access to the highest ranks of organizations), and people change jobs and careers with more alacrity and less social stigma. (p. 11)

The career landscape has also been altered through globalization, technological advancement, diversifying workplaces, and the increasing use of contingent workers, affecting how individuals choose to move through their careers.

Although there is empirical evidence to support many career theories (e.g., Brown & Lent, 2021; Robertson et al., 2021), CD theory has several shortcomings, including:

1. Most CD theories were developed to explain and inform how children and young adults develop a sense of career identity and vocation.

2. Career theories were predominantly developed in the Western world, meaning they may have limited usefulness in describing or informing career decisions in other cultures.
3. Career identity has been assumed to be unidimensional or a fixed, unchanging construct where a unitary, autonomous, and stable self moves through a chosen career when in reality, the self is multi-dimensional and changes over the lifespan (Alvesson, 2010).
4. CD theory has a racial and gender bias that has persisted since the early developments of career theory, meaning that the theories, models, and instruments may not be valid for predicting the career interests of women, people of color, or other groups who were not represented when the theories were tested. Further, Gedro (2017) looked at gender and age research in HRD and concluded that career theories are masculinized, homogenous, and linear, disregarding the intersectionality of age and gender.
5. Race is rarely discussed in career theory except in empirical studies that were analyzed based on race.
6. Few theories take an intersectional perspective meaning they fail to consider how the intertwined identities of gender, race, social class, gender identity, and other positionalities influence career choice and experience.

Gedro (2017) charged CD theory with being a middle-to-upper-class construct and argued that career choice and experience are shaped by the ways people's identities change over time through a range of human experiences from gradual processes such as aging to transformative moments such as struggling with addiction, realizing sexual orientation or gender identity, experiencing relationships, and enduring hardships. She problematized and challenged "the Western capitalist orthodoxy" (p. 6) underlying career success for the ways it diminishes career success into:

> [S]omething that can be measured in the three-dimensional, material world through metrics such as one's position on an organizational chart, one's salary and benefits and perks, and one's social status in a given sociological milieu (manifested through membership at country clubs; sending children to particular exclusive primary, secondary, and then higher education schools that signal the extent to which the family is resourced). (p. 6)

An important critique made by Gedro (2017) is that traditional career and identity development are heterosexist because it is assumed that gender identity occurs along a chronological, linear trajectory. This is an incorrect assumption, for example, when a GSM person's identity development does not necessarily synch with the heteronormative definition of chronological development.

Gedro (2017) urged that HRD professionals would be wise to understand career development as a self-directed process where people with less visible identities may have more challenges and decisions around career choice and that relationships and jobs are shorter term making it more challenging to forecast appropriate training and investment in people by organizations.

CHAPTER SUMMARY

Chapter 3 began with Lewis' (1947) quote about the need to "see something through things" rather than to "see through things," an apt description of theory. The chapter summarized key dominant career development theories, noting significant contributions, relevance for adults, and critiques. Structural career theories focus on determining the ideal fit between the person, job, and work environment. In contrast, developmental theories focus on how adults learn and evolve across their career lifespan and make meaning about their career choices and experiences. The chapter also summarized career metaphors to offer a different way of understanding career development theory. The chapter closed with critiques of career development, noting its shortcomings for diverse adults.

4. Exploring critical, intersectional adult career development

4. Recognize mindsets and practices that impinge intersectional, equitable CD.
5. Connect criticality and intersectionality to socially just CD.

A TALE OF TWO WORKERS' PARENTAL LEAVE

Critical career issues can best be understood by comparing the career experiences of two people with very different social positions and career paths and the subsequent choices they face. This section profiles the respective pregnancy work experience and parental leave of Latavia Johnson, a Walmart employee, and Adam Isserlis, a Facebook Communications Manager.

Latavia Johnson, Walmart

Latavia Johnson, a Walmart employee, wrote about her experience working for the largest private employer in the US when she became pregnant:

> I worked in the Bakery Department at Wal-Mart in Granite City, Illinois, as a cake decorator. When I found out I was pregnant, my doctor told me I had a high-risk pregnancy and that I could no longer lift over 25 pounds on the job. I brought my doctor's recommendation to my manager, and she told me she needed to see a doctor's note. I brought her a note that same day, but instead of giving me lighter duty work, she told me that I didn't need to come back to work until my restrictions were lifted.
> I was making only $8.85 an hour and living at home with my mother. When I started, I was happy the store would give me 40 hours each week. But soon they started cutting back my hours until I was only getting around 25 hours per week. With an infant at home and another baby on the way, I was already struggling to help my mom pay rent, keep up with car payments and put food on the table. Needless to say, when Wal-Mart told me to stop coming to work because of my pregnancy complications, I didn't have any money saved.
> For the next three months, I was out of work. I kept calling to ask my managers if they could put me somewhere with lighter duties and give me some hours so I could support my son. They refused to give me any work. (Johnson, 2015, paras 4–6)

Johnson joined Respect the Bump, an organization that fights pregnancy discrimination. Through their support, she was able to return to work with the Walmart pregnancy policy and was reinstated to her regular schedule. Still, she continued experiencing cuts to her hours and receiving smaller paychecks, making it difficult to support her family. Plus, she was also under pressure to lift heavy objects. Johnson resorted to taking unpaid pregnancy leave due to the struggles she experienced at Walmart. Johnson (2015) concluded, "No woman should have to choose between her pregnancy and a paycheck, or fear that she will lose her job at the moment she needs it most" (para. 12).

Adam Isserlis, Facebook

Adam Isserlis was Facebook's Communications Manager in the corporation now known as Meta at the time of this story. Gillet (2015), writing an article on progressive paid parental leave policies, wrote about his 2013 experience in the company:

> After his daughter's 5 a.m. feeding during the first few months after she was born, Adam would lie back in bed with his newborn child resting on his chest, and the two would doze off together. Thanks to Facebook's parental-leave policy [which provides at least four months of paid parental leave], the first-time father says he enjoyed innumerable "magical" moments like these that helped him foster a bond with his new daughter ... "That's the way this was presented to me here at Facebook," he says. "It's like, 'Things will come and go, and we'll handle them, we'll deal with them, but you should be with your family'—that's a really important and wonderful thing." (p. 707)

Although pregnancy support and parental leave should be provided to all employees, these two cases exemplify very different experiences with different career impacts. Adam, a White man in a prestigious company with a good position, did not have to worry about parental leave regarding his long-term employment prospects. Latavia needed to work in a job that discriminated against her and endangered her child to provide for her family. Latavia's and Adam's cases illustrate that people experience different treatment based on their intersecting identities, such as gender, race, class, and education, and as a result have different choices when it comes to careers.

Parental Leave Career Perils and Promises

This chapter focuses on critical, intersectional approaches to adult CD. The stories of Latavia and Adam illustrate how people are treated differently in their careers based on race, gender, social class, whether they have a good or bad job and other factors. The stories illuminate the need to consider people's identities and positionalities and how they affect CD. Mothers, in particular, experience wage penalties for childbirth (England et al., 2016; Kramer et al., 2023). More than one in five pregnant workers are in low-paid employment, and these workers are more likely to stand, perform repetitive activity, walk extensively, and engage in heavy lifting or physical exertion throughout the workday, putting them at higher risk of pregnancy complications (Harwood & Heydemann, 2019). These working conditions often force women into a position where they must choose between their jobs and the health of themselves and their babies. Further, these workers tend to be Black women and Latina as they are disproportionately represented in low-wage jobs.

Workplaces are gendered, and the image of the ideal worker is a White man who is solely devoted to their work (Acker, 1990), which puts anyone looking different or prioritizing family at a disadvantage. Gupta et al. (2008) showed that raising children often creates career trade-offs between being effective at one's career and parenting. Although Adam had a significantly more privileged experience than Latavia in the cases profiled in the previous section, Kelly et al. (2014) found that supervisors' and managers' expectations to show work devotion and minimize breaks from work are higher. Men also tend to take less parental leave due to gendered workplace norms and virtue signaling of their work commitment (Kramer et al., 2023). Marriage, caregiving, and childcare require workers to make decisions that influence their employment and career trajectory (Budig & Lim, 2016). Kramer et al. (2023) summarized, "Many working individuals, and especially women, are forced to make multiple and difficult decisions, such as whether to have a child, the timing of having children, and whether to use work–family accommodations" (p. 206). To further accentuate the disparity in parental leave, about 78% of US workers are allowed up to 12 weeks of unpaid leave (US Department of Labor, n.d.c.). However, only 12% of workers have paid leave benefits (De Silver, 2017).

Considering how diversity impacts people's careers is imperative in creating equitable access and opportunity. Sisco (2020) studied CD and self-preservation among Black US professionals and concluded when organizations "[choose] to disregard race and adopt a colorblind lens, our racialized systems reproduce disparities and maintain social division" (p. 431). Sisco (2020) urged human resource professionals to take an active and critical approach to understand "… how the workplace operates as a racialized system can inform the necessary action needed to constitute sustainable social change within corporations" (p. 433). This chapter foregrounds career justice and equity issues and underscores the importance of understanding discrimination and injustice in CD and choice. Later in the book, Chapter 8 will explain how active measures can be taken to transform organizational policies and practices so everyone can access career learning, choice, and development.

CRITICAL CAREER DEVELOPMENT

Rethinking Adult Career Development introduces Critical Career Development (CCD) as a practice and theory of rethinking adult career development. CCD challenges the efficacy of CD theory and practice with the goal of making the career lifespan more equitable, just, and accessible to all career explorers, sustainers, and changers while also making workplaces more inclusive and fairer. CCD applies a lens of critique to theories and practices of CD, drawing, for example, on critical theory, critical management studies, critical HRD, and liberation theories such as feminism, queer theory, and critical race theory, among others. Table 4.1 briefly defines the ideas providing a basis for critical CD.

Table 4.1   *Critical principles or theories, definitions, and implications for adult career development*

Critical principle or theory	Definition	Implications for adult career development
Critical theory	Critiques social conditions and assumptions people hold (viewed as "false consciousness") and how they contribute to injustice and sustain unequal power relations based on positionalities such as race, gender, class, age, sexual orientation, physical ability, and other identities and positionalities. Critical theory challenges what privileged groups profess as "truth," and those in power create dominant public discourse to manipulate how people think and act. Critical theory serves to create emancipation and elimination of oppression in society.	Examines and critiques how race, gender, age, sexual orientation, gender identity, disability, and other positionalities and identities affect people's ability to have a fulfilling career and full access to learning and advancement opportunities. It challenges purported "truths" such as "women do not want to relocate or travel."
Critical management studies (CMS)	Critical management studies emerged in the 1990s and critiques the "truths" that tend to preserve power among managers and executives, typically White heterosexual men. CMS aims to realize workplace equity and justice for workers and hold managers more accountable for how their actions impact the lives of workers and other stakeholders (Alvesson & Willmott, 1997).	CMS challenges the uncritical promotion of White heterosexual men into positions of power and management and seeks to create more justice and equitability by making structural changes to the recruitment, development, and advancement of workers and measuring success at creating equity.

Critical principle or theory	Definition	Implications for adult career development
Critical HRD (CHRD)	Critical HRD emerged in the early 2000s and mirrors CMS's aims in the context of human resource activities and how they create inequity and injustice in organizations. CHRD challenges HRD theories and practices that privilege managers and productivity at workers' and other stakeholders' expense. CHRD advocates for socially conscious and humanly sustainable organization practices.	Some key problems CHRD addresses are treating workers more like commodities than humans; privileging management and shareholder interests above all others, such as employees, communities, families, customers, and the environment; unquestioning acceptance of managerial power and dominance; and adopting traditional organization structures and reward systems (Bierema, 2010).
Feminism	Feminism is concerned with eliminating bias and discrimination against women and other marginalized social groups by making the workplace, politics, economics, and society more equitable and just.	Working to minimize or eliminate gender bias and other discrimination in the career exposure and decision-making processes, ensuring workplace equity through policies that create more equitable recruitment, hiring, development, and promotion of employees, and holding leaders accountable for results.

Critical principle or theory	Definition	Implications for adult career development
Critical race theory (CRT)	Critical race theory grew out of a legal movement in the 1970s that critiqued extensive delays in the progress of civil rights litigation and racial reform. CRT confronts the role of law in upholding White supremacy. Today CRT is discussed in the context of other fields including education, sociology, and women's studies among others to understand the theoretical and practical implications of racism. CRT is considered *oppositional scholarship*, that is, it challenges the experience of White people as the normative standard (White supremacy).	When organizations have effective policies at recruiting Black men, for example, yet the culture is characterized by a lack of support and repressiveness toward Black people, this toxic culture often drives the Black men and other marginalized people to leave (Cornileus, 2013; Wicker, 2021). CRT serves to help people affected by racism tell their stories that challenge false, racist assumptions. Organizational proclaimed "neutrality" towards historically excluded groups further strengthens racism as it benefits White people materially and psychically (Wicker, 2021). CRT counters dominant narratives by helping those affected by racist workplaces to name their reality, which helps toward meaning-making and racial healing.

Critical principle or theory	Definition	Implications for adult career development
Queer studies	Queer studies differs from queer theory (an analysis within queer studies that challenges how we socially construct categories of sexuality) and emerged approximately 30 years ago. It is a multidisciplinary field grounded in critical theory that explores power relations related to sexuality and gender identity with a focus on LGBTI (lesbian, gay, bisexual, transgender, and intersex) individuals. Queer studies confronts how ideologies of sexuality privilege heterosexuality as the norm and how intersectionality further marginalizes gender and sexual minorities (GSM).	Working to ensure gender equity among GSM in the career exposure and decision-making processes is crucial, as well as making the workplace friendly to GSM workers. Key strategies include establishing and enforcing LGBTQ+ (lesbian, gay, bisexual, transgender, queer, and others) non-discrimination policies; ensuring hiring policies and practices avoid unconscious bias; training about the policies and accountability for upholding them; supporting the LGBTQ+ community; extending benefits to partners of LGBTQ+ workers; and communicating the organization's commitment to inclusiveness (Blackman, 2019).

Note: See Merriam and Bierema (2014) for a full discussion of these theories in the context of adult learning.

A main premise of *Rethinking Adult Career Development* and CCD is viewing CD as a contested process. Contested career processes may be the pursuit of work that fulfills a personal career goal while simultaneously hurting individual self-interest, such as a Black woman pursuing her dream job in a racist environment that blocks access to the development and promotion of Black women. CCD involves naming and discussing topics often not broached in CD conversations, such as sexism, racism, and other marginalizing structures, and recognizing that experiencing a satisfying, affirming career should be the norm and a human right, not a privilege for an elite group, often White straight men.

CCD considers how social dynamics of management power and abuse, sexism, racism, heteronormativity, colonialism, asymmetrical power relations, environmental exploitation, political corporate action, ableism, performativity, and other isms contributing to unjust workplaces affect CD. This book does not just consider factors making CD contested. It also offers strategies for promoting equitable, just CD for individuals, career counselors, advisors, leaders, and organizations.

CCD applies a Freirean (Freire, 1973a, 1973b) "critical consciousness" to career theory and practice—understanding how structural oppression, such as poverty, colonization, or lack of access to education or opportunity, creates inequities in work and life, as introduced by Brazilian Paulo Freire who developed a critical pedagogy to teach impoverished, poorly educated Brazilians how to challenge the system. Diemer and Blustein (2006) defined critical consciousness as "the capacity to recognize and overcome sociopolitical barriers" (p. 220), for instance, understanding how structural racism and inequitable access to resources create social injustice and how to take individual or collective action to change the system. CCD is a thread of critical human resource development (CHRD or critical HRD). Bierema (2009) defined critical HRD as challenging four outcomes of masculine rational HRD (a patriarchal culture valuing aggressiveness, profit, and performance) that questions the (a) Privileging performativity or focus on money, (b) Commodifying workers or treating them like expendable resources, (c) Being beholden to stockholders instead of stakeholders, and (d) Ignoring power relations like sexism and racism (Bierema et al., 2024). CCD challenges prevailing career theories and CD development for career explorers, sustainers, and changers. Byrd (2018b) urged a call to action and a duty to respond to social injustice by breaking the silence about injustices in organizations and developing mindsets to promote social justice and build strong human relations. She recommended social justice as a progressive workplace norm that privileges inclusivity, safety, and security, developing to full capacity, and engaging democratically. Developing critical consciousness requires learning. A good place to begin this journey is by assessing diversity intelligence, as described in Box 4.2.

BOX 4.2 TIPS AND TOOLS FOR CAREER DEVELOPMENT

Diversity Intelligence

Hughes (2018) defined diversity intelligence (DQ) as "the capability of individuals to recognize the value of workplace diversity and to use this information to guide thinking and behavior" (p. 374). To assess your level of DQ, you can visit this website (note there is a cost): https://www.dive rsityintelligencellc.com/. The instrument measures diversity knowledge, workplace training and education perceptions, individual behavior, and an overall DQ score.

ENGAGING WHITE MEN IN EQUITY EFFORTS

Rethinking Adult Career Development addresses challenging CD issues that regularly go under-discussed or undiscussed in most circles. Although the world has grown up learning systems of racism, sexism, capitalism, and other isms, often there is hesitancy to talk about them out of fear of offending someone, looking stupid, appearing bigoted or ignorant, or being unsure what to say. Singh (2019), in her introduction to *The Racial Healing Handbook,* explained that inequitable systems continuously reflect societal value back to dominant groups (e.g., White people), while people of color experience a world that does not value them in the same way, evident through lack of access to neighborhoods, schools, communities, and careers—realities hurting their health and well-being. The same could be said for other identities such as gender, age, sexuality, disability, or religion. All people learn stereotypes from the time they are born and internalize and act on them without much conscious thought. Singh (2019) also lamented that people do not talk about race, making understanding it and identifying when racist things occur more challenging. She advocated that *everyone* needs to "heal from racism" by "unlearn[ing] the stereotyped racial messages you internalized about your own race and the race of others" (p. 2).

It is important to understand the words of Parris (2021): "White men are not the enemy—the lack of social fairness and equality is the enemy" (para. 8). By sensitivity, he means awareness of others' experiences and how you as a person are perceived. Zheng (2019) observed that although most leaders outwardly support organizational diversity, equity, and inclusion (DEI) efforts, some White men leaders do not see a role for themselves in these initiatives. Yet, if workplaces and society are to become more equitable and just, it takes *everyone*. Reasons for this reaction to DEI by White men include not feeling wanted in the discussion and process, being uncomfortable identifying their privilege or feeling attacked. As Zheng (2019) explained,

> One of the functions of privilege is rarely having to think about privileged identities as "identities." In America, historical power inequities make it so women, people of color, religious minorities, disabled people, and LGBTQ+ people are constantly reminded of their differences while men, white people, able-bodied people, straight people, and cisgender people can go their entire lives without thinking actively about their masculinity, whiteness, abled bodies, heterosexuality, or cisgender status. For privileged leaders, seemingly innocuous workplace comments can be some of the first times they explicitly think about their race, gender, or sexuality. These leaders may hear mentions of a group they belong in, find those parts of their identities more salient than ever, and sensing critique, get defensive. (para. 6)

To engage in this important work, Zheng (2019) recommended dominant group members frame identity as a place for inquiry and curiosity to build insight while keeping the long-term goal of equity as value central to this work. People need to feel safe to have these conversations, which requires skill and facilitation. Cultural humility—interest in other cultures and willingness to learn from them—was introduced in Chapter 2 as an alternative to cultural competence and is a foundation of socially just career development. It is also a powerful tool for privileged individuals and groups to engage in important conversations about equity and justice. Weldon-Caron (2022) explained,

> Cultural competency is finite, with an endpoint in knowledge development, whereas cultural humility is dynamic and ever-evolving. Cultural humility allows for a continuous growth process. Competency signifies that one has knowledge of other cultures, and that knowledge informs their views of those different from themselves which can lead to stereotyping. (p. 44)

Taking a cultural humility approach to recognizing and challenging power differentials in organizations that impede CD can increase sensitivity and accountability for leaders and the organization to create more equitable practices and policies. Box 4.3 shares tools to help cultivate an inclusive mindset helpful in this work.

BOX 4.3 TIPS AND TOOLS FOR CAREER DEVELOPMENT

Cultivating an Inclusive Mindset

Whether you are a career explorer, sustainer, or changer, or helping another navigate career development, developing an inclusive mindset is crucial for career success in an ever-diversifying global work context. Tulshyan (2022), in her book *Inclusion on Purpose*, offered multiple strategies for creating a culture of belonging in the workplace. An important step is overcoming defensiveness and acknowledging your privilege. Often thinking about, for example, how being White might be beneficial as a leader might be a reflection that makes the White leader uneasy. Yet, oppressive systems are not about the White CEO. They are about systems that perpetuate privilege and marginalization. Tulshyan frames inequity in the following way:
1. The problem isn't men, it's patriarchy.
2. The problem isn't White people, it's White supremacy.
3. The problem isn't straight people, it's homophobia.

4. Recognize systems of oppression before letting individual defensiveness stop you from dismantling them. (p. 26)

Tulshyan (2022) outlined steps for developing an inclusive mindset in *Inclusion on Purpose*. The steps follow the acronym BRIDGE and are as follows:

1. **Be** uncomfortable.
2. **Reflect** on what you don't know.
3. **Invite** feedback.
4. **Defensiveness** doesn't help.
5. **Grow** from your mistakes.
6. **Expect** that change takes time. (p. 42)

How can you be more aware of your privilege and practice the BRIDGE framework in your career and use it in ways supportive of others?

All members of a workplace are important to building inclusive, equitable cultures. White people, especially White men, are more likely to be in positions of leadership with the power to set an example and orchestrate change, which is a key reason they are important to equitable CD.

INTERSECTIONAL CAREER DEVELOPMENT

A key component in developing a critical perspective of CD is understanding intersectionality. This section opens with a career story that captures important issues of intersectionality. Next, intersectionality is defined and discussed in terms of career implications.

An Intersectional Career Development Story

Erica is a Black Woman on a human resource development career path in a US corporation. Her career was going well, primarily due to her recent promotion to a director role. Despite her success, the culture felt unwelcoming to Erica. She had grown accustomed to being the only Black person, although she worked with other White women. Throughout her career, Erica has contended with people mistaking her for an executive assistant or server. She regularly sits in meetings where her ideas are seldom heard until a White man repeats them, and she is held to higher standards than her White counterparts. Erica decided to raise these issues with her boss, a White man. After she explained her experience, Erica's boss told her, "You are overly sensitive and need to show some humility." He also advised, "You should watch your tone because it comes off as angry and ungrateful for your success." Erica knew that Black women were often "tone policed" [a tactic privileged people use to focus on the way something is being said versus the actual content of the message, especially when issues of racism are raised (Saad, 2020)]. Erica also noticed her decisions were scrutinized and questioned more than her peers. Although her organization professed diversity, equity, and inclusion, Erica found the pledges and actions hollow as she tried to advance in a system that tried to erase, silence, and mischaracterize her. Although she seemed to be doing well regarding her recent promotion, Erica was unsure what her next opportunity would be or who would support her. A couple of months later, she'd had enough when a project she had been lobbying for was given to a less qualified, lower-performing peer director. Erica retreated to her office and began plotting her exit.

Erica's case is unfortunate but not unusual. According to Lean In (2020), Black women face several challenges in their careers, including (a) They are significantly underrepresented in leadership roles and less likely to be promoted, (b) They are less likely to receive the support and access necessary for advancement, and (c) They face more day-to-day workplace discrimination. If organizations hope to stem the exodus of Black women, they need to (a) Commit to Black women's advancement, (b) Address bias in hiring and promotions, and (c) Create an inclusive workplace. Effectiveness at these and other equity-oriented interventions requires an understanding of intersectionality.

Defining Intersectionality

The development of intersectionality was shaped by Black feminism and the term was coined by Kimberlé Crenshaw (1989) to portray the complex and unique experiences of women of color that could not be explained by a single-axis framework of either gender or race. Black feminism (Collins, 1990, 2022), also known as womanism, Afrocentric feminism, and Africana womanism (Collins, 1990, 2022), evolved out of Black women's frustration that feminist theory and activism privileged White, middle-class women. Black feminism focuses on Black or African American women's experiences and how racism and sexism intersect to marginalize and oppress them. Black Feminist Thought (Collins, 1990) is a diverse and complex idea acknowledging that Black women are not a homogenous population. Yet, it provides a common ground for the exploration and understanding of Black women's experiences and intersecting oppressions through (a) Acknowledging the dialectical relationship of African American women's oppression and activism; (b) Resisting oppression; (c) Celebrating the intersecting identities of race, gender, class, sexuality, citizenship, and other positionalities; (d) Confronting everyday racism at work, in housing, schools, shopping, and other social interactions; (e) Experiencing segregation; and (f) Working for equity.

Although the interlinking positionalities of gender and race served as the initial foci for exploring Black women's subordination, scholars expanded the meaning of intersectionality, not limiting its focus to Black women or to the intersection of only gender and race (Cho et al., 2013). Intersectionality recognizes the existence of people's multiple social identities and the complex ways they intertwine, interconnect mutually, and are socially constructed (Bowleg, 2008; Collins & Bilge, 2020). Intersectionality plays out in CD in the myriad ways people access career role models and career information and how inequity is created when people lack equal access to the same information, education, and opportunities that set them up for productive, fulfilling careers. Box 4.4 discusses the global gender pay gap, a situation exacerbated by intersectionality.

▮▮ BOX 4.4 ADULT CAREER DEVELOPMENT BY THE NUMBERS

The Global Gender Pay Gap

The gender pay gap—GPG (Belli, 2018; Ketkar et al., 2021; Payscale, 2023) averages US$.83 that women earn for every US$1.00 men earn, worsening by race and geography. The gap equates to US full-time, year-round women workers losing an average of US$398,160 more throughout their lives than men peers, and for Black, Latina, Native, Hawaiian and Other Pacific Island women, an average of US$1,000,000 over their lifetimes (National Women's Law Center, 2023, para. 1). Of note,

> This "lifetime wage gap" exists across the country: in every single state, career losses for women of all races working full time, year-round compared to men of all races working full time, year-round based on today's wage gap would amount to hundreds of thousands of dollars—and in 12 states women's career losses would amount to more than half a million dollars. (National Women's Law Center, 2023, para. 2)

According to Payscale (2023), the top five jobs with the highest gaps are bartenders, restaurant servers, physicians and surgeons, religious professionals, and drivers or sales workers. Ketkar et al. (2021) observed that GPG mitigating factors making achieving gender parity difficult in G20 nations include financial resources, public spending capacity, cultural norms, and gendered beliefs. They recommended systemic treatment of the problem to include: passing pay transparency legislation; mandating data-driven gender budgeting; providing and endorsing parental leave; promoting women in science, technology, engineering, and mathematics (STEM); engaging industry in initiatives to hire and advance women; and eroding gender biases in organizations.

Globally, the pay gap is even worse. The World Economic Forum's (2023) Global Gender Gap Index Framework measures (a) Economic participation and opportunity, (b) Educational attainment, (c) Health and survival, and (d) Political empowerment. According to the 2023 report, the gender gap is lifelong for women:

> On average, over the past 17 years, the gap has been reduced by only 0.24 percentage points per year. If progress towards gender parity proceeds at the same average speed observed between the 2006 and 2023 editions, the overall global gender gap is projected to close in 131 years, compared to a projection of 132 years in 2022. This suggests that the year in which the gender gap is expected to close remains 2154, as progress is moving at the same rate as last year. (para. 35)

The top five countries out of 146 in the 2023 report with the smallest GPG included: Iceland, Norway, Finland, New Zealand, and Sweden. The UK ranked 15th between Costa Rica and the Philippines, and the US ranked 43rd between Colombia and Luxembourg. The bottom five countries out of 146 were Pakistan, Iran (Islamic Republic of), Algeria, Chad, and Afghanistan.

Are you, as a career explorer, sustainer, or changer, aware of your peers' annual salaries? Is there equitability? Although wage transparency is becoming more common in some countries and cultures, it is a right protected for private sector workers under the US National Labor Relations Board. Several US states have passed laws prohibiting employers from firing or punishing workers who share their salaries (Rosenfield et al., 2023), yet often people are afraid or unwilling to share such information.

Understanding intersectionality is important in supporting equitable and just CD. Yet, common mindsets and practices in workplaces and society work against it.

MINDSETS AND PRACTICES THAT IMPINGE ON INTERSECTIONAL, EQUITABLE CAREER DEVELOPMENT

Social justice refers to how wealth, privilege, and opportunity are distributed in society. McWhirter and McWha-Hermann (2021) identified five marginalizing conditions that restrict progress toward social justice: group bias, forced movement of people (e.g., refugees), poverty, unemployment, and lack of decent work. CD research and practice have only addressed these issues superficially or not at all.

Intersectional research and practice are beginning to emerge in HRD and adult education literature (e.g., Bierema, 2020a, 2020b; Greer et al., 2023; Monaghan & Isaac-Savage, 2022; Sim et al., 2023; Sim & Bierema, 2023a, 2023b; Sim & Jeong, 2023). Despite this understanding of how identities interact to influence social interactions, some mindsets and practices work against promoting equity and justice in society, especially in CD. This section discusses the mindsets and practices that can work against equitable career development, including intersectional invisibility, colorblindness, multiculturalism, implicit bias, and meritocracy.

Intersectional Invisibility

Intersectional invisibility is "the general failure to fully recognize people with intersecting identities as members of their constituent groups" (Purdie-Vaughns & Eibach, 2008, p. 381). Tefera et al. (2018) explained an "intersectional approach is fundamentally oriented toward analysing the relationships of power and inequality within a social setting and how these shape individual and group identities" (p. viii). Black women's career experiences become invisible if viewed in the same ways White women's career experiences are considered. Intersectionality provides a vital lens to assess organizational and social dynamics on three levels by (a) Illuminating how subordinate identities are marginalized and invisible, (b) Revealing the complexity of power structures created by racism, sexism, or other isms, and (c) Identifying the gap between subordinate identities and how they are influenced by the people and context around them, recognizing that no single social identity provides a complete explanation of a person's life (Ramdeo, 2023).

> Paradoxically, intersectional invisibility renders Black women simultaneously invisible and hyper-visible, meaning that their accomplishments and potential are easily overlooked by the majoritarian group members, yet their minimal representation within the workspace places them under greater scrutiny than those around them. (Smith et al., 2019; Ramdeo, 2023, p. 5)

Smith et al. (2019) defined constructs of intersectional invisibility using the management literature on how individuals manage multiple marginalized identities in the workplace. People who hold dual+ marginalized identities at work tend to face challenges and stigma, such as women juggling pregnancy and parenthood, lesbian, gay, and bisexual parents, and women from historically excluded groups. Table 4.2 builds on Smith et al.'s (2019) definitions of intersectional invisibility by adding career implications.

Table 4.2   Definitions of intersectional invisibility, definitions, and career implications

Construct	Definition	Examples of potential career implications
Intersectionality	The intertwined and reproducing effects of multiple identity groups that can create disadvantage and cancellation.	The combination of race, class, gender, sexuality, and other identities and how they affect career outcomes.
• Intersectional disadvantage	• The effects of multiple subordinate group memberships creating combined inequities and disparities.	• Being a woman from a marginalized or historically excluded group combines to impede career progress, as in Erica's career story in this chapter.
• Intersectional canceling effects	• The neutralizing effects of one subordinate identity group on another subordinate identity group.	• Being a woman might cancel out being a Black or Latina or lesbian or vice versa.
Outsider within	Being regarded as outsiders when working in predominantly high-status spaces such as White- and men-dominated spaces.	A lesbian is viewed as other and excluded from socializing or important work discussions.
(In)visibility	• Visibility is the extent to which an individual is fully regarded and recognized by the dominant group. • Invisibility is the experience of marginalized group members whose authority, potential, and recognition are overlooked and dismissed by the dominant group.	• A Black woman is a valued member of the team who is highly regarded and considered for opportunities and promotions at the same rate as her peers. • Marginalized members' ideas are ignored, they are not considered for opportunities or promotions, and their stature is unequal to their dominant peers.
Hypervisibility	Members of multiple subordinate groups experience higher scrutiny for their work and contributions than members of the dominant group.	Members of multiple subordinate groups experience lower performance ratings, are overlooked for opportunities and promotions, and are judged more harshly by peers or subordinates than the dominant group.

Construct	Definition	Examples of potential career implications
Intersectional invisibility	Members of multiple subordinate groups do not fit prevailing stereotypes, making them difficult to categorize and easy to overlook.	The combination of race, class, gender, sexuality, and other identities does not fit stereotypes, and the person is not considered for opportunities due to these dynamics.
Benign intersectional invisibility	When people belong to multiple subordinate identity groups, it may create positive interactions with others with multiple subordinate identities and create unfamiliar perceptions by the dominant group that are not bound by stereotypes tightly associated with their subordinate identity groups. Intersectional identities may also cancel each other.	Mothers of mixed races and sexuality share an affinity for the challenges of navigating a career and parenthood that is likely not understood by people who are not parents nor men who are not responsible for the bulk of the childcare.
Hostile intersectional invisibility	The negative interactive effects of belonging to multiple subordinate identity groups such that the dominant group perceives them as a combination of stereotypes, thus subject to compounded negative stigmas.	The same mothers as discussed under benign intersectional invisibility begin lobbying for more paternal leave benefits and flexibility, which challenges patriarchal practices that benefit White men, which causes resentment and backlash.
Agentic visibility tactics	Strategies to gain visibility as credible leaders.	A Black woman creates tactics to be seen in her organization by volunteering for high-profile projects, seeking mentors, developing new knowledge and skills, or other strategies to amplify her visibility.

In addition to intersectional invisibility, Smith et al.'s (2019) study of Black executive women found they experience an "outsider within" phenomenon where they simultaneously encounter opportunities and benign and hostile constraints. At work, this status manifested as exclusion from informal White networks, despite the women's credentials and accomplishments. In their communities, they experienced a similar dynamic as they were often different from the people in their communities due to education, income, and status, meaning they navigated work and community life without fully belonging to either. The intersectional context of the workplace often makes Black women recipients of dual stigma. For instance, stereotypes of women and Black people affected what assignments they would be given (e.g., racist decisions like not being sent to clients who did not want Black people in their offices or gendered stereotyping about their appearance or emotions). They also did not receive substantive performance feedback important to their development and advancement. The women also reported race and gender barriers that prevented them from fully understanding organizational politics. The professional context saw that the Black women were heavily invested in their professional selves and advancement, despite the perpetual biases. They sought professional support from sponsors and mentors to help them navigate the organization's culture. The women reported family support and self-assurance as sustaining them during their careers.

Colorblindness

Colorblindness is another mindset that works against intersectionality. Adopting a "colorblind" stance means minimizing race and assuming it should not and does not matter in workplace interactions, policies, and decisions (Plaut et al., 2018). Colorblindness is endorsed by White people more often than people of color. Perhaps its appeal protects the ego of people who perpetrate racism by bolstering an egalitarian self-image and a belief one cannot be prejudiced. Although professing to be "colorblind" is viewed as virtuous by some White people, it often justifies inequality. It can be used to rationalize the status quo and functions to reduce sensitivity to racism and the lived experience of historically excluded and marginalized people. Yet, Emerson (2017) reported that when organizations downplay diversity it reduces the engagement of historically excluded and marginalized workers and increases their perception of bias from White colleagues. She profiled Deloitte which abolished employee resource groups (ERGs) in 2017, a move toward colorblindness that was widely criticized. The company was trying better to integrate White men into its diversity and inclusion efforts yet removed an important space for workers who faced discrimination and created inequity in the process. Emerson (2017) concluded, "Ultimately, while including everyone in organizational diversity efforts is important, a colorblind approach isn't the best path. Race, gender, and other demographics are not just 'hot political topics,' ... They are important identities that require recognition and deserve space" (para. 10). Colorblind strategies can help communicate equal opportunity and cultural commitment to fairness, can represent a vision for equality, and can be useful if they focus on commonality without dismissing the experiences of marginalized groups (Plaut et al., 2018). Yet, they lack a strategic and intentional approach to workplace equity.

Multiculturalism

Multiculturalism is a mindset of valuing and acknowledging racial group membership with the view that it should be recognized and respected (Plaut et al., 2018). According to Plaut et al. (2018), minority groups tend to endorse this approach more often than majority groups, perhaps because the stance can threaten majority group members. It is inconclusive whether a multicultural perspective leads to more or less stereotyping. However, White people who value multiculturalism show less prejudice and engage in less prejudicial behavior than those adopting a colorblindness ideology. It has also been shown to positively impact interracial interaction, engagement, performance, and detection of discrimination (Plaut et al., 2018). Multiculturalism is a poor strategy when it sparks threat or hostility in White people or it encourages preference for stereotypical members of a racial group over counter-stereotypical members of the racial group. It is also a poor strategy when the representation of people of color is low, and it can create an illusion of fairness and non-discrimination. Multiculturalism is an advisable strategy when it encourages more positive interracial interactions and leads to less behavioral prejudice and greater ability to detect racial incidents. Supportive White people help create an engaged, less biased workplace and improve the organization climate for diversity, equity, and inclusion with this mindset (Plaut et al., 2018).

Implicit Bias

Bias or stereotyping are mindsets permeating workplaces and society and involve harboring a favorable or negative prejudice against a person or group as compared to another person or group (e.g., biases may be based on gender, race, age, gender identity and expression or other identities and positionalities) (Byrd, 2018a; Collins, 2017; Davis et al., 2020; Trusty et al., 2023).

Bias results in unfairness when it manifests in stereotyping, decisions and actions that inhibit or help the individual or group. Implicit bias is a prejudice that a person may not be aware that they hold. Byrd (2018a) explained,

> Social cognition is recalling a stereotype, bias, or unfavorable opinion about a social group and activating that perception during social or work-related encounters. A state of unconscious bias that is often held in check by members of the dominant group can be psychologically projected upon a marginalized person who now has a position of power. (p. 291)

Often, decisions about who gets hired or promoted are shrouded in implicit bias targeted at individuals, and these decisions accumulate to create systems of inequity. Claiming a person is a "cultural fit" for example, might signal the hiring committee's comfort level with a job candidate who is similar to them. When organizations hire on "fit," they tend to perpetuate the homogeneity of the workforce since it is often a code for "similar to us." Saying someone is "not a cultural fit" absconds hiring committees and authorities from confronting possible implicit biases.

McFadden (2022) offered that if implicit bias is viewed as "unconsciously held negative assumptions, discrimination could be described as their more active counterpart—the action or decision that builds off unconscious bias" (p. 389). Bierema (2020b) defined types of implicit bias and how they manifest in thought or discourse. "Bandwagon bias," for example, is believing something because others in an immediate work or social group do. This type of bias is not uncommon in hiring decisions when someone might think, "Well, no one seems to think that candidate is qualified, so I guess I don't either." "That candidate" is likely from a marginalized or historically excluded identity.

McFadden (2022) provided a historical review of implicit bias and associated training and noted it is often eschewed as high-status groups (e.g., White men) feel threatened by such training that may be poorly designed and facilitated in ways that assign guilt and blame, which is not constructive. He emphasized that highlighting that a person has an implicit bias does not mean they are a bad person, especially since biases can be culturally bound. He critiqued implicit bias programs as often targeted at individuals to consider how structural bias is embedded in the organization. McFadden (2022) emphasized:

> Movements such as Black Lives Matter and #MeToo have prompted many organizations, and the individuals within them, to more closely investigate the role of systemic and institutional discrimination moving beyond the "one bad apple trope" to examining how organizations themselves contribute to inequality and prejudice. (p. 391)

Bias can take other forms, such as access and treatment. Access bias is the stereotyping and structural inequities embedded in recruitment, selection, evaluation, and promotion practices and policies that exclude women and historically excluded and marginalized workers in their careers (Bertrand & Mullainathan, 2004). Treatment bias reflects the culture and climate created by access bias (Kanter, 1977; Turco, 2010) as well as implicit stereotypes that impede women and historically excluded people from establishing career-enhancing developmental relationships and networks (Castilla, 2008).

Women and historically excluded and marginalized workers encounter access and treatment bias across their careers. This is compounded when people have intersectional positionalities (e.g., gender and race) that place unreasonable expectations on them to (a) Demonstrate competence, (b) Adopt simultaneously masculine- and feminine-enough postures to meet cultural expectations, (c) Balance family with tenure and promotion expectations, and (d) Contend with implicit biases held by women and men in both the hiring and career trajectory (Williams et al., 2014). Treatment bias may also manifest through tokenism and well-intentioned attitudes like colorblindness that subsequently lead to self-limiting career beliefs and aspirations for women and people of color (McCoy et al., 2015). Box 4.5 shares information on taking the Implicit Bias Association Test.

BOX 4.5 REFLECTIVE PRACTICE

The Implicit Bias Association Test

The Implicit Bias Association Test (IAT) was developed to measure brain associations when encountering various images. This tool can help you, as a career explorer, sustainer, or changer, become more aware of your own implicit bias. If you discover something you did not expect as you work through these exercises, try asking yourself questions about it from a place of curiosity. Questions such as, "What is behind this result?" or "Where did I learn this?" might be effective starting points.

According to the website:

> The Implicit Association Test (IAT) measures attitudes and beliefs that people may be unwilling or unable to report. The IAT may be especially interesting if it shows that you have an implicit attitude that you did not know about. For example, you may believe that women and men should be equally associated with science, but your automatic associations could show that you (like many others) associate men with science more than you associate women with science. (Project Implicit, n.d., para. 2)

You can learn more and use the tool here:
https://implicit.harvard.edu/implicit/takeatest.html

The Myth of Meritocracy

Meritocracy is a mindset and practice embracing the idea that people's career advancement should be based solely on their performance and talent with no regard for identities or positionalities like race, gender, class, sexuality or others. Amis et al. (2020) suggested meritocracy "... implies a social system in which individual advancement and the allocation of rewards in organizations and society more broadly are based on an individual's capabilities and performance rather than on family connections, seniority, race, gender, or class" (p. 196). Amis et al. (2020) conducted an integrative literature review across the social sciences to assess which organization practices exacerbated social and economic inequity. They found five major practices emerge as central in this phenomenon: hiring, role allocation, promotion, compensation, and structuring (formal and informal decision-making, coordination of activities, and allocation of resources).

Van Dijk et al. (2020) underscored work's role in rising social inequities, explaining, "Whereas the conventional view of workplaces as meritocracies suggest that work is a conduit for social equality, we unveil the ways in which workplaces contribute to the accumulation of social inequality" (p. 240). Van Dijk et al. developed a model of cumulative social inequities in the workplace to show "how initial differences in opportunities and rewards shape performance and/or subsequent opportunities and rewards, such that those who receive more initial opportunities and rewards tend to receive even more over time" (p. 240). They concluded that meritocracy cumulatively exacerbates social inequalities, legitimates social inequalities, and manifests through day-to-day events and interactions in the workplace. How does meritocracy hurt workers? "Initial inequalities increase over time because workers with an initial advantage have increasing access to resources and opportunities, whereas those with initial disadvantages have diminished access to resources and opportunities" (p. 241). The adage of "the rich get richer, and the poor get poorer" parallels the outcomes of workplace meritocracy. Their model shows how the mechanisms of meritocracy work at multiple levels as summarized in Table 4.3.

Table 4.3   Van Dijk et al.'s model of cumulative social inequality in the workplace

Level of meritocracy	Characteristics of meritocracy
Individual Opportunities and rewards affect how the worker functions and performs, which influences subsequent opportunities and rewards. There are two aspects: knowledge, skills, and abilities (KSAs); and motivation.	*Knowledge, skills, and abilities (KSAs):* A worker comes to their job with KSAs, but those with more initial opportunities and rewards will cumulatively benefit more from them over time.
	Motivation: Workers receiving more opportunities and rewards will have stronger motivation. Lower motivation levels negatively affect performance.
Didactic The assumption that differences in performance, opportunities, and rewards between workers originate from work evaluators' assessments of and responses to a worker's competence and associated status.	*Status beliefs:* Status is the level of respect, prominence, esteem, and influence attributed to people. The higher-status people are perceived to have increased the level of attention and support they receive in their jobs.
	Stereotypes: Workers subjected to negative [positive] competence perceptions and attributed status perform worse [better] and cause others to evaluate their performance as worse [better], which decreases [increases] their opportunities and rewards and, consequently, confirms and reinforces status and competence attributions.
Network Differences in job performance and in opportunities and rewards derive from differences in social capital (resources available within a worker's social network, such as training or mentoring), which differs between social groups.	*Homophily:* Forming connections with and sharing the opinions and behaviors of others who are similar in terms of demographics, history, status, values, or other characteristics. Dominant groups will tend to benefit from this affiliation which results in more opportunities and rewards and further accumulation of social capital.
	Reciprocity: The expectation that other people will reciprocate a favor. Disadvantaged groups will have less capacity to reciprocate for favors, putting them at a further disadvantage.
	Capital correlations: Gaining access to one form of capital tends to facilitate access to other forms, contributing to further homogenization and stratification of social networks.

Level of meritocracy	Characteristics of meritocracy
Organizational Systems at the organizational level affect how performance evaluation translates into opportunities and rewards.	*Segmentation:* Organization and occupational. *Organizational segmentation* is the capacity to offer wages, bonuses, stability, and nonmonetary benefits. *Occupational segmentation* depends on core versus peripheral work and is based on power differentials. For example, professional and unionized workers have more employment security and benefits than restaurant workers. Membership in these different occupational groups is often related to social group membership.
	Winner-take-all structures: Opportunities and rewards are disproportionately granted to the highest performers in an organization and those with the strongest talents.
	Meritocratic ideology: The extent to which organizations endorse the principle that opportunities and rewards ought to be distributed on the basis of performance.

The implications of meritocracy are several, including that it exacerbates and legitimizes social inequities over time (Van Dijk et al., 2020). Workers who benefit from merit-based opportunities and rewards also benefit from non-merit-based advantages including higher status and more access to social capital. Conversely, those receiving fewer rewards due to performance lags and lower status may not gain access to training or other assistance that can help them rebound. Thus, their motivation diminishes, they secure less status, and they lack access to networks that could enhance their social capital and create a more inequitable situation for them. Legitimization of social inequities in the workplace occurs because meritocracy creates performance differentials between workers that are erroneously attributed to individual qualities when they are influenced by opportunities, rewards, and status that are context-based. A person's accumulation of KSAs is also influenced by the legitimization of inequities where the privileged worker has access to mentoring, coaching, and feedback that may be unavailable or substandard for workers with less status. The creation of social inequities through meritocracy occurs through the day-to-day accumulation of privilege and marginalization that is created by this mindset and practice, not by major career events such as promotions, life events, or work accomplishments. This dynamic can be illustrated in the number of men who get promoted to full professor in university positions as compared to women. According to Spoon et al. (2023), a census of 245,270 tenure-track and tenured professors in US-based PhD-granting departments using the person-environmental fit as a framework found that women leave academia at a higher rate than men at every stage of their careers. Although women and men are hired at similar rates, women represent 44% of tenured faculty and only 36% of full professors. The reasons women leave are gendered and they reported work climate most often as the reason. The authors concluded,

> Our findings indicate that gender incongruences are real, substantial, and universal in academia, even in disciplines with larger proportions of women, such as health and education. The dominant incongruences for women arise from workplace climate, including dysfunctional leadership, feelings of not belonging to the department or university, harassment and discrimination. As a result, workplace climate is a major reason that women faculty leave academia, at every career age, but especially for tenured women ... Such incongruences highlight the way departmental and institutional policies and norms tend to reflect, accommodate, and reinforce the traditional overrepresentation of white men from more privileged backgrounds, thereby driving gendered attrition over a career and inducing a substantial, asymmetric loss of overall talent and scholarship. (p. 7)

Workplace equality depends on understanding intersectionality and the mindsets and practices working against it. Recognizing how these dynamics function at individual, group, and organizational levels is important when making career choices and engaging in career development.

CHAPTER SUMMARY

Chapter 4 explored neglected topics in career development: critical perspectives and intersectionality. Understanding critical perspectives and intersectionality is useful for creating more just, equitable, and inclusive workplaces and societies and helping individuals consider career choices not only as individual acts but as ways of responding to and resisting prevailing social forces. This chapter has emphasized that social justice is fixing the oppressive system, not fixing the oppressed individual. "A social justice perspective suggests that systems that perpetuate inequalities in career development and that disempower individuals need to be changed or demolished" (McDonald & Hite, 2016, p. 193). To this end, how can CD better advance social justice? How can career choice and development more effectively promote social justice for individuals, groups, organizations, and society? Gedro (2017) urged:

> As the construct or paradigm of organization career, protean career, boundaryless career, encore careers, and re-careers become more and more prevalent in career development theory and practice, so should the fields of Human Resource Development and Management develop an ability to flex in the ways they respond to the needs of stakeholders. (p. 95)

Critical, intersectional CD serves all stakeholders and strives to build a critical consciousness about the mindsets and practices that obstruct equitable careers for all and to create more equitable pathways for career development and choice for *everyone.*

5. Interpreting career development as adult learning and change

Blustein and Duffy (2021) summarized the psychology of work theory (PWT)—sentiments that align with key principles of adult education:

> PWT offers practitioners both an orientation toward enhancing the *dignity of all work* as well as specific recommendations to implement the multifaceted goals of *fostering individual well-being* and *fostering systemic change* (p. 229, italics added for emphasis)

This chapter aims to examine career development (CD) as a process of adult learning (AL), development, meaning-making, and change.

The chapter introduces PWT and compares it to adult education (AE). Next, the chapter reviews the characteristics of adult learners with implications for work and CD. Change is discussed in relation to learning and work. AL theories are evaluated in terms of how they apply to CD. The chapter concludes with a discussion of adult identity development and ways of using CD theory pragmatically to the career challenges adults face.

As a result of reading this chapter and completing the exercises, you, the reader, should be able to:

1. Compare PWT to AE.
2. Understand how characteristics of adult learners shape work and career learning.
3. Interpret how AL theory applies to work and career learning.
4. Appraise how identity shapes career choice and development.
5. Apply CD theory to typical challenges adults face in their careers.

When thinking about career development (CD), images of researching different job titles, trial and error, or perhaps changing careers might come to mind. Yet, the process of CD is less of a technical question about "What should I be when I grow up?" and more of a lifelong learning and meaning-making process that evolves with the person within their context. Learning and meaning-making take many forms, such as formal education, planning, unexpected events, crisis, opportunity, loss, joy, and leaving a legacy. Most adults work during their lifetimes, both in the workplace and domestic sphere. Everyone deserves decent work and to be treated with dignity but finding that match is not always easy. Box 5.2 offers the opportunity to reflect on behaviors that may be career derailing.

☙ BOX 5.2 TIPS AND TOOLS FOR CAREER DEVELOPMENT

Know Your Strengths, Weaknesses, and Learning Development Goals

As an executive coach, I often tell my clients, "You get hired for your skills and fired for your behavior." Think about that reality. The most brilliant accountant will have difficulty advancing if they are a jerk. Marshall Goldsmith's (2010) *What Got You Here Won't Get You There* is a very insightful book. Goldsmith illustrated that a person's skills, behaviors, and attitudes instrumental in reaching a certain career level may not be the same as those needed to advance to a higher level. The book profiles 20 derailing behaviors that are common among leaders. He and Helgesen wrote a follow-up book in 2018, *How Women Rise*, describing women-specific derailing behaviors. Although I disagree that derailers are gender-specific, both books are good resources to help people name what holds them back in their work and life and create more productive behaviors.

There is an overemphasis on strengths in the US workplace, and although strengths are important to develop and hone, weaknesses get people in trouble. As a career explorer, sustainer, or changer, I urge you to do a realistic and truthful assessment of your major derailer at work. Are you a poor listener? Do you fail to give your team timely feedback? Are you afraid to delegate? Do you know how to set a clear expectation? If you are not sure, ask yourself, a trusted friend, or a colleague these two questions:
1.   What is the one thing that derails me in my work?
2.   What would be a game-changer for me in my career if I changed it?
Once you have named your weakness or derailer, develop a learning and development plan to address it.

PSYCHOLOGY OF WORK THEORY AND ADULT EDUCATION

This chapter is about the learning adults experience in their work and careers, an aspect of adult education (AE). Bierema et al. (2024) defined learning as "a process of transforming the basis of one's knowledge, skill, and attitude to create the potential for behavioral change" (p. 140). Yet, the notion of a "career" has been critiqued for being "embedded in an ethos of self-centered individualism and in an ethnocentric conception of the self" (Richardson, 1993, p. 48). Richardson argued that "work" connected more to adults' social roles, responsibilities, and communities (Blustein & Duffy, 2021). As an alternative, the Psychology of Working Theory (PWT) emerged based on arguments (Blustein, 2001, 2006) for more inclusive terminology that includes all adults who wish to work since the notion of a career "implied a level of volition and intentionality that arguably is to the prevailing experience for most workers around the globe" (Blustein & Duffy, 2021, p. 201). Despite "work" being considered more inclusive, Blustein and Duffy did not advocate doing away with the term "career," explaining

> ... we are comfortable with using the terms work and career; However, we propose that they should not be used interchangeably. In PWT, work is the broader concept, encompassing a wide array of activities and projects—as well as caregiving work—that is performed by people to meet needs for survival as well as higher order needs such as social contribution, interpersonal connection, and self-determination. A key attribute of our conceptualization of working is its integral connection to human activities that are essential to the existence, survival, and well-being of most adults across the globe throughout the eons. By contrast, vocational psychologists generally refer to career as "a sequence or collection of jobs one has held over the course of one's work life." (Lent & Brown, 2013, p. 8 as cited in Blustein & Duffy, 2021, p. 204)

The central precepts of PWT include work being a significant influence on individual and community well-being, being influenced by social, economic, and political forces, and affecting marketplace and caregiving contexts. Psychological and systemic interventions should consider people who work and those who want to work (Blustein et al., 2019; Blustein & Duffy, 2021).

PWT shares similar values with AE, especially since work-based learning is the most significant learning endeavor most adults will undertake during their lifetime. The conceptual foundations of PWT are rooted in social justice, similar to AE, to describe work-related experience and behavior that would inform change from individual to system levels. AE's early goals were to promote effective functioning for people as family members, workers, and citizens. Both approaches are interdisciplinary and value critical consciousness for adults to make informed choices in their lives and work, as described in Chapter 4, rooted in Freirean philosophy. PWT research has examined decent work—providing physically and interpersonally safe work with reasonable hours that promote balance; championing organizational values compatible with family and social values; compensating adequately; and ensuring access to health care (Duffy et al., 2016). Like AE, PWT research has examined economic constraints and marginalization and how they impact people's access to work. Finally, PWT also examines need satisfaction or how well people's needs for self-determination (autonomy, relatedness, and competency), survival, and social contribution are met through work. Translating PWT to practice also parallels the values of AE, including fostering empowerment, skill building, and critical consciousness in ways that enhance adults' capacity to learn, change, and thrive within a work context. PWT is also attuned to intersectionality and power relations, also important concepts in AE.

Certain learning and career theory principles apply to adult CD. Constructivism was introduced in Chapter 3 as people's creation of meaning from experience. Adults build work and careers that are personally meaningful and self-managed. To have meaningful careers, individuals must reflect on their experiences and make the necessary changes to keep their work or career aligned with their values and interests (Patton, 2000; Savickas, 2000). Career adaptability emphasizes making career changes without great difficulty to fit new or changing circumstances. It involves both an ability to cope with the predictable tasks of CD, such as preparing for and finding a job, as well as a future orientation that allows individuals to improve the match between their internal job description and the external world continuously (Plimmer et al., 2000; Savickas, 1997). Career adaptability "involves planful attitudes, self- and environmental exploration, and informed decision making" (Savickas, 1997, p. 254). Planned happenstance is a theory that helps individuals develop skills to recognize, create, and use chance in CD. Closely related to both constructivist notions of CD and career adaptability, it requires individuals to exercise curiosity to explore new learning opportunities, persist despite setbacks, meet changing attitudes and circumstances with flexibility, optimistically view new opportunities as possible and attainable, and take risks by being proactive in the face of uncertain outcomes (Mitchell et al., 1999). Box 5.3 details US adult learning participation rates.

▮▮ BOX 5.3 ADULT CAREER DEVELOPMENT BY THE NUMBERS

Adult Learning in the Workforce

This box contains summaries of research on AL from the National Center for Educational Statistics (NCES—see https://nces.ed.gov/).

The NCES conducts periodic surveys on *Participation in Adult Education and Lifelong Learning*. Results from the 2001 survey concluded:

> In 2001, the overall participation rate in formal AE during the 12-month period prior to the interview was 46 percent. About 92 million adults participated in one or more types of formal educational activities during this period. (p. vi)

The rate shifted from 40% to 45% during the 1990s, and a more recent survey has not been conducted.

During 2005, the breakdowns of adults taking specific programs, classes, or courses included (see https://nces.ed.gov/programs/digest/d19/tables/dt19_507.40.asp):

- Informal learning activities for personal interest: 70.5%
- Career or job-related courses: 27%
- Personal interest courses: 21.4%
- Basic skills/general educational development (GED) classes: 1.7%
- Part-time post-secondary education: 5%
- Apprenticeship programs: 1.2%
- English as a second language (ESL) classes: 0.9%

Informal learning is common among adults and is defined as learning outside a classroom or traditional, formal setting. Much of AL is self-directed, planned, and controlled by the learner. Work-related learning is the second highest area, where activities like workplace training occur.

Workplace training is a thriving industry, with *Training* magazine reporting in its annual Training Industry Report that US expenditures were US$10.1 billion in 2023, averaging US$954 per employee (Freifeld, 2023).

UNDERSTANDING ADULT LEARNING AND CHANGE

This section provides an overview of AL theory, focusing on its relevance for work and careers. The first section describes the characteristics of adult learners with implications for work and CD. Next, change is discussed as a primary motivator and outcome of learning. Then AL theories are profiled with implications for CD.

Understanding Adult Learners

Bierema (2019) observed, "Adult learning might be the most overlooked learning process across the lifespan" (p. 4), noting much more attention is paid to children's learning as they advance through primary and secondary school and, for some, through higher education. The same could be said for work and career learning, as non- and pre-adults tend to be its recipients. Bierema (2019) offered principles of AL which are summarized with implications for work and CD in Table 5.1.

Table 5.1   *Characteristics of adult learners and implications for adult career development*

Adult learning characteristic	Definition	Adult work and career development implications
Adult learning is distinguishable from children's learning	AL is distinguishable from children's learning in at least three ways: 1) Reflective capacity—An adult's ability to hold contrary thoughts and examine them simultaneously; 2) Experience—Adults have a rich repertoire of experiences that have taught them lessons and helped them develop values and assumptions about the world; and 3) Critical thinking—The ability to recognize and test assumptions, beliefs, and actions, and possibly change mindsets, thoughts, or actions.	Adults are likely to weigh work and career choices differently than children: 1) Reflective capacity—Assessing the pros and cons of job choices, people, and organizations. Questioning oneself about work performance, such as, *"How open am I to feedback?" or "What am I afraid of?"* are hallmarks of reflection. 2) Experience—Adults build expertise at work, yet this same deep knowledge may prevent them from seeing new ways of doing things, leading to career stagnation or lower performance. 3) Critical thinking—Rethinking values related to a career or shifting time used to be more flexible and adaptable, as occurred during the pandemic.

Adult learning characteristic	Definition	Adult work and career development implications
Learning helps adults cope with change	Change is often an impetus for learning in adulthood and few changes can be mastered without learning, and few lessons can be lasting without change. Change can be either planned or unplanned. Sometimes change creates identity crises and may force adults to question who they are, what they want, and whom they can trust. Change may also spur reflection on what they are giving back to others.	Planned change: A person plans to attend graduate school or change jobs. Unplanned change: A person gets fired; they weather a merger and acquisition that changes their work and culture; they have an unexpected failure; or they have an unanticipated traumatic event that derails their work. An unplanned change such as job loss or the pandemic might result in a values assessment and changes in knowledge, career direction, or organization.
Adult learning is life-centered	Adults are not usually motivated to learn something unless it is relevant to their life or work. They are life-centered, not subject-centered in their learning. Few adults would sign up for golf lessons unless they intended to play golf, for instance.	An aspiring promotion seeker was not motivated to seek help with leadership and interpersonal skills until they became aware the issues were hurting advancement prospects. This is also why compulsory training is usually ineffective. Adults are not motivated to participate unless the learning can be connected to relevance in their work or personal lives.
Experience is a key learning asset	Adults learn through life encounters, challenges, relationships, travels, and work. Sometimes experience can be a barrier to learning new ways of thinking and being that are at odds with what they already know.	Work and career experience is a tremendous resource for future learning and sharing with others. For example, the shift to remote work during the pandemic allowed adults to draw on their experience of doing their job and apply it in a new context. Some CEOs' push to return to in-person work might indicate their pre-pandemic experience is an obstacle to relearning how to run a business or conduct work in the aftermath of the pandemic, where remote work and flexibility are in high-demand among workers.

Adult learning characteristic	Definition	Adult work and career development implications
Adult learners tend to be risk-averse	Adults may be cautious in learning settings, particularly when they feel unsafe. They tend to seek the preservation of self-esteem and maintenance of self-efficacy. This means that adults fear making mistakes and looking "stupid" in front of their peers and will remain silent and withdrawn if uncomfortable in the learning setting.	Some people may avoid taking risks in their current work or stretching toward new assignments or promotions out of fear of failing or erring. They play it safe, although may regret it later.
Learning should be active and self-directed	Engaging learners in active learning such as discussions, practice, or teaching others is superior to passive learning activities such as lecture, reading, or demonstration. Passive learning strategies are poor at promoting the retention or transfer of learning.	The majority of learning adults engage in is self-directed. That is, the learner plans, controls, adjusts, and evaluates the learning themselves. For example, imagine if an adult were seeking to improve their leadership skills. They might read books, watch videos, take a lesson, observe peers or bosses, and solicit tips from trusted advisors. As the learner, they have designed and implemented the learning plan.
Learning is potentially transformational	Learning and change are intertwined and sometimes learning changes the essence of a person. This type of learning does not add to the repertoire of skills or knowledge a learner already possesses, but rather it shifts how they see themselves in the world. Transformative learning is grounded in change and change-producing learning. It does not change the information a person knows; it changes their self-perception. Transformative learning can be gradual or sudden.	A woman professional might not be conscious of gendered power relations in her organization until she notices she keeps being passed over for a promotion by less-qualified men. Suddenly she begins to observe how other women are being treated and how sexist the culture is. She becomes interested in women's rights at work and challenging the patriarchal culture. The woman, who was never interested in feminism and wouldn't consider herself a feminist, is now shifting her priorities and identity.

Appreciating Change and How it Relates to Work and Career

Change is the ongoing adaptation to the environment, which sometimes results in transformation. People change their minds, their circumstances shift, and they experience crises. Change is often unwelcome, and it takes many forms in work and careers. Impermanent change might be doing an internship, taking a position temporarily, or deciding a job is a poor fit after a few months. Transitional change occurs as adults navigate career moves, perhaps into new roles or organizations. Sometimes change is reversible, such as trying a new position and returning to the old one. Permanent change is lasting: A job ends, colleagues change, or the environment shifts. Finally, change can be transformational in ways that change how a person sees their work or career. The pandemic was the impetus for such transformation for many workers who used the opportunity to assess their work and make decisions that reflected new insights and value shifts in the pandemic's aftermath. Some people even changed careers. Change is not just an individual phenomenon. Organizations also encounter change through leadership reshuffling, market shifts, product innovation, competition, and crisis. The COVID-19 pandemic was a dramatic experience in the need and capacity to radically change personal and professional behavior overnight, proving that change does not need to take a long time or planning in some instances and can occur rapidly on a global scale.

Lewin (1947) developed a three-step model of change that involved (a) Unfreezing, (b) Moving, and (c) Refreezing. Unfreezing occurs when people or organizations grasp a need to change and decide to make one. Unfreezing is metaphorical for transferring from one state to another and may be brought on by a problem, opportunity, crisis, new knowledge, or feedback. For example, if a person is fired, they will experience a crisis, perhaps of identity, and need to regroup and find a new position. Suddenly being on the job market and needing income creates the impetus for change. Moving, step 2, is taking action to change. The person who was fired decides to use the opportunity to develop new skills and enroll in either a certificate or degree program to better position them for future employment. The person may also undergo a personal transformation in how they view themselves and their career. Moving involves engaging in actions to transform and sustain the change. Refreezing involves measures to cement and sustain the change to ensure it is permanent. Although the fired individual has engaged in skill building, they also need to safeguard that any previous behaviors that might have contributed to their firing are corrected and replaced with more productive behaviors. Box 5.4 shares data on the types of learning adults undergo at work as they learn and change during their careers.

▮ BOX 5.4 ADULT CAREER DEVELOPMENT BY THE NUMBERS

Adult Learning in the Workforce

This box contains summaries of research on AL from the National Center for Educational Statistics (NCES—see https://nces.ed.gov/). The latest *Adult Training and Education Survey* by NCES:

> … collected data about adults ages 16 to 65 who are not enrolled in high school. The survey focused on nondegree credentials and work experience programs. Nondegree credentials included two types of work credentials–certifications and licenses–and postsecondary educational certificates. Work experience programs included internships, co-ops, practicums, clerkships, externships, residencies, clinical experiences, and apprenticeships. Characteristics of adults were also collected, including level of education, labor force and employment status, earnings, job sector, and occupational field. (para. 1)

The total number of completed ATES questionnaires was 47,744, representing a population of 196.3 million. Here are selected findings from the report (Cronen et al., 2017):

Nondegree credentials:

- In 2016, a total of 27% of adults reported having a nondegree credential—that is, having a postsecondary certificate, a certification, or a license.
- These work credentials were more prevalent among adults with college degrees than those with less education. For example, 48% of adults with a graduate or professional degree had a work credential compared to 5% with less than a high school education.
- Most work credential holders reported that their most important credential was for their current job (85%) and that they prepared for their most important work credential by taking classes from a college, technical school, or trade school (67%).

Work experience programs:

- Overall, 21% of adults reported completing a work experience program.
- Work experience programs can include a range of characteristics. Overall, 11% of adults completed a work experience program in which they were *paid*; 6% completed a program that *lasted one year or more*; 14% completed a program that was *part of an educational program after high school*, and 9% completed a program that included both *instruction, training or classes* and *evaluation by a co-worker or supervisor*.

- Among adults who reported completing a work experience program, the most prevalent program field was health care (26%), and the second-most prevalent field was teaching (13%).

Usefulness of nondegree credentials and work experience programs:

- A majority of adults reported that their most important work credential was beneficial for getting a job (82%), keeping a job (80%), remaining marketable to employers or clients (81%), and improving work skills (66%).
- Among adults who reported completing a work experience program, 64% found them to be very useful for getting a job, 66% thought they were very useful for improving work skills, but only 37% considered them to be useful for increasing their pay.

Interpreting Career Development through Adult Learning Theories

Adult learning (AL) is the process of adults attaining discipline or contextual knowledge, skill, and expertise. AL in CD is concerned with job preparation for work contexts such as becoming a lawyer within a corporation. Adult development is an accumulation of systematic behavioral change over time as a person engages with the world through relationships, experience, schooling, and trial and error. Adult development in career terms might be the corporate lawyer's interests and priorities shifting over time to practicing law in non-profit organizations. The theories in this brief overview are presented chronologically, representing how theory developed historically. The first group of theories focuses on adult learners' distinguishing characteristics and learning preferences. The second group of theories shifted away from learner description to understanding the process of learning itself—what happens in the hearts, minds, and bodies of adults when they learn. The third body of theory considers the environment or social context where AL occurs and uncovers how social inequities and injustice affect whether learners are privileged or marginalized in their learning encounters.

Adult learning theory describing the learner

AL theory emerged during the mid-20th century when scholars such as Knowles (1980, 1984) popularized andragogy—distinguishing adult from child learning. Houle (1961) identified adult motivation to learn as related to achieving specific goals, engaging in social activity, or learning for the sake of learning. Tough (1989) studied AL projects to discover that adults were self-directed learners. The work of Knowles, Houle, and Tough led to the development of self-directed learning theory (Brockett & Hiemstra, 1991; Garrison, 1997; Grow, 1991)—the idea that adults design, organize, manage, and evaluate their learning projects that are outside formal education, such as learning to bake sourdough bread or learning a new language. Next, theories began emerging to describe what happens when adults learn.

Adult learning theory describing the learning process
Transformative learning emerged in the late 20th century (Cranton, 2016; Mezirow, 1978, 1991; Taylor & Cranton, 2012) and is the process of change that dramatically and fundamentally shifts how an adult sees themselves in the world (Merriam & Baumgartner, 2020), such as how the COVID-19 pandemic changed many adults' perceptions of their work and careers. Experiential learning is learning by doing (Boud & Walker, 1991; Dewey, 1938; Fenwick, 2003; Knowles, 1984; Kolb, 1984; Lindeman, 1961; Marsick & Watkins, 1990). For example, a person cannot learn how to be a good public speaker until they practice public speaking before an audience. Reading books and observing others might be helpful cognitively and affectively, but they will not help someone hone their skills as a speaker behaviorally. Merriam and Baumgartner (2020) identified five lenses through which experiential learning is understood (a) Constructivist—making meaning from life's encounters, (b) Situative—engaging with a community of practice and learning by doing, (c) Psychoanalytic—the need for a learner to surface unconscious fears and desires, (d) Critical—the need to resist dominant and oppressive social norms, and (e) Complexity—learning through networks of relationships focused on challenging problems that lack clarity or clear answers.

More contemporary AL theory and process descriptions emerged in the late 20th and early 21st centuries. Embodied, spiritual, and narrative learning theories understand learning as dwelling in and constructed and interpreted by the learner (Merriam & Baumgartner, 2020). Embodied learning (Amann, 2003; Lawrence, 2012) is knowing through the body or senses and the experiences of the heart, body, and mind (Merriam & Baumgartner, 2020). For instance, a person may know they are feeling fear or anger in their body before it registers in their brain. Spiritual learning (English et al., 2003; English & Tisdell, 2010; Graves, 1977; Tisdell, 2003) is a lifelong process of meaning-making and mindfulness, similar to, but different from, religion. It focuses on the soul in building the capacity for thought and action). Narrative learning (Rossiter & Clark, 2007) uses stories to construct meaning related to the self, others, and the world. Eastern and indigenous perspectives of learning are ancient, although they emerged in AL literature in the late 20th century as a counter to the rational, objective biases of Western educational theories that advocate personal freedom, separate people from nature, and view dominant Western knowledge as universal and valid over all other ways of knowing (Merriam & Baumgartner, 2020).

Adult learning theory describing the learning context
Another shift in AE theory was to trouble social context, social injustice, and inequality. Critical theory, postmodern, and feminist learning are contemporary theories that critique power relations, focusing on how the intersection of race, class, gender, and other positionalities affect the distribution of resources leading to privilege and oppression in society. Critical theory critiques social and economic structures and the power they create (Merriam & Baumgartner, 2020). Brookfield (2012) suggested a framework for critical theory in AE—and I have added examples: (a) Challenging ideology or the givens of everyday life—Such as refusing to use the term "mankind" to represent all humanity, since half of humanity is womankind; (b) Contesting hegemony through opposing it—Hegemony is people's acceptance of unjust social practices that hurt them such as voting for a candidate that will not protect their interests; (c) Unmasking power through collective discourse to recognize and oppose it—Countered by joining a union or activist group and sharing stories and collective action; (d) Overcoming alienation through reclaiming freedom and creativity—Deleting social media accounts from unethical platforms and finding more affirming spaces for engagement; (e) Individually and collectively learning liberation from dominant ways of thinking—Making acquaintances with people different from one's culture and joining their cause; (f) Reclaiming reason and applying it widely, particularly with concern for values to live by—Refusing unrealistic standards of beauty; and (g) Practicing democracy by realizing its limits and engaging in it—Volunteering in the community to help a political or social cause. Postmodernism explores shifting power, knowledge, space, and time globally (Giroux, 2006). The term VUCA introduced in Chapter 2 captures the postmodern world that needs adaptive approaches to learning and problem-solving. Feminist pedagogy is a diverse arena of theory and activism, and when applied to AL is concerned with women and other marginalized groups' learning that raises their consciousness and activism in an unjust world (hooks, 1994; Lee & Johnson-Bailey, 2004; Tisdell, 1995). Generative learning (Nicolaides, 2023) focuses on adults learning to "become" amid a VUCA context that requires learning through inquiry, being vulnerable, humble, and willing to question ways of knowing, doing, and being, and being open to what emerges.

Illustrating Adult Learning Theory's Relevance to Career Development

Before delving into this section, complete the activity in Box 5.5 to reflect on major work or career milestones. Table 5.2 provides a definition of major AL theories and their relevance to CD. As you read the theories and examples, consider how they apply to you as a career explorer, sustainer, or changer.

⌣ BOX 5.5 REFLECTIVE PRACTICE

Tying Adult Learning Theory to Your Own Work or Career Development Story

Take a few minutes and write a brief story capturing the history of your CD. Alternatively, plot your CD along the continuum provided in this box from your earliest memory to today, noting major educational accomplishments, jobs, promotions, and other significant moments.

Earliest	Present Day
Career	
Memory	

Next, make some notes, either in the margins of your story or on the timeline, of what theories applied to your experience. Review AL theory in Table 5.2 and see which theories describe your learning process at the time.

Table 5.2   *Adult learning theory definitions and career development applications*

Adult learning theory	Definition	Career development application
Andragogy	Lindeman (1961) was the first to use the term "andragogy" (the art of teaching adults), and Knowles (1984) propagated the term. Knowles (1980, 1984) proposed certain assumptions about AL: 1. People's self-concept shifts from dependence toward self-direction as they develop and mature. 2. Adults' cumulative life experience is a rich learning resource. 3. Adult readiness to learn relates to their tasks or social roles. 4. Adults are motivated to learn by timely, relevant knowledge application rather than subject-centered. 5. Adults are internally motivated to learn. 6. Adults need to understand the rationale and value of learning something.	The principles of andragogy align with adult career learning by: 1. Focusing on career-relevant learning, such as seeking certifications or specialized training to better perform in one's current role or advance. 2. Using career experience to apply to adults' work and learning and comparing future learning to their current knowledge. 3. Connecting learning to work and social roles. For example, adults may not be interested in leadership training until they aspire to move into a leadership role or improve as a leader. 4. Engaging in career learning that immediately applies to their work tasks or goals, such as improving team leadership skills when asked to lead a project. 5. Recognizing adults are self-motivated and internally driven to learn, rather than being inspired by the boss telling them to. 6. Understanding when adults learn something, they need to know how it is relevant to their work or the organization, such as how a tool might enhance teamwork.

Adult learning theory	Definition	Career development application
Self-directed learning	Knowles (1975) defined self-directed learning (SDL) as adults taking the initiative (with or without others' help) to diagnose their learning needs, formulate learning goals, and identify resources for learning, choosing and implementing appropriate learning strategies, and evaluating the results (p. 18).	A person might engage in career SDL by diagnosing their learning needs, such as preparing for advancement. They formulate learning goals that include attending company-sponsored leadership development and furthering their education. They identify resources for learning, including reputable training and master's degree programs, and ultimately select one. They choose appropriate resources as they learn, which may be human or material such as mentors, peers, networks, university personnel, professional associations, library or internet sources. They hone their academic skills to succeed in the program. Eventually, they graduate and use that milestone to evaluate the results as satisfactory, as well as to achieve their career goal when that eventually occurs. Note that although learning is self-directed, adults often seek the help of others or enroll in formal courses.

Adult learning theory	Definition	Career development application
Experiential learning	Experiential learning enhances knowledge from life and work encounters, such as formal training, observation, or mistakes. Prior life experience shapes people's values, expectations, knowledge, skills, and attitudes. Learning can also be designed to be experiential in that it simulates real life. Importantly, not all experiences are educative; some can miseducate, such as fake news or faulty instruction. Although there are several models of experiential learning, Kolb's (1984) learning cycle is highly applicable to CD. The cycle illuminates how knowledge is created through the transformation of experience through stages of concrete experience, reflective observation, abstract conceptualization, and active experimentation.	Kolb's (1984) learning cycle might be reflected in career learning in the following ways for you as a career explorer, sustainer, or changer: 1. Concrete experience—Ability to involve yourself fully, openly, and without bias in a learning experience, such as becoming immersed in learning to lead your team. 2. Reflective observation—Ability to reflect on and observe your experience from many perspectives, such as reflecting on how a meeting went and how you influenced interaction or impinged the discussion. You might also ask others for feedback. 3. Abstract conceptualization—Ability to create concepts that integrate your observations into logically sound theories. Imagine you received the feedback that you interrupt too often and listen poorly. You might begin to analyze why you behave this way and question why you are not always aware of your behavior. You also decide to learn more about how to improve your communication skills. 4. Active experimentation—Ability to use your theories to make decisions and solve problems. You use the feedback, your observations, and learning to experiment with more effective meeting leadership and interpersonal communication, and the cycle repeats.

Adult learning theory	Definition	Career development application
Transformative learning	"Transformational learning shapes people; they are different afterward, in ways both they and others can recognize" (Clark, 1993, p. 47). Transformational learning (TL) does not change a person's knowledge but rather how they see themselves in the world. TL causes people to question their assumptions and beliefs, take new perspectives, and act on them. Mezirow (1978) suggested TL begins with a "disorienting dilemma" or a significant personal event such as a tragedy, trauma, loss, or other event that triggers change. Accumulated experience over time can also serve as a triggering event.	Mezirow suggested ten phases that occur in TL: Experience a disorienting dilemma; Engage in self-examination or questioning of beliefs; Critically assess past assumptions and knowledge; Recognize shared experiences; Explore new options for action; Plan a course of action; Acquire knowledge; Try new roles; Build confidence; and Reintegrate the new self into life. For example: (1) First, a *disorienting dilemma*: after numerous incidents of sexist treatment in the workplace, (2) a woman employee begins to *question her assumptions* about equality in the workplace. (3) She critically *assesses the assumptions* she held before the initiation of her learning (that is, that men and women are treated equally in the workplace). (4) She begins to *recognize other women who share her discontent* with their experience of sexist treatment and want to do something about it. (5) The women gather to *explore options for new roles, relationships, and actions.* (6) They collectively *plan a course of action*, such as forming a women's network and bringing sexist practices to management's attention. (7) They *acquire knowledge and skills* for implementing the plans through reading, networking, and dialoguing. (8) They *try new roles*, such as supporting each other in meetings and strategically representing women's interests in the organization. As they experiment with roles, they begin to (9) *build confidence* in their new roles and relationships and (10) *reintegrate* this new, more gender-conscious way of being into their daily lives (Mezirow, 1991).

Adult learning theory	Definition	Career development application
Embodied learning	Embodied learning is also known as embodiment, somatic learning, and embodied cognition (Merriam & Bierema, 2013). It engages the whole body in the learning process, not just the mind, to also include the physical, emotional, cultural, and cognitive aspects of learning. Sometimes it is referred to as tacit knowing or a gut feeling— something a person may intuitively know but not be able to explain why.	When dealing with a difficult problem at work, two colleagues decide to walk outside and talk through the issues. Physical movement, such as walking, engages the senses and the body physically and qualitatively and impacts the quality of learning because the environment affects perception, the light is different, and the people and objects encountered along the way factor into the experience. When walking, senses are heightened, usually making people more creative. It may also enable difficult conversations more readily than sitting in an office. During the walk, the pair share their perspectives on the problem, discuss how they each might be helping and hurting the issue, and return to the office with clearer heads and some ideas for the next steps. Practices such as yoga, meditation, tai chi, or mindfulness can also strengthen the mind-body connection and help people in their careers and life.

Adult learning theory	Definition	Career development application
Spiritual learning	Western learning theories have rationalized the mind and learning. Spirituality is a counter to such thinking and is often imagined as soul, grace, flow, life force, or something beyond the self (Merriam & Bierema, 2013). It is an inner journey of discovery and can help adults construct knowledge and meaning while working (Tisdell, 2001). Spirituality is also expressed in social movements. Spirituality in AE has been studied in adult development—especially identity development, social action and justice movements, and the workplace. You et al. (2021) defined workplace spirituality as experiencing a sense of purpose and meaning in one's work and feeling a sense of connectedness with work colleagues and the community. They noted spirituality is a highly personal and philosophical construct, although it tends to involve a sense of wholeness, connectedness at work, and deeper values.	Ellen was a devoted environmentalist whose life purpose was to live lightly on the earth and minimize wastefulness. Career-wise, she wanted to work for an organization that shared her values and was committed to the triple bottom line of human, environmental, and economic success. She aimed for and was hired by Patagonia, an outdoor gear maker that is deeply committed to sustainability through its environmentalist practices and activism. The company's core mission is to save the planet and build its products to ensure function, repairability, and durability. The founder and former CEO, Yvon Chouinard, famously declared in 2000, "Earth is our only shareholder." The company is known for leaders with a spiritual connection to their work and the intentionality of the people who chose to work there due to its mission. The company has transparency in its environmental performance and charitable standards and uses recycled material extensively in its production process and is working toward a goal of eliminating its use of fossil fuels. The company also engages in the conservation of vulnerable land, protecting plants and animals. It also follows fair labor practices and works with suppliers to improve their wages. The company has also been known to take activist stances like pulling its products, for instance, when a resort co-owner in Jackson Hole, Wyoming, held a fundraiser for US Representative Marjorie Taylor Greene. The company is committed to cutting its ties with "anti-democratic conspiracy theorists" said CEO Ryan Gellert (Tong & Hagan, 2021, para. 3). They also turned off paid advertisements on Facebook and Instagram in this quest. The CEO explained, "If you are a business and your sole reason for existing is making money and offering product to as big a slice of humanity as possible, I suppose that does make sense ... That's not our reason for being" (Tong & Hagan, 2021, para. 9).

Adult learning theory	Definition	Career development application

Narrative learning	Narrative learning is learning through stories that occur in at least three ways (Clark, 2010):
	
	1. People learn from hearing stories on the news or internet and from family, friends, and co-workers.
	2. People tell stories and can play the roles of the listener and the actor where meaning is being made from an experience.
	3. People recognize how the narratives are positioned in the stories, which can be critical and emancipatory.
		To apply narrative to a career, consider your career story as a career explorer, sustainer, and/or changer. According to Jarr and Hunderman's (2021) article for the National Career Development Association (NCDA), this constructivist approach to CD can help turn life experience into career aspirations with actionable goals. They referenced the story of Nigerian novelist Chimamanda Ngozi Adichie (see Box 5.6), whose early stories did not reflect her experience or culture. They offered exercises for developing a career story:
		
		1. The Seven Stories Exercise:
		  a. Make a list of 25 life experiences that you enjoyed, did well, and made you proud.
		  b. Select seven experiences from the list of 25 and rank them from 1–7 in terms of their importance.
		  c. Write a paragraph about each of the seven experiences. What was the context? Who was involved? Did you act alone or with others? What was done and achieved? What made it enjoyable?
		  d. Analyze your stories.
		  e. From your analysis, identify potential career paths you might enjoy.
		
		2. The SOAR Method (How to structure a short story about yourself):
		  f. S—The situation or circumstance in which you were involved;
		  g. O—The opportunity that existed for, first, your organization, then for you;
		  h. A—The actions you took;
		  i. R—The results of your action.

116

Rethinking adult career development

Adult learning theory	Definition	Career development application
Eastern and indigenous learning perspectives	These ancient theories, yet relatively new to AL, share themes of interdependency, community, holism, and informal learning. Identity, self-concept, and esteem are only developed and enhanced in relation to others. It is everyone's responsibility to teach and learn within the community. Learning serves more than just the mind, as it also includes the body and spirit. Finally, learning is informal, situated in daily life (Merriam & Baumgartner, 2020).	Here are some strategies for honoring different perspectives in the CD process summarizing ideas from Merriam and Baumgartner (2020, pp. 276–286): 1. Focus on holism in the career such as mind-body connection, engagement with nature, and the whole of the universe. 2. Imitate the virtues of another person in your life and work, particularly when one does not know how to act in a certain situation. 3. Enjoy and engage in holistic learning daily, including connecting with nature. 4. Make people a central focus and value, with the good of the community in mind. 5. Accept responsibility to share knowledge with others. 6. Embark on a career that is responsible to society and elevates the community. 7. Become a lifelong learner. 8. Engage in participatory learning through ritual, spiritual work, recreation, storytelling, poetry, and teaching.

Adult learning theory	Definition	Career development application
Critical theory, postmodern, and feminist learning	These contemporary approaches critique power relations focusing on how the intersection of race, class, and gender affects the distribution of resources leading to privilege and oppression in society. These theories also examine the nature of knowledge and truth and the construction of meaning and learning.	Bierema et al. (2022) proposed a model of critical feminist developmental relationships (e.g., mentoring, networking, or coaching)—an invaluable CD resource if the relationship dyad is effective. They suggested that dismantling systemic oppression through these relationships depends on an effective developmental relationship as a foundation that builds the capacity to navigate cultural and organizational dynamics that preserve unjust organizational practices and policies. Integrating criticality into developmental relationships involves interpreting the context, naming what is occurring, and acting for change, for example, a mentor and mentee dialogue about injustices and how to mutually interpret and act on racism, sexism, or other isms within the culture in ways that value cultural diversity, engage in cycles of reflection and action, challenge the status quo and act for change on individual, team, system, and community levels. Shoukry (2016) studied emancipatory coaching dyads and found they used tools of retelling narratives using consciousness-raising and naming of the lived experience of oppression, surfacing mindsets and assumptions about structural contributors to oppression, and creating ways of fighting back through learning new mindsets and behaviors of resistance and change.

Adult learning theory	Definition	Career development application
Generative learning	Nicolaides (2023) implored, "the field of AE is grappling with how adults learn in a world being recomposed by a global pandemic and the *Ruptures* that have emerged from its influence" (p. 8, italics in original). She offered generative learning as a strategy for keeping pace with the rapid rate of change and described it as a process of "*learning to become*" (p. 8). She described three aspects of generative knowing as ruptures, in-scending, and awaring.	1. Ruptures occur when the unknown is met with learning, and the learner faces complexity, ambiguity, and the unfamiliar in their career, such as during the COVID-19 pandemic. This state of rupture is frightening and unrooting, where the temptation is to cling to how the world was pre-pandemic, a phenomenon that can shut down learning. People who managed ruptures well during the pandemic used the time as an opportunity for change and new learning about how, where, and when to do their work. 2. In-scending follows rupture and involves learning that includes sitting with the unknown and making meaning out of the situation. During the pandemic people engaged in in-scending might have asked, "What am I feeling?" "What don't I understand?" or "How can I behave most ethically?" 3. Awaring is the culmination of generative knowing when new learning inspires action. The pandemic provided workers with a unique opportunity to reevaluate their work lives and make changes. For example, some people quit their jobs for more flexible and humane workplaces. Others changed careers entirely, enrolling in school or shifting to new career paths in new organizations. Others dropped out of the workforce completely. People who failed to learn from the pandemic are those demanding a return to work as if the pandemic never occurred, with face time in the office, long hours and commutes, and toxic work cultures.

BOX 5.6 TIPS AND TOOLS FOR CAREER DEVELOPMENT

The Danger of a Single-Story: TED Talk by Chimamanda Ngozi Adichie

Narrative learning was one of the AL theories profiled in this section. As a career explorer, sustainer, or changer, listen to Chimamanda Ngozi Adichie's (2009) TED Talk about the importance of not having or believing a single story about yourself, places, or others. Visit

> https:// www .ted .com/ talks/ chimamanda _ngozi _adichie _the _danger _of _a _single_story or search for "The danger of a single story."

Questions for reflection:
1. What does her message mean as you think about your story or the important stories you have heard or retold related to your or others' careers?
2. How does power show up in your stories?
3. How is what you believe about your career dependent on a single story?
4. What stories form you?
5. How might you want to change your story?

FORGING ADULT AND CAREER IDENTITY

So far, this chapter has introduced AL and change and linked them with the psychology of work and CD. The last section connects adult and identity development to work and careers. This section begins with an overview of adult identity development and links it with identity and CD, considering the important ways intersectionality affects adult work and career identity. The chapter concludes with pragmatic applications of CD theory (Yates, 2022) that examine the key content of CD—identity and environment, and key processes of CD—career learning and psychological resources—a melding of work, career, and AL theory and practice.

Linking Identity and Adult Career Development

Identity, according to Gedro (2017), includes self-concept, and individual, personal, and social identity. She noted, "Individual identity is concerned with the self; Personal identity is concerned with the extent to which one person relates or identifies with another person; And social identity refers to the way that an individual perceives membership in a group or organization" (p. 23). Personal identity might be synonymous with "personal brand" in the sense that it is the combination of unique attributes, goals, and desires of a person that are not shared with others and not necessarily connected with group memberships (Gedro, 2017). Identity is also influenced by group membership and how people self-categorize or identify in terms of the groups they belong to and the roles they assume since personal identity represents relationships between and among people (Gedro, 2017). People will often describe their identity as "I'm a mother," "I'm a corporate accountant," "I'm a graduate student at the University of Georgia," or "I am a nonprofit executive director," all indicators of how they are in relationship with family, work colleagues, classmates, or community members. People build relationships out of personally identifying with attributes of other people, developing connections, and seeing themselves in new ways through the relationship, such as mentoring (Gedro, 2017).

The notion of "self-concept" is foregrounded in traditional CD theories (e.g., Gottfredson, Super, Holland). People develop their careers based on their self-concept, and it is undeniable that their identities influence this development. Also, one's identity can directly influence CD. Gedro (2017) illustrated this connection: "How do gender dynamics impact a CD relationship? When working with a single mother with a high school education, who is re-entering the workforce, to what extent does the identity of the career developer impact the effectiveness of the relationship?" (p. 33). Gedro (2017) continued, "To ignore identity, to pretend it does not exist or to shy away from discussing it, perpetuates a tacit mythology that the world of work is based upon merit, and that it is not impacted by dominant paradigms, populations, and identities" (p. 34). Gedro concluded, "Identity, however, should be contained for use only in limited ethical, responsible, and transparent ways and not in ways that limit the potential of the employee" (p. 43).

Connecting Intersectional Identity and Career Development

People have multiple social identities, such as gender, race, sexual orientation, social class, age, (dis)ability, religion, and other positionalities. The identities intersect (e.g., gender*race) and shape people's unique experiences, as described in Chapter 4. Kimberlé Crenshaw (1989), a Black feminist and a leading scholar of Critical Race Theory (CRT), coined the term "intersectionality" in her article "Demarginalizing the intersection of race and sex: Black feminist critique of antidiscrimination doctrine, feminist theory and antiracist politics." She thought her unique, oppressive experiences as a Black woman could not be explained by the single axis, either "gender" or "race," and said, "the intersectional experience is *greater* than the sum of racism and sexism" (Crenshaw, 1989, p. 140, italics in original). The oppressive experiences cannot be just the sum of the system of oppression (e.g., sexism + racism), because social identities are not separable and independent. Intersectionality posits that identities are mutually constitutive, interrelated, and intersecting. Thus, intersectionality interrogates the "interlocking" systems of oppression (e.g., sexism*racism).

Intersecting identities impact one's CD. Statistics show that multiply marginalized groups are more likely to be disadvantaged in the workplace. Only 1.2% of CEOs in Global Fortune 500 companies are women of color, and 21.6% of Black people with disabilities are unemployed, compared to 11.2% of White people with disabilities and 11% of Black people with no disability (United States Bureau of Labor Statistics, 2016). Also, gendered ageism, "discriminatory actions, whether intentional or unintentional, that are based on the intersection of gender and age" (Jyrkinen, 2014, p. 176) may systematically disrupt and restrict older women's CD. Appearance and attractiveness, which disproportionately matter for women, oppress older women more than older men (Gedro, 2017). Jyrkinen (2014) found that older women tended to live up to the entrenched ideal of beauty in the workplace (e.g., young, slim) and "felt obliged to 'keep up their looks' in order to be successful in their careers" (p. 182). Besides these examples, multiple identities, which are fluid and intersecting, shape people's experiences and CD. More importantly, power imbalance exists across the identities, and interlocking systems of oppression reinforce the power structure, which disproportionately influences multiply marginalized groups. CD professionals need to understand the effects of identities in CD and try to question CD practices and programs that buttress the gap between historically privileged groups and marginalized groups.

Identity is the meanings attached to a person by themselves or others that are usually connected to the person's social roles, plus any idiosyncratic character traits or personal identities they exhibit—they are social constructions people hold and portray in terms of how they wish to be regarded in society (Sealy & Singh, 2010). Gedro (2017) explained that career identity is a subset of identity in that it is influenced by the priority a person puts on work and their organization concerning their personal identity or self-image. Walker (2013) defined career insight as holding realistic views of the self and work context in relationship to career goals and using the information to make career choices. They viewed this process as a self-monitoring feedback loop. Walker (2013) also defined career resilience as coping with a suboptimal work context or recovering from career challenges.

Gedro (2017) identified key aspects of adult identity, including that it is fluid, drawing on queer theory illuminating,

> It provides such a powerful way to think about how categories, labels, language, customs, conventions, dress, speech, mannerisms, and expectations have the power

to put people in boxes that may or may not fit their own sense of self. These social constructions of identity can shape who people conceive themselves to be; The act of forming one's own sense of self, of identifying, creating, and manifesting career choices, represents a daunting yet exciting way to think about life itself. (pp. 47–48)

Identity is also constructed—much like learning is constructed—through people's frames of experience, cognition, and engagements with role models, different social contexts, and other social dynamics. This means that career explorers, sustainers, and changers, along with their helpers, need to be cognizant of identity-facilitating factors—supportive context, positive experiences, and self-confidence, as well as impeding factors—stigmatized identity, negative experience, and difficult contexts (Gedro, 2017). Identity is constantly being interpreted and reinterpreted, often as internal and interpersonal dialogue. Gedro (2017) explained that the binarized construction of identities (e.g., straight or gay, woman or man) are ways the dominant culture regulates identity. This is one reason White, straight men enjoy privilege in many organizational cultures and society through their easier access to jobs, housing, and cultural and social functions (Gedro, 2017). Gedro emphasized,

> Although it mostly rests on the constructions of sexuality, gender expression, and gender identity, Queer Theory is useful and important as a template for this argument that identity is a social construction, and that identity is not power-neutral. Identity is a contested construct ... Identity is a continuous process that is reshaped and reformed over the life (and work) course. There are some identities that have privilege built into them, and some identities that have marginalization built into them, and there are some identities that are perhaps somewhere in between. (p. 49)

Gedro also argued that identity is contested and negotiated terrain between the person and the organization, a point that has been argued throughout *Rethinking Adult Career Development*. This terrain becomes contested due to the blurring of lines between life and work, a dynamic accentuated by the COVID-19 pandemic. Given the age of the protean and boundaryless career, how far a worker should be identified with and loyal to an organization is debatable, yet people's identities are shaped by the organization's culture and how the culture frames identities (Gedro, 2017). The extent to which organizations welcome and support non-work identities is visible by whether they provide onsite daycare, gyms, cafeterias, work-from-home technology, employee affinity groups, or invite the inclusion of these identities at work. Problematically, when identities are not recognized by a culture, such as racial or sexual and gender identity minorities, people will feel pressure to suppress those identities (Gedro, 2017).

Integrating Identity Crisis, Adult Development, and Career Development

Adults' ability to construct meaning is a fundamental marker of adulthood, especially since life presents ongoing developmental tasks and challenges. Adulthood has at least three recurring themes of development that repeat over and over in adulthood. Erikson (2001) identified these developmental dilemmas as related to identity, collegial intimacy, and generativity.

(Re)Interpreting identity: Who am I?

The term "identity crisis" or "midlife crisis" refers to the developmental challenge of identity. As already described, identity incorporates the traits and characteristics that make a person unique and shapes their self-concept, self-image, self-esteem, and individuality. An identity crisis can be brought about by any major life change that requires a person to resolve identity issues such as a promotion, achieving a milestone like graduating from a degree program, getting fired, or contending with a personal emergency. Adults successfully address identity issues when they begin to adjust, embrace, and reincorporate the change into their lives. Characteristics of effectively navigating this adult developmental challenge include:

- Articulating qualities most central to the self, especially during change. For example, being able to state, "I am _____."
- Developing a core self-image that provides continuity and sameness.
- Building a sense of "inner firmness" or resolve in one's individuality.
- Realizing strong values and beliefs that relate to social and work roles.
- Finding a vocation.
- Resolving the main identity learning dilemma: Identity is called into question during change, raising the question, "Can I be faithful or live up to my identity?"

For example, Jane was recently unexpectedly divorced and found herself working full time after being a stay-at-home mom for many years. Jane saw herself as a mother and homemaker and was unhappy to shift her focus and energies to something that felt unnatural. She was also unsure about herself around her work colleagues and questioned her experience and capacity to contribute. Jane enrolled in a master's degree program to feel more confident in her work role and upgrade her skills. Although she was excited to learn, Jane initially felt out of place among the students. As she progressed through her program, Jane began to feel clearer about herself and could see how her identity as a mom translated to her new role. She recognized her talents and developed new skills. She realized she had a lot to learn but felt more comfortable and aligned with herself and her values as she adjusted to her new life and career path.

Developing collegial intimacy: How is my interpersonal competence?
Collegial intimacy is building high-quality, trusting relationships with professional contacts such as peers, supervisors, mentors, supervisees, and others in the workplace. Betzler and Löschke (2021) defined "collegial" (colleagues) as sharing two of the same: (a) Work content or activity domain, (b) Institutional affiliation or common purpose, and (c) Status or responsibility level. Work is accomplished through relationships with others, making it crucial to develop skill at collegial intimacy. Betzler and Löschke (2021) found that a person must be proficient at their work to be considered a good colleague, and people are likely to be better colleagues when their work is regarded as valuable. Characteristics of collegial intimacy include respecting another colleague's identity without imposing the self; willingness to take risks, make compromises, sacrifice, and keep commitments; and the ability to work cooperatively, compete effectively, and seek and offer help. Good colleagues have influence and are influenceable. They form lasting relationships and earn trust. The most considerable aspect of this developmental dilemma is what happens when trust and integrity are challenged. Feltman (2021) defined trust as "choosing to risk making something you value vulnerable to another person's actions" (p. 9) and distrust as "what is important to me is not safe with this person in this situation (or any situation)" (p. 11).

For example, as people age, their beliefs become stronger. Joe has been around his company for a long time and strongly feels that in-person communication is superior to any other mode of connecting. Between the pandemic and technological advances to allow remote meetings and connecting, the younger workers tease him and pressure him to "get with the 21st century and hold a meeting on Zoom." These remarks initially hurt Joe, yet he valued his relationships with the team. He opted to reflect on how his views and behaviors impacted himself, others, and the organization and concluded he needed to be more flexible. Joe might have damaged his relationships with the team if he decided to dig in his heels. Managing collegial intimacy is about how people's views and actions interact with their colleagues. Preserving collegial intimacy creates a constant tussle over wills and demands integrity, compromise, negotiation, and influence if people are to manage relationships and preserve trust effectively. When people experience failure in this realm, it can cause feelings of being unloved, unliked, unlovable, and unlikeable. These dynamics tend to repeat themselves as conflict ensues with parents, significant others, children, friends, co-workers, and society, and are a developmental challenge that is part of living, particularly in how to effectively resolve events that threaten relationships.

Fostering generativity: Am I ready to care for and nurture the next generation?

Generativity is a person's desire to give back or leave a legacy by engaging in activities that promote the well-being and sustainability of the next generation of beings and the earth. Although it is sometimes associated with aging, generativity is not tied to chronological age. Most people want to ensure their lives have meaning and importance—one that makes a lasting impression on their families, profession, friends, community, or the environment. Some people will realize generativity through their work or career. Others through volunteering, engaging in activism, mentoring, philanthropy, or other activities that are intended to leave the world a better place. Characteristics of generativity include: realizing a desire to contribute to a cause or organization; worrying about the continuation of institutions one cares about; or recognizing ideas whose survival is important. Learning in this dilemma is how best to pass along ideas and values to the next generation. Box 5.7 explores work and career identity.

BOX 5.7 REFLECTIVE PRACTICE

Work and Career Identity: A Deep Dive

This box contains deeply personal questions about work and career identity for you to devote reflection time as a career explorer, sustainer, or changer.

1. How would your colleagues describe your work or career identity or your personal brand? If you're unsure, think about times when you've been asked to help with a project, task, or assignment; what did that person want your help with specifically? Are there discrepancies in how you versus your colleagues view your identity?
2. How would your friends or family describe you? How is this similar or different from your work or career identity? Is there any overlap?
3. If you could design your perfect job, what would it look like? How could you adapt your professional identity to match that role?
4. Create a mind map of all your work, career, and/or personal projects you are passionate about. Are there any that you are especially proud of? What areas do you want to improve upon?
5. Take a few minutes to write down your "elevator pitch." How would you describe what you do, what you are passionate about, and/or what you want to do with your career in less than two minutes?

6. List the different "hats" you wear (i.e., parent, student, friend, partner, coach, mentor). Which of these do you want to emphasize in your work or career identity? Which do you want to be known for?
7. What sets you apart from your colleagues? If asked in an interview, "of all the candidates who applied to this job, why should we choose you?," how would you respond?
8. What work, career, or personal accomplishments are you most proud of?
9. If you could accomplish anything in your field, what would it be? What are the potential barriers preventing you from doing so?

CHAPTER SUMMARY

This chapter began by reflecting on Blustein and Duffy's (2021) quote about enhancing the dignity of work and worker well-being—things most workers want for what will occupy a large portion of their time and energy. This chapter connected adult education and adult learning theory to career development theory. Adults are continually making meaning out of their career experiences. Learning and change are continuous, fundamental processes that will serve you well as a career explorer, sustainer, or changer. As Krishnamurti (1992) observed,

> There is no end to education. It is not that you read a book, pass an examination, and finish with education. The whole of life, from the moment you are born to the moment you die, is a process of learning. Learning has no end and that is the timeless quality of learning. (p. 82)

6. Connecting career development with meaning in life and work

⌐ BOX 6.1 CHAPTER OVERVIEW AND LEARNING OBJECTIVES

Annie Dillard (2013) famously said:

> How we spend our days is of course, how we spend our lives.

Dillard's quote is powerful in its truth that life is composed of little things people do daily that add up to the totality of their lives, perhaps without them noticing. It is not the big promotion or recognition that occurs once in a while. It is the daily thoughts, mindsets, and interactions that compose a life or a work life. Many people either have friends, or themselves, who say, "Things will slow down next week (or next month, or next year), and then I will be able to ... ." The next week, month, or year will never change unless the person consciously tries to shift something.

One of my dearest friends and I used to run regularly. We would recount our workday, trials, and triumphs as we ran. The conversation often turned to her toxic colleagues and her unhappiness in her work situation. I moved across the country, and although we remained in touch, we no longer had these runs or personal conversations. I moved back to the same city eight years later, and we resumed our regular runs and check-ins. One day, shortly after we continued our tradition, she started complaining about her work situation. I stopped in the running path, looked at her, and said, "Your work complaints haven't changed in eight years! What are you going to do about it?!" We both laughed the moment off, and I forgot about it until a few weeks later when she told me how startling my observation had been to her. She had been spending her days in an unhappy, untenable work situation, but they became how she spent her life. She decided to quit and use her talents in other ways, much to her life's happiness and work satisfaction.

This chapter aims to examine how adults derive meaning and purpose from their lives and work by discussing theoretical perspectives and presenting practical strategies for connecting work and meaning. The chapter defines theoretical perspectives on career calling, meaningful work, and volition. Next, other ways of interpreting life purpose, including right livelihood and ikigai, are introduced. Discovering how meaning and purpose in life and work are achieved is discussed. The chapter concludes with some practical exercises to help individuals determine their purpose.

As a result of reading this chapter and completing the exercises, you, the reader, should be able to:

1. Define the significant concepts of meaning in life and work.
2. Describe and apply right livelihood and the Japanese philosophy of ikigai to your life and work.
3. Explore theoretical precepts of purpose in life and work.
4. Engage in multiple exercises and activities to discover meaning in life and work.

THE MEANING OF WORK IN ADULTHOOD

Dik et al. (2021) asked, "Why do you do the work you do? ... Beyond a paycheck, does or will your work offer a sense of happiness, satisfaction, self-esteem, contribution, success, personal growth, or meaning? At its best work can produce outcomes like these" (p. 237). People want to do meaningful work, but, sometimes, determining what that is and finding it is challenging. Especially when there may be self or familial pressure to get a job to pay off educational loans and be self-sufficient, or the individual encounters systemic barriers such as racism, sexism, ableism, heterosexism, or other marginalizing dynamics. Sometimes people chase money at the expense of their happiness. This chapter is about finding out what gives your life a sense of meaning and purpose. Box 6.2 poses questions for reflecting on what matters in work or a career.

BOX 6.2 REFLECTIVE PRACTICE

Questions to Consider When Reflecting on a Work or Career Calling

As a career explorer, sustainer, or explorer, consider the following questions and use them as a springboard to test whether you are in your career calling or if more exploration and change is in your future.

1. What is your current career?
2. What is your ultimate career?
3. What meaning do you derive from work?

4. What external factors, if any, have affected your career or career plans?
5. Who are your career role models? Why?
6. Who can be helpful to you for your next career steps?

Career theory can often seem individualistic, mechanistic, and careerist. Careerist culture is when a person is focused on what's next: the next promotion, raises, or recognition, and it is not necessarily related to job performance. Similarly, careerism is advancing one's career, oftentimes at the cost of one's integrity. There is nothing wrong with striving for advancement, but perhaps a more important question is: What is a career in service to? How are the days becoming the work or life? Is the career in service of the self or a larger purpose? These questions are pertinent to the meaning of work in adulthood.

Work involves performing a job or fulfilling assignments for wages or salary, task completion through sustained effort or continuous repeated activity, physical or mental exertion for a purpose, producing desired results, or exerting influence. Work also fulfills humans' need to be part of something bigger than themselves and often gives people a sense of purpose. Adult learning theory has long articulated that adults are more motivated to learn when they find the topic meaningful and purposeful, and work is no exception. Yet, the COVID-19 pandemic allowed many individuals to reflect on the meaning of work in their lives, often reorient priorities, and seek new work that is better aligned with their values, goals, and life balance needs. Sixty-six percent of workers are reported to have reconsidered their purpose in life during that time (Dhingra et al., 2021).

Work has multiple meanings historically. Most adults will work during their lifetime. Do you, as a worker, know how much time that is? See Box 6.3 for the numbers.

ıl BOX 6.3 ADULT CAREER DEVELOPMENT BY THE NUMBERS

How Much of Your Lifetime Will You Spend Working?

How much time will you, the reader, spend working in your lifetime? Based on a lifespan of 80 years*:

• The average person will work approximately 90,000 hours during their lifetime (Tan, 2022) or about 13 years or 4,821 days, plus 1 year of unpaid overtime. This is about 24% of the total lifespan.

- 33 years or 12,045 days are spent in bed: 26 years sleeping and 7 trying to fall asleep!
- 1 year and 30 days is spent on romance; 4.5 years or 1,583 days eating.
- 3 years, 1 month, and 3 weeks will be spent vacationing or 1,146 days.
- 1 year and 4 months is spent in exercise, although 6x longer is spent watching television and 2x longer on social media.
- People spend 12x more time working than socializing.
- Random time is spent in:
  - Queuing: 235 days.
  - Laughing: 115 days.
  - Getting ready: 136 days for women; and 46 days for men.
- What's left? Eight years and 2 months or 2,997 days. How will you spend those days, weeks, months, and years?

*Numbers are based on Campbell (2017) unless otherwise cited.

Exploring the Historical Meaning of Work

Understanding career development (CD) requires appreciating the role of work in adults' lives. The idea of a vocation dates at least to the 16th century when religious leaders Martin Luther and John Calvin rejected the prevailing notion that earthy occupations should be devalued and instead developed the idea that work can hold spiritual significance (Hardy, 1990). Freud argued that "work is the individual's link to reality" (Yesilyaprak, 2012, p. 112). Work has different meanings in different cultures and was once a means of survival and still is for most people striving to care for the welfare of themselves and loved ones. The Greek word for "work" has the same root as "sorrow" or a curse (Berger, 1963; Hardy, 1990). An early Judaic view of work was drudgery by which one could atone for original sin (Beatty & Torbert, 2003). The notion that "idleness was akin to sinfulness" grew from the early Christian tradition and was the prevailing view through the Middle Ages (Beatty & Torbert, 2003). Work was a means of spiritual purification. The Reformation marked a change in the view of work. Martin Luther viewed work as a means of serving God, and John Calvin added the idea that the results of work (i.e., profit) should be used to finance new ventures to build profit and return on investment. Calvin's belief in predestination preceded the belief that people were obligated to God to achieve the highest level possible in the most rewarding occupation. This allowed striving for upward mobility to become more acceptable. The Reformation gave rise to what is known as the "Protestant work ethic," which became the basis of contemporary capitalism and industrialism. The principle valued independent effort, self-sufficiency, frugality, self-discipline, and humility. Oates (1971) explained,

> The so-called Protestant work ethic can be summarized as follows: a universal taboo is placed on *idleness*, and *industriousness* is considered a religious ideal; waste is avarice, and *frugality* is a virtue; *complacency* and *failure* are outlawed, and *ambition* and *success* are taken as sure signs of God's favour; the universal sign of sin is *poverty,* and the crowning sign of God's favour as *wealth*. (p. 84, italics in original)

The notion of an occupation replaced work as a means of determining status at the turn of the 20th century as the setting of work moved into large cities and industry, and workers developed a career ethic (working to get ahead, climbing the career ladder, making oneself marketable). Career progress can be fleeting in an era of downsizing. Some have argued that the "career has died" (e.g., Rifkin, 1995) and that a new ethic is needed for the 21st century. A self-fulfillment ethic is predicted where people "work to live" rather than "live to work." The COVID-19 pandemic ushered in a transformation on the career landscape, facilitating what some refer to as the "Great Resignation."

In contrast, others attempt to shift the discourse by calling it the "Great Rethink," as discussed in Chapter 2. Whatever it is called, workers have rethought work and know they want out of toxic environments without support or flexibility. Expectations are high for remote, flexible organizations and a reimagining of work that includes more life balance and human sustainability. Organizations privileging cultures of belonging and engagement are attracting and retaining workers for their healthy organizing practices (Byrd, 2022; Shuck & Rose, 2013; Valentin, 2013). Work satisfaction has been linked to feelings of career commitment and work meaningfulness (Duffy et al., 2014). This section examines work as a calling, meaning, and volition.

Understanding Work as Calling, Meaningful Work, and Volition

Dik et al. (2021) wrote a chapter in *Career Development and Counseling: Putting theory and research to work* (Brown & Lent, 2021) and discussed emerging perspectives in CD that focused on calling, meaning, and volition. These three concepts are different ways of understanding how people connect purpose with their work and should be of concern to organizations since a McKinsey Purpose Survey concluded that 85% of frontline managers and workers are unsure or disagree that they can live their purpose in their daily work (Dhingra et al., 2021).

Work as calling

Bellah (1985) proposed a tripartite work orientation framework suggesting people have one of three orientations toward their work, (a) Job—working for a paycheck, (b) Career—working to advance, and (c) Calling—working to do something meaningful and fulfilling. This section focuses on calling, as Dik et al. (2021) explained, that the research has focused on calling rather than looking at the three orientations. Dik and Duffy (2009) distinguished between a vocation and a calling. They defined vocation as "an approach to a particular life role oriented toward demonstrating or deriving a sense of purpose or mean-ingfulness, and that holds other-oriented values and goals as primary sources of motivation" (p. 428). They defined calling as:

> A transcendent summons, experienced as originating beyond the self, to approach a particular life role in a manner oriented toward demonstrating or deriving a sense of purpose or meaningfulness and that holds other-oriented values and goals as primary sources of motivation. (p. 427)

They imply that most people have a vocation, although adults may be on a quest to find one or both.

Given the amount of time adults work and years in work (approximately 18–65 years or longer), finding fulfilling work is often an important goal. Duffy and Dik (2013) connected the notion of living out a calling to the career lifespan in a literature review highlighting over 40 studies. A calling originates from a sense of destiny or degree of fit with a particular career, although, historically, it was considered to have more of an external source, such as a higher power or social needs (Duffy et al., 2014; Dik & Duffy, 2009). A more contemporary definition is "a calling represents a career that is personally meaningful and prosocial in nature ... People who endorse a calling view it as an integral part of their life meaning and actively use their job to help others" (Duffy et al., 2014, p. 605). Dik et al. (2021) observed that published studies on work as a calling have increased over the past 15 years, with at one time fewer than ten published papers available, but there are now over 500.

The notion of calling fits with several CD theories, according to Dik et al. (2021), including person-fit theories in terms of encouraging people to modify work environments to maximize alignment with their values, interests, and strengths (Hansen, 2013). Super's (1980) developmental theory considered the broader context where career decisions occur and encouraged people to connect their occupational actualization with purpose and meaning. Social cognitive career theory (Lent, 2013) links personal, behavioral, and envi-ronmental variables to well-being and meaningfulness through developing self-efficacy, outcome expectations, and personal goals. Career construction theory (Hartung & Taber, 2013) purports meaning-making through narrative or career stories that help connect people's work with matters of the heart. Finally, the psychology of work theory (Duffy et al., 2016) posits that decent work promotes a sense of fulfillment in one's work. When adults feel a sense of calling in their work, there are many positive effects, including organization and career attachment, lower burnout and turnover, effective performance, career success, professional competence, employability, lower absenteeism, dedication to work, and good organization citizenship that on the whole benefits both people and organizations (Dik et al., 2021).

The majority of calling research has been on adults. A career calling is also perceived as a career or organizational commitment, work meaning, occupational identity, person-job fit, work engagement, occupational self-efficacy, and job satisfaction, with most pronounced feelings when people have actualized the career to which they feel called (Duffy et al., 2014). The inability to live out a career calling may create dissatisfaction. Work as a calling theory (WCT) "frames perceiving a calling as a predictor of work outcomes, positive and negative, with living a calling positioned as the key mediating variable" (Dik et al., 2021, p. 245). According to Dobrow & Tosti-Kharas (2011), calling predicts positive career results, including clarity of professional identity, self-efficacy, and insight. However, the negative aspects of calling have been sparingly researched. It has been found that career calling makes people less receptive to career advice over the long term and can cause people to become stuck in certain career paths despite advice to the contrary. Duffy et al. (2014) studied a diverse group of working adults to understand the link between living a calling and the variables of career commitment, work meaning, and job satisfaction at three points over six months. They used structural equation modeling to test hypotheses that living a calling would predict their variables over time. Counter to their hypotheses, living a calling was more of an outcome of the three variables than the cause of them. Dik and Duffy (2009) called for CD researchers and practitioners to explore processes of developing, experiencing, and promoting meaningfulness and purpose at work, with relevance for creating more inclusive and cross-culturally relevant career and work constructs.

Meaningful work

"Contemporary social science scholarship on meaningful work begins with the assumption that work is an important pillar of a fulfilling life" (Dik et al., 2021, p. 246). Yeoman et al. (2019) described meaningful work as creating a personal sense of import in an individual with ethical and moral significance beyond the person. Meaningful work is difficult to quantify as it depends on individual values, capabilities, and interests within a particular social context. Factors such as access to decent work and positionalities of gender, race, class, and other identities also impact meaningfulness to the worker. Meaningful work differs from calling in that it lacks a "transcendent summons" (Dik et al.,

2021, p. 248). People who feel their work is meaningful have higher commitment, well-being, and career satisfaction (Dik et al., 2021).

Chalofsky (2003) reviewed the literature and found three aspects of meaningful work described as overlapping and intertwining into "integrated wholeness" or "The idea of people needing to bring their whole selves (mind, body, emotion, and spirit) to their work" (p. 78). The three parts include (a) A sense of self—awareness of one's values, beliefs, and life purpose, and the context where people feel safe to bring their whole selves to work; (b) The work itself—the opportunity to realize one's life purpose through the work in a way that brings continuous learning, challenge, and growth; and (c) A sense of balance—equalizing the mind, body, spirit, and community with the work or achieving live balance. Chalofsky urged, "One approach that needs to be utilized and developed further is the concept of crafting or sculpting work. This approach shifts the emphasis from fitting the worker to the work to fitting the work to the worker" (p. 80).

Volition

Volition is the degree to which a person perceives they have the freedom to choose a career path (Dik et al., 2021). Although many people may have a calling to work, they may lack the resources and power to pursue their true passion (Blustein, 2006). This perspective on work focuses on the privilege to make career choices at work.

> Although highly privileged people might certainly feel constrained in their career choices (e.g., a highly paid White male bound by "golden handcuffs" to an unsatisfying job), the systemic oppression of those with marginalized identities (e.g., women, people of color, LGBTQ and trans populations) was the driving force in work volition's theoretical development. (Blustein, 2006; Dik et al., 2021, p. 253)

Volition is not about systemic barriers faced by historically excluded and marginalized people: it is about how people perceive their work choices with knowledge of the obstacles. For example, Sumner et al. (2018) discussed how an adolescent's sense of purpose was affected by experiencing marginalization from racism, segregation, and discrimination, noting the dearth of research on how the development of youth is affected by these oppressions. They explained marginalization can hurt the formation of a positive and coherent identity and cause social isolation and restricted access to power sources. Still, it can also prompt youth to reflect, form close bonds with others experiencing injustice, and spur them to leverage collective power for social change. Sumner et al. offered potential opportunities for developing purpose among marginalized youth, such as supporting broad career exploration and ways to engage in civic and cultural work that addresses oppression in their social group. Building on social support among family, friends, teachers, and others is also important as it is a strong predictor of purpose.

Volition is theoretically aligned with the psychology of working theory (PWT) and its description of decent work as discussed in Chapter 5. Williams et al. (2023) scrutinized contemporary CD research for prioritizing people who enjoyed power, privilege, and volition; usually White middle-class workers in the US. They studied 241 Black workers using a PWT model that looked at general ethnic discrimination and racial microaggressions. They found that marginalization predicted volition and perceived access to decent work.

Dik et al. (2021) offered practical implications for integrating calling, meaningful work, and volition into CD. Table 6.1 takes their advice and adds questions for consideration in making career choices. Although their advice is wise, it is focused on the individual and how a career counselor might help them. The activity offers individual and organizational questions to address these aspects of work and CD aspects.

RIGHT LIVELIHOOD

Calling, meaningful work, and volition are not the only ways to understand purpose in people's work lives. Right livelihood originated as a Buddhist principle about work that comes from the Noble Eightfold Path—a process of growing and experiencing rich and fulfilling lives by cultivating *wisdom* through right view and right thought, upholding *morality* through right speech, right action, and right livelihood, and *meditating* on right effort, right mindfulness, and right contemplation (Whitmyer, 1994a, 1994b). Right livelihood is:

> Mak[ing] a living in ways that avoid deceit, treachery, trickery, and usury. Five occupations are specifically condemned: trading in arms, living beings, flesh, intoxicants, and poison ... In short, a Buddhist practicing "right livelihood" can do no work that might hurt living beings or the environment. (Whitmyer, 1994b, p. 12)

Whitmyer (1994b) observed Western culture in the 20th century has "expanded beyond the meaning of the Buddhist idea of doing no harm, to include the ideas that work should make a difference in the world, benefit the community, and be personally fulfilling" (1994b, p. 15). Box 6.4 offers practical applications of right livelihood to work and CD.

Table 6.1   Integrating calling, meaningful work, and volition into career choices for individuals, leaders, and organizations

Advice to integrate calling, meaningful work, and volition (Dik et al., 2021)	Questions and activities for individual consideration in making career choices	Questions and activities for organizational consideration in supporting worker career choices
Consider existential issues of importance in career decisions.	• How does this work contribute to things I care about? • What legacy can I leave through this work?	• How well does the organization's mission, culture, climate, and values resonate with workers? • Do you know what your people care about?
Primarily focus on eudaimonic well-being (existential, purpose-driven happiness), and secondarily on hedonic well-being (pleasure-driven happiness) (Grant et al., 2018).	• Do I know what my purpose in life is? (eudaimonic) • How engaged, thriving, intrinsically motivated, dedicated, and absorbed am I in my work? (eudaimonic) • How satisfied am I with my job, and committed to work, and how do I feel about it? (hedonic) • What makes me happy? Do I spend enough time doing it? (hedonic)	• What mechanisms do we have to help workers reflect on their purpose and connect it with the organization's mission? Orientation is a good place to begin. (eudaimonic) • How well do managers and leaders connect people to their purpose? (eudaimonic) • How can we find more opportunities for people to connect to their purpose in their daily work? (eudaimonic) (Quinn & Thakor, 2018)
Consider how your work is generative and contributes to the greater good.	• How aware or mindful am I from moment to moment? Awareness has been linked to finding meaning in work (Lysova et al., 2023).	• How well does this organization articulate its impact on the greater good?

Advice to integrate calling, meaningful work, and volition (Dik et al., 2021)	*Questions* and activities for individual consideration in making career choices	*Questions* and activities for organizational consideration in supporting worker career choices
Reflect on how you integrate calling, meaning, and volition into your own life and work (Nice, 2023).	Nice (2023) recommended adding "MAGIC" to your life: • Mirror: *How did I get to my current situation? What are the positives and improvement options?* • Aspirations: *Who is the person I want to see in the metaphorical mirror? What does success look like to me in the next year?* • Goals: *What are my goals and milestones to achieve my aspirations?* • Ideas: *What is the action plan?* • Commitments: *How can I hold myself accountable for the plan?*	• *How often do teams and leaders reflect?* For example: • Identify pluses and deltas (changes) for projects and challenges. • Discuss things the team should stop, start, and continue. • Learn to ask good questions. • *How well do leaders model reflective practice?* • *Do we give our workers paid reflection time?* For example: • Establish a 4-day work week to encourage reflection and creativity. • Provide workers with sabbaticals.
Try job crafting (finding new ways to frame and enjoy your current work to make it more meaningful) (Tims et al., 2022; see Chapter 7 for more information).	• *Do I love my work?* If the answer is no, it might be time to reflect on seeking more meaningful work. • *How can I reframe how I perceive my work?* • *How can I develop better working relationships?* • *How can I change my mindset about my job?*	• *Where is there room for flexibility and autonomy in job descriptions?* • *How can we help leaders support work redesign for job crafting?* • *How can the organization promote trust, transparency, and relationship building?*

Advice to integrate calling, meaningful work, and volition (Dik et al., 2021)	*Questions* and activities for individual consideration in making career choices	*Questions* and activities for organizational consideration in supporting worker career choices
Seek life balance or the maintenance of harmonious boundaries between your personal and work life in ways that amplify health and well-being.	• *How well do my priorities align with a healthy life balance?* • *What boundaries do I need to set or revise?* • *How can I practice "paying myself first"?* (The practice of ensuring you have ample sleep, exercise, and other supports to be your best). • *Am I getting enough rest?* • Headlee (2020) suggested in her book, *Do Nothing*: challenge your perceptions, take the media out of your social, step away from your desk, invest in leisure, make real connections with others, and take the long view.	• *Do we offer interventions to support life balance?* For example: • Employee leave policies. • Workplace social support. • Helping workers manage healthy boundaries. • Encouraging wellness behavior. • Training supervisors to support family, personal, and work demands (Hammer, 2021).

Advice to integrate calling, meaningful work, and volition (Dik et al., 2021)	Questions and activities for individual consideration in making career choices	Questions and activities for organizational consideration in supporting worker career choices
Consider how to address barriers that prevent realizing volition. Barriers negatively impact your career path such as race, ethnicity, gender, socioeconomic status, (dis)ability, sexual orientation, and other identities (Duffy et al., 2012).	• *Am I getting assigned "office housework"?* (behind-the-scenes tasks that are important, but do not raise my profile). Tulshyan (2018) recommended: preparing your answer so saying no does not catch you by surprise. When saying no, offer to do another high-value task instead. Collect evidence to show how often and to whom this phenomenon is occurring. If you cannot say no, make sure it is clear the extra work you are taking on. • *Do I effectively "manage up"?* (understanding how your boss communicates, when it is good to check-in on work, and build a trusting relationship so you can create space to discuss what matters) (Henry, 2013, 2019).	• *How is poverty, marginalization, and stigmatization impacting workers' career progress in this organization?* • *How well are our DEI (diversity, equity, and inclusion) efforts helping diminish and eliminate career volition barriers?* • *How well are we equipping people to be allies, mentors, and supporters of affected workers?* • *Is work being assigned fairly?*
Cultivate critical consciousness by understanding how structural oppression such as poverty, colonization, or lack of access to education or opportunity create inequities in work and life (see Chapters 4 and 7 for more information).	• *How are social inequities and structural barriers affecting me or others?* • *How can I build critical consciousness?* According to Pillen et al. (2020): • Prime yourself to reflect. • Name disorienting dilemmas. • Take time to be introspective. • Revise frames of reference. • Develop agency for change. • Take action.	• *How are social inequities perpetuated in this organization?* • *How are we engaging everyone in addressing them?* Byrd (2018b) recommended: • Breaking the silence about organization injustice. • Developing mindsets to promote social justice and build strong human relations.

BOX 6.4 TIPS AND TOOLS FOR CAREER DEVELOPMENT

Right Livelihood

How does right livelihood apply to your work as a career explorer, sustainer, or changer? The Blog "Buddha's Advice to Laypeople" at Livelihood (n.d.) offers practical advice:

1. Discern right and wrong livelihood—Right livelihood is respectable, honorable, and harmless work. Two people could hold the same position, and each person's approach to livelihood could be present in the case of one person carrying out their tasks with honesty and integrity and the other doing the opposite.
2. Ensure the end-product of your work is wholesome—Regardless of position, your work can benefit yourself and others because your care for other beings shines through. Truthfulness is also an important characteristic of wholesome work. Right livelihood is not being put in a position to lie. Wholesomeness is also doing a fair day's work for a fair day's pay.
3. Separate unethical from unpleasant tasks—Most jobs have unpleasant aspects, such as firing someone for cause or doing something difficult. Although firing someone is unpleasant, it can be done with care, humanity, and high ethical standards.
4. Pay attention to how your work makes you feel—If work makes you tired or irritable regularly, you have cause for concern. How other people feel about their work also rubs off on you. Is the vibe negative or positive? For example, many healthcare workers left their positions in the wake of the pandemic because the demands, low staff, and stress felt bad and had health consequences.
5. Make career changes mindfully—If and when you decide to change your work situation, consider how the change will disrupt others close to you, like family and co-workers. Make a harmless transition.
6. Strike a balanced livelihood—balance income and expenditures and how you enjoy what your income brings you.
7. Be conservation-minded—Take care of and protect the things you have since a safe and cozy home and life is not a privilege everyone enjoys.

Krishnamurti (1992) urged in his book *On Right Livelihood*:

> Is it not necessary for each one to know for himself [sic] what is the right means of livelihood? If we are avaricious, envious, seeking power, then our means of livelihood will correspond to our inward demands and so produce a world of competition, ruthlessness, oppression, ultimately ending in war. (p. 1)

He continued, observing love for work and love in life create possibilities:

> You have to find out for yourself what you really want to do, and not rely on your father, on your grandmother, on some professor, or anybody else to tell you what to do. And what does it mean to find out what you really want to do? It means finding out what you love to do, does it not? When you love what you are doing, you are not ambitious, you are not greedy, you are not seeking fame, because that very love of what you are doing is totally sufficient in itself. In that love there is no frustration, because you are no longer seeking fulfillment. (p. 23)

Finding a calling or right livelihood sounds like a good idea, but how does one do it? The next section delves into how to find purposeful, meaningful work as a career explorer, sustainer, or changer.

DISCOVERING MEANING AND PURPOSE IN LIFE AND WORK

Part of determining a satisfying career path is discovering what drives you as a career explorer, sustainer, or changer. Discovering your life purpose or key driver is crucial to understanding yourself. Do you know what it is? Have you ever thought about it? This chapter introduces theoretical precepts and practical tools for discovering meaning in life or the fulfillment of one's life passion as a clue to a fulfilling career. Passion is a strong inclination toward something a person likes and values in which they invest time and energy (Bronk & McLean, 2016). This section features models, theories, and tools for understanding how people derive meaning in life.

Ikigai

Most people want great careers, and work can present a twisting path. What is a career, anyway? What is its meaning, and what drives you as a career explorer, sustainer, or changer? The Japanese philosophy of ikigai translates as "reason for being." "Iki" ("icky") means life, and "gai" ("guy") means value or worth, an idea introduced in Japanese literature by Kamiya (1966), meaning a sense of "life worth living," "feelings of well-being," "purpose in life," or "reason for living" (Sartore et al., 2023, p. 387). Others have likened ikigai to self-actualization (Bilash, 2019; Hikmawan et al., 2020). Medical research has found that people lacking a sense of ikigai were more likely to have increased risks of all-cause mortality (Cohen et al., 2016; Sone et al., 2008), whereas people with a clear igikai experienced improved health (Nakanishi, 1999) and longevity (Sone et al., 2008).

Although igikai means finding your bliss in Japanese culture, the Westernized version has interpreted ikigai as a process of discovering a dream career.

> In Japan, the desire for ikigai is considered universal (Kamiya, 1966; Nakanishi, 1999) and may contribute to meet seven needs: (1) Survival, (2) Growth and Change, (3) Future such as life goals and dreams, (4) Influence (being necessary to others), (5) Freedom of choice, (6) Self-fulfilment or personal development through one's potential (autonomous growth), and (7) Meaning of life (a sense of value and worth of one's own life). (Sartore et al., 2023, p. 388)

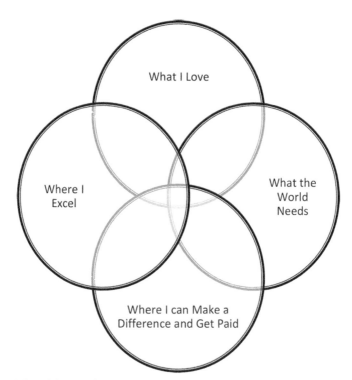

Source: Adapted from Kudo (2018), Perry (2021), Winn (2014).

Figure 6.1   Ikigai model

Figure 6.1 captures how the concept integrates (a) where a person excels, (b) what a person loves, (c) what the world needs, and (d) where a person can make a difference and get paid.

Vanderheiden and Mayer (2021) linked ikigai with transformative pedagogies noting that research on adult education and ikigai was scant. They attempted to contribute toward developing a corresponding model, emphasizing that transformative education and ikigai are holistic in how they regard people as whole selves who are learning and developing continuously. They also noted that personal deconstruction and reconstruction occur with a temporal dimension—how time affects a person's learning and growth, relationships, and communities of practice. They further connected the phenomenon of disorienting experiences from life events and transformational learning that reinforces life purpose.

Kumano (2006, 2012), in an attempt to formalize ikigai, created a hierarchal model containing key aspects of the principle being life affirmation, goals and dreams, meaning of life, existential value, a sense of fulfillment and commitment (Sartore et al., 2023). See Box 6.5 for an exercise to discover your ikigai.

BOX 6.5 TIPS AND TOOLS FOR CAREER DEVELOPMENT

Discovering your Ikigai

Jot down your reflections as a career explorer, sustainer, or changer in the first blank row in Table 6.2. Next, write down how the categories relate in the second blank row according to your passions, values, vocation, and profession.

Table 6.2   Discovering your ikigai

What I Love: I get lost in my work, feel great excitement about doing it, and experience a strong emotional connection with my work.	Where I Excel: Work that gives me a sense of efficacy (I'm good at it) and causes others to seek my expertise on work topics, job tasks, and my ability to excel.	What the World Needs: My work is in high demand and valuable now and likely in the future.	Where I can Make a Difference and Get Paid: My work is compensated comparably to others doing similar work, and the job market is competitive. I do or expect to make a good living at my work.

Passions: What you Love + Where You Excel	Values: Where I Excel + What the World Needs	Vocation: What the World Needs + Where I can Make a Difference and Get Paid	Profession: Where I can Make a Difference and Get Paid + What I Love

Understanding the Theoretical Underpinnings of Meaning in Life

It has been said, "The two most important days in your life are the day you are born and the day you find out why" (Campbell, 1973). The notion of meaning in life—MIL or "life purpose"—is the phenomenon of living a profound, purposeful life as Victor Frankl (1985) described in his book *Man's Search for Meaning*. The process of discovering meaning in life or one's life purpose involves identifying a global schema to understand life, such as "to be respected," "to give back," or "to educate." Life mission theory (Ventegodt et al., 2003) claims that having a life purpose is core to human existence and one that can be articulated in words such as "I help" or "I design." They described life mission as realizing one's purpose, a gift to the world, true nature, existential duty, life path, or key talent. MIL is also referred to as "a calling" (Dik & Duffy, 2009), "finding your why" (Sinek, 2017), "why it matters" (Corbett & Chloupek, 2019), "internal driver" (Chloupek, 2023), "raison d'être"—the French expression referring to the reason for existing—or "ikigai", a Japanese principle of "the reason we get up in the morning" (Garcia & Miralles, 2016, p. 9), as discussed earlier in this chapter.

A sense of meaning or purpose is a lifelong motivator. Having a sense of meaning has been linked to improved health (Czekierda et al., 2017) and lower mortality across the lifespan (Hill & Turiano, 2014). MIL also drives adult learning. Living a profound life in this sense means one that is evocative of meaning and significance to the person. Damon et al. (2003) defined purpose as "a stable and generalized intention to accomplish something that is at once meaningful to the self and of consequence to the world beyond the self" (p. 121). Meaningfulness is "the sense made of, and significance felt regarding, the nature of one's being and existence" (Steger et al., 2006, p. 81). MIL has two facets: (a) The presence of meaning in life (Steger et al., 2006) and (b) The search for meaning (Steger et al., 2008). Box 6.6 raises existential questions that get at MIL.

☼ BOX 6.6 REFLECTIVE PRACTICE

Wong's Important Questions

Wong (2012) identified the five most important and enduring questions people can ask themselves about the meaning of human existence as:
1. Who am I?
2. Why am I here?
3. Where am I going?
4. What is the meaning of suffering and death?
5. How can I find significance and happiness?

Spend some time reflecting on these questions and dialoguing about your answers with a trusted friend or family member.

V. E. Frankl (1946, 1955, 1958, 1959), an Austrian psychiatrist and psychotherapist who survived imprisonment in a Nazi concentration camp during the Second World War, founded logotherapy, or a stream of psychotherapy concerned with the human search for meaning as a core life and motivational force. Frankl found meaning and purpose in the direst of conditions and, through his survival, sought to help understand the role purpose has in people's lives. Through his clinical practice and research, Frankl reported a new neurosis that represented over half of his caseload that was attributed to a lack of purpose in life which created an existential crisis, a sense of no meaning in personal experience, that was manifested in boredom (Crumbaugh & Maholick, 1964). Crumbaugh and Maholick (1964) defined "'purpose in life' as the ontological significance of life from the point of view of the experiencing individual" (p. 201) and developed a "Purpose in Life" instrument (PIL) to assess the degree to which a person experienced a sense of purpose. Box 6.7 offers examples of meaning and purpose in life.

☼ BOX 6.7 REFLECTIVE PRACTICE

Finding Meaning and Purpose in Life

Just as humans seek meaning in work, they also seek to find a sense of meaning and purpose in life. This quest is as long as humanity and takes multiple forms in scientific inquiry, hemispheric philosophical perspectives, religious perspectives, and popular culture. Various viewpoints on the meaning of life:

- Realizing one's potential.
- Living a long, healthy life.
- Seeking wisdom and knowledge.
- Doing good or doing the right thing.
- Attaining eternal life and union with God (common across multiple religious traditions).
- Loving and finding joy in life.
- Being powerful.
- Believing life is meaningful, making it special.
- Knowing life's meaning is not possible for humankind.

Which one(s) do you relate to as a career explorer, sustainer, or changer?

A sense of life purpose is larger than a career calling and is derived from believing life is meaningful and is also known as "meaning in life" or MIL. Meaning in life might include a religious tradition or spiritual quest. Everyone has a key driver or life purpose, and each one is unique. Allan and Duffy (2014) described a calling as "a personally meaningful career that works toward the greater good and originates from a source external to the self" (p. 451).

George and Park (2016) explained a tripartite view of life purpose as "[T]he extent to which one's life is experienced as making sense, as being directed and motivated by valued goals, and as mattering in the world" (p. 206). They identified three conditions of their definition: (a) Comprehending or making sense out of one's life, (b) Discovering life purpose, and (c) Mattering.

Comprehension is "the degree to which individuals perceive a sense of coherence and understanding regarding their lives" (George & Park, 2016, p. 206). When comprehension is lacking, life may seem meaningless, fragmented, and incoherent. When comprehension is high, well-being is enhanced by minimizing daily uncertainty, experiencing a greater sense of clarity about decisions to make and actions to take, and having a higher capacity to make meaning about challenging life circumstances and manage life difficulties as they arise.

Purpose is the extent to which people view their lives as directed and motivated by valued life goals that provide a sense of direction and engagement with life. People lacking a sense of purpose may feel aimless with little to look forward to. Higher purpose impacts well-being with a daily focus on value goals and their pursuit, more positive emotions because of working toward life purpose, perceived alignment between life goals, core values, and identity, and better ability to adjust goals in the face of obstacles.

The third condition, mattering, is "the degree to which individuals feel that their existence is of significance, importance, and value in the world" (George & Park, 2016, p. 206). When mattering is low, people may feel like their existence is irrelevant, and few would notice if they ceased to exist. Mattering can impact well-being by helping to buffer death or existential anxiety and provide greater equanimity when faced with situations that threaten one's sense of existential value. Although meaning in life (MIL) constructs have been critiqued for being ambiguous and unclear conceptually, their convergence is around exploring how humans understand themselves, their environments, and their relationship to the environment through sense-making (George & Park, 2016).

Theoretical Approaches to Meaning in Life

Life purpose theory is derived from at least six theoretical approaches, including Maslow's hierarchy of needs, logotherapy, terror management theory, hope theory, narrative psychology, and self-concordance theory. Each will be briefly defined and discussed.

Maslow's hierarchy of needs: beyond self-actualization

Maslow (1943) introduced his hierarchy of needs based on the premise that unfulfilled needs influence human behavior and that when needs are satisfied, they are no longer a source of motivation. Maslow's hierarchy begins with physiological needs (air, water, food, shelter), and moves up the shape of a pyramid to safety and security (safe community, job security, health insurance), social activity (love and belonging through relationships), to esteem (ego needs include recognition and respect), and finally self-actualization. It was long inferred that self-actualization emphasizing the self was the highest need to be satisfied. Yet, in *Farther Reaches of Human Nature* (1971), published one year after Maslow's death, his later thinking revealed what Maslow termed in the book as "Beyond Self Actualization" (p. 42). Green and Burke (2007) noted that the term self-actualization is assumed to focus inwardly on the self, with the goal of betterment and growth. Still, per Maslow's later views, the term would more accurately be known as "'selfless actualization' indicating human development beyond the self in self-actualization" (p. 119). Greene and Burke (2007) continued:

> Maslow's message is that to achieve peak experience people must move from self to other. Social justice, generativity, and transformative thinking and acting are all concepts that could be associated with this orientation [selfless actualization]. The fundamental idea is that people must move to a focus and concern for other people to achieve the highest level of human nature. People who move beyond self-actualization "are without a single exception, involved in a cause outside of their skin: in something outside of themselves some *calling* or *vocation*" (Maslow, 1971, p. 42; Greene & Burke, 2007, p. 120, italics added for emphasis)

Greene and Burke (2007) proposed a sixth stage to Maslow's hierarchy of selfless actualization that they noted is necessary in a complex, ambiguous world with uncertainty and upheaval. They recommended the following six actions toward selfless actualization: (a) Educate through art to encourage creative and introspective expression; (b) Understand how to think in, work with, and manage polarities; (c) Provide structures and cultures to encourage and stimulate individuality, autonomy, and initiative; (d) Engage in dialogues on ethics, offer opportunities for dialogues on spirituality and its relationship to the world; (e) Practice sense-making, invention, and connectedness, and (f) Be keenly aware of and accept reality, in an honest and calm way. As they concluded, selfless-actualization "is increasingly important in a world that is more interconnected and interdependent and this in need of strategic cooperation rather than strategic self-interest" (pp. 126–127).

Logotherapy

Developed by psychiatrist and psychotherapist Victor Frankl after surviving Nazi concentration camps in the 1940s, logotherapy is grounded in "Logos" which means word, reason, or motivation where:

Logotherapy = Meaning + therapy, or a search for life purpose

Logotherapy is based on the premise that humans are called to, in Frankl's words, a "will to meaning" (literal translation from German), or a drive to find a sense of meaning and purpose in life. Frankl (1985) captured this sentiment observing, "There is nothing in the world, I venture to say, that would so effectively help one to survive even the worst conditions, as the knowledge that there is a meaning in one's life" (p. 126). Frankl's model was borne out of adversity and how humans can use spiritual resources to withstand difficulty. This happens through turning focus outward, away from the self to other people, or what he called "dereflection," as in turning the reflective gaze away from oneself. Another principle is a paradoxical intention or wishing for the most feared thing. For example, if one is afraid of speaking publicly, they might seek it to combat their fears by volunteering to speak at work or in the community. Finally, Socratic dialogue, asking open-ended questions that encourage reflection and assumption testing, was used by Frankl to process self-discovery. The role of a career helper or coach in this sense is to listen closely to words and point out patterns to help the career explorer, sustainer, or changer realize their meanings and answers.

According to Frankl, life's meaning can be discovered in three different ways (with CD examples added): (a) By creating a work or accomplishing some task such as work projects or career milestones; (b) By experiencing something fully or loving somebody such as a peak career experience like a promotion or recognition or building fulfilling personal relationships; and (c) By the attitude that one adopts toward unavoidable suffering such as opting to see the positives in a career that is unfulfilling or building skills to move on to a more fulfilling organization or career. Today, logotherapy is evident in cognitive-behavioral therapy and positive psychology and is used in career counseling, coaching, and other helping professions.

Terror management theory
The notion of terror management theory (TMT) (Greenberg et al., 1986) sounds rather morose and is based on the realization of one's mortality. The brighter side is that it is based on a human's "sense of enduring significance" (George & Park, 2016, p. 213) through mattering that helps people cope with their anxieties about mortality. The reality of death creates anxiety and fear that humans mitigate by striving to feel significant and part of something larger than themselves. This sense is known as generativity in adult development terms, as discussed in Chapter 5, or the drive to give something back to the next generation. This consciousness can motivate people to leave a legacy or mark, or contribute to their family, work, community, or society. This drive is not necessarily age-driven, although may become more pronounced as people age or face debilitating or life-ending challenges.

Hope theory
Hope theory (Snyder, 1994) is based on how people aspire to certain goals and then find ways to achieve them bolstered by their ability to believe in their capacity to make necessary changes and achieve their goals. In Snyder's (2002) words, "Hope is defined as the perceived capacity to derive pathways to desired goals and motivate oneself via agency thinking to use those pathways" (p. 249). As people are more successful at realizing their goals, they become more confident and able to achieve more challenging goals, as this is a self-perpetuating cycle. According to Snyder (1994), hope is a positive, motivated state and cognitive process characterized by goal-directed thinking or direction based on seeking goals, pathway thinking or the capacity to find routes to desired goals, and agency thinking or the motivation to use the pathways to the goals. Of course, with little or no hope, the opposite might occur, where a person could spiral downward into despair and hopelessness.

Narrative psychology
Narrative psychology (Baumeister & Wilson, 1996; McAdams, 1996) is also a theoretical framework that helps understand life's purpose. Narrative involves constructing stories to make meaning of life experiences. Narrative or storytelling was discussed in Chapter 5 as a tool for discovering a career path. Connecting a career path to meaning and purpose will yield a more satisfying

work life. Meaningfulness in narrative is derived through identifying a sense of purpose, believing in one's ability or efficacy to achieve it, the value of the purpose to the individual or others, and a sense of positive self-worth. Craig and Snook (2014) wrote in the *Harvard Business Review* that the first step in discovering purpose is to "mine your life story for major themes that reveal your lifelong passions and values" (p. 5) and use that to develop a concise statement of purpose in your language. Follow their steps in Box 6.8.

⸜ BOX 6.8 TIPS AND TOOLS FOR CAREER DEVELOPMENT

Mining your Life Purpose through Analyzing your Life Story

As a person in search of purpose, consider Craig and Snook's (2014, p. 6) questions adapted for reflection after you reflect on the major threads and themes of your life story:

What did you especially love doing as a child, especially before people started telling you what you should and should not be doing? Recall a moment or feeling when doing this activity as a child.

What have been your most challenging life experiences? How have they shaped you as a person?

What do you enjoy doing in life that makes you feel full of purpose?

Once you reflect on the questions, share them with others, such as peers or family members who know you well.

Eventually, take a shot at crafting a concise purpose in your own words:

My purpose is _____

Self-concordance theory

Self-concordance theory describes how the selection and attainment of goals enhance well-being (Allan & Duffy, 2014). Self-concordant goals are derived from a person's values and interests and tend to be pursued with more sustained effort over time, which increases the likelihood of goal attainment and meeting human needs of competence, autonomy, and relatedness (Allan & Duffy, 2014). Allan and Duffy surveyed adults to see whether career goal self-efficacy (CGSE) mediated the relationship between calling and life satisfaction and whether intrinsic, extrinsic, self-transcendence, or physical self-goal aspirations had an influence. They found a partial mediation between calling and life satisfaction. Additionally, for people high in calling, the mediation only existed for those with high self-transcendence goals or low physical-self goals, suggesting people with callings may need to have self-transcendence goals and avoid physical-self goals in order to build confidence in their ability to achieve career goals.

DISCOVERING YOUR PURPOSE IN LIFE

This section provides a curated collection of exercises that help discover purpose or meaning in life. As a career explorer, sustainer, or changer, use this section to discover or confirm your key life purpose. What motivates you to get up every morning, pursue your goals, and live out your life's purpose? Meaning in life (MIL) or purpose in life (PIL) is not "to make money for my family," but a more fundamental drive such as "to be respected," "to serve," or "to educate … ." How do you discover PIL? Several tools that are featured in this section are useful in narrowing it down. You may not need to use all of these tools to discover your PIL. Yet, most people do not take time to stop and reflect on the culture of hustle that can subsume work and life. You cannot let hustle conflict with finding time to reflect on PIL. Block an afternoon, day, or weekend, and take measures to devote the time to yourself in a quiet, comfortable place. Any of the following activities will help you structure the reflective time. To get the most out of this section, ensure you have the time to reflect on each exercise that resonates with you. You may find something more relevant to your current work and career needs, which is perfectly fine.

Work and Career Values Exercise

The Work and Career Values Exercise provides an opportunity to identify things you value most in your work as a career explorer, sustainer, or changer. Follow the steps as prompted:

1. Work through the checklist in Table 6.3 and rate the importance of each work value to you by ticking the appropriate column. Try to complete the checklist quickly and honestly. Remember you are choosing what is most important to you in a job right now; your values may alter over time and with changing circumstances.

Table 6.3   *Work and career values exercise*

Work value	Very important	Somewhat important	Not important
Steady income with good benefits			
Chance for advancement; increased pay			
Doing a variety of tasks			
Having an established routine of work			
Respect and recognition			
Friendly fellow workers			
Pleasant physical surroundings			
Expectations by boss clearly defined			
Being in charge/supervising/ managing/having authority			
Persuading others			
Motivating and inspiring others			
Teaching/training others			
Flexible hours; control over own time			
Regular hours (little overtime)			
Leaving my mark on the world			
Chance to use my own ideas/ creative expression			
Working as part of a team			
Working on my own			
Being my own boss			
Chance to use my initiative			
Working on one project at a time			
Time and energy left for outside activities			
Opportunity to learn new things			
Working for a cause; being of service to others			
Having clearly defined tasks			

Work value	Very important	Somewhat important	Not important
Spirit of competition; chance to be successful			
No responsibility			
Producing a tangible product			
Having responsibility			
Working with details, data, numbers			
Working with things/machines			
Working with people			
Working with ideas			
Challenging work			
Job security			
Good salary			
Seeing results of work; accountability			
Opportunity to use my special skills/knowledge			
Working with an organization/ people of high integrity			
Producing high-quality work			

2. Step 2: Now, look through the completed checklist. Of the items you've rated as very important, pick the three most important to you now. Discuss your choices with a confidant if convenient. As you rank your top values, consider how well your current job "fits" with what you selected.
3. My Top 3 Work Values:
    i.
    ii.
    iii.

Once you have determined your top three values, assess how well they are being met in your current work.

Take a Solo Retreat

A solo or personal retreat is a period you can set aside that you do not usually make time for in the hustle of life and work. The benefits of a solo retreat are a change of pace, quiet time for reflection and to gain perspective, goal setting, boundary defining or redefining, renewal, reconnecting with the self, or finding clarity. Here are some steps to planning a solo retreat:

1. Designate a time and place that is comfortable, safe, and peaceful where there will be no interruptions.
2. Set your intention for the time (e.g., goal setting, perspective gaining, PIL discovery).
3. Structure your time. Plan for indulgences such as your favorite tea, meditation, or yoga. Move. Plan your meals.
4. Be flexible.
5. Take time afterward to debrief and understand what you became aware of or decided.
6. Repeat as needed!

Reflect Using Various Exercises

Reflection is a key adult learning process and crucial to discovering PIL. This activity can be accomplished through reflecting on life lists, "focus on five", naming life mantras, key life stories, and naming values. The activities are outlined in this section.

Reflect on thought-provoking questions of self-discovery:
Answer or journal about the following questions:

1. What would you do even if you didn't receive a salary for it?
2. What do friends, family, and colleagues say you excel at in life or work?
3. What do friends, family, and colleagues say you should try in life or work?
4. What legacy do you want to leave in this world?
5. What does your perfect day look like?
6. What sets your soul on fire?
7. Who do you admire most and why?

Make "life lists"
Think about your life and work. Make a long-term list of personal goals. Write down things you love to do, list things you do with relative ease, things that scare you, things you want to do or see, people you want to meet, and other things that are important for you to do or experience. Refer to the list periodically to edit it as necessary and track how you are doing in accomplishing your life goals.

Focus on five

This activity was featured in Angela Duckworth's *Grit: The power of passion and perseverance* (2016), which she adapted from billionaire Warren Buffett, who may have taken it from Alan Lakein:

1. Write down a list of your top 25 goals (or more). Although the prospect seems daunting, list all your current projects at home and work.
2. Write down a list of the 25 things you *want* to do but feel there is no time to do.
3. Next, review your lists and identify the most appealing goals.
4. Narrow the list to the *five* highest-priority objectives. Circle them or write them down.
5. Review the goals you *did not* choose. These should be avoided as they often distract you from your ultimate goals even more.
6. You can also take a more numerical approach as outlined in Table 6.4.
7. Write a personal mission statement or career plan.
8. Write down your life philosophy in 100 words.

Table 6.4   Focus on five

	Goal	Interest 1= low 10= high	x	Importance 1= low 10= high	=	Total
1.			x		=	
2.			x		=	
3.			x		=	
4.			x		=	
5.			x		=	

Reflect on key life stories

1. Listen to feedback from trusted individuals.
2. Create a personal or professional "board of directors" (see Stelter, 2022).
3. Create a lifeline of key events in your life history that shaped you as outlined in Chapter 5.
4. Do life visualization by reflecting on:
    a. What things were you drawn to and fascinated by as a kid?
    b. What senses do you live through the most (sight, sense, sound, taste, touch)?
    c. What did/do you daydream about?
    d. What aspirations or goals are going unfulfilled?

Name values

Conduct a values exercise, identify causes or charities that matter to you, and identify injustices that bother you. See Brown (2024) for more resources to reflect on values.

Discover your "why it matters" (WIM)

Corbett and Chloupek (2019) defined WIM as the motive, the reason, or the thing that drives you as a person. Their book is chock-full of self-guided exercises to help you define your WIM. Although the Corbett and Chloupek (2019) text is an excellent application of practical activities to identify life purpose, the text's major shortcoming is failing to link WIM to theory and how people might better understand the human psyche and the developmental need to make meaning of experience and continue learning and changing in the pursuit of life purpose.

The model focuses on four points for reflection to help you build awareness: (a) The people places, and things that you've been exposed to in your life; (b) Evidence of the choices that you make through words, stories, and your key strengths and weaknesses; (c) What excites you and how you express your passions for life; and (4) Your essence or what is at your core and heart as a person. Corbett and Chloupek (2019) explained, "Your why it matters represents what drives you and can be distilled into a phrase that represents you" (p. 1). Examples of typical WIM statements are presented in Table 6.5.

Table 6.5   Examples of why it matters

To commit	To be right	Is it worth it?	To keep the peace
To get through it	To accomplish	To be enough	To be a problem-solver
To be respected	To appear brilliant	To be a catalyst	To be unique
To get it right	To succeed	To be a guiding	To educate
To be seen	To be in control	light	To encourage
To be admired	To be included	To be relevant	To make people happy
To know needs	To be liked	To be perfect	To prove competence
To be creative	To be needed	To be rewarded	To provide
To be heard	To be noticed	To be the expert	accomplishment
To fill a need	To play	To be understood	To stay in comfort zone
To fit in	To protect	To be worthwhile	To be a dominant force
To get it done	To shine	To be above	To be stable
To win	To succeed	average	To teach
To belong	To challenge	To belong	To serve
To be free	To be real	To connect	To learn
		To be competent	

Source: Adapted from Corbett and Chloupek (2019, p. 65).

Find your why

Sinek (2017) designed this approach for either individuals or teams. The steps to the individual process include (a) Gathering stories and sharing them; (b) Identifying themes in the stories; and (c) Drafting and refining a Why Statement. Sinek recommends the following format:

To _____ so that _____ (p. 35).

The book offers multiple strategies for approaching the process. Like the WIM approach, the book lacks theoretical grounding.

Identify your internal driver

Chloupek (2023) explained,

> Think of your internal driver (ID) as your driver's license. It gives you permission to steer your own course and make choices that align with your values and aspirations. When you know what drives you, you can take ownership of your life and create the road map that reflects your unique vision and goals. This can give you a sense of empowerment even in the face of challenges and setbacks. (p. 1)

This approach is divided into three parts: (a) Awareness or building insights into your behavior and why you do what you do, (b) Core behaviors or the evidence about how your behaviors are both working for you and perhaps working against you according to your ID, and (c) Core connections show how your ID impacts your personal and professional relationships. This book is also a self-guided reflection and discovery of your ID. Like WIM and Find Your Why, this approach lacks a theoretical foundation.

CHAPTER SUMMARY

Chapter 6 explored how adults derive meaning from their lives and work by discussing theoretical perspectives and presenting practical strategies for connecting work and meaning. The chapter defined theoretical perspectives on career calling, meaningful work, and volition. It covered other ways of interpreting purpose, including right livelihood and ikigai. Discovering meaning and purpose in life and work was discussed, and the chapter concluded with some practical exercises to help individuals determine their purpose. Krishnamurti (1992) summed up life's purpose as a labor of love: "To bring about a radical change in the ways of our life, there must be expanding awareness, and a great depth of feeling which is love. With love everything is possible" (p. 172).

7. Appreciating work and career challenges based on positionality and intersectionality

⊔ BOX 7.1 CHAPTER OVERVIEW AND LEARNING
OBJECTIVES

Maya Angelou wisely said in 2013:

> I think you must struggle for betterment for yourself and for everyone. It is impossible to struggle for civil rights, equal rights for blacks, without including whites. Because equal rights, fair play, justice, are all like the air: we all have it, or none of us has it. That is the truth of it. (Rolfes, 2014, para. 9)

Angelou's brilliance is in her observation that no one is equal until everyone is equal. Adults have a human right to decent work, fair pay, and a humanly sustainable work culture and climate. Everyone in the workforce has a responsibility to support and advocate for these rights.

Rethinking Adult Career Development has focused on the realities of career development (CD) for adult workers. Chapter 7 examines work and career challenges connected to people's positionality and intersectionality. This chapter explores identities that often intersect to understand career challenges based on gender, age, race, socioeconomic status, gender identity and sexuality, and disability.

As a result of reading this chapter and completing the exercises, you, the reader, should be able to:

1. Define the major challenges faced by various demographic populations, including gender; age; race and ethnicity; social class and poverty; lesbian, gay, bisexual, transgender, queer, questioning intersex, asexual+ people; and disability.
2. Appreciate how work and career challenges may compound with intersectionality.

Rethinking Adult Career Development has underscored the problem that work and CD are not equitable for all people desiring decent, stable, fulfilling work. Positionality is how a person's identities, such as gender, race, class, disability, and others, combine and intersect to influence how people engage with and experience society. Gedro (2017) discussed the metaphor of "closet" as "hiding or concealing of an aspect of one's identity" (p. 61). Although often referring to concealment of gender or sexual minority status, Gedro explained,

> With respect to several aspects of identity that I highlight, such as recovery from alcoholism, formerly incarcerated status, perhaps even military and veteran status, it is useful to think about concealment and disclosure in a more nuanced way. The closet represents a fixed discrete image. A closet has a door (which is ostensibly opaque). With respect to these different aspects of identity, it is perhaps more accurate to think of a person in a shadow. A shadow can be dark or semi-transparent. One can move in and out of the cover of a shadow; And be visible or invisible. (p. 61)

Positionality also works similarly in that although some identities are readily visible, others are not.

CAREER HEADWINDS AND TAILWINDS

People encounter challenges in life and work. Work is an expression of identity that is fluid, constructed, multidimensional and matrixed, often recognizable and detectable, and value laden (Gedro, 2017). Identity has both benefits and costs:

> Identity capital is the benefit of having an identity that results in a gain in the market space of work. Identity cost is the loss, or marginalization that occurs as a result of having a stigmatized identity that is known or suspected by others. (Gedro, 2017, p. 13)

Chugh and Bock (2018) cited antiracist educator Debby Irving's (2016) use of the metaphors of headwinds and tailwinds to explain how people have different capital costs in life. If you have flown east to west and west to east, you may have noticed flying from east to west took longer. This is due to prevailing winds. Headwinds impede westward travel, and tailwinds accelerate eastward travel. Chugh and Bock explained,

> Headwinds are the challenges—some big, some small, some visible, some invisible—that make life harder for some people but not for all people. When you run against a headwind, your speed slows down and you have to push harder. You can feel the headwind. When you have a tailwind pushing you, it is a force that propels you forward. It is consequential but easily unnoticed or forgotten ... The invisibility of headwinds and tailwinds leads us to vilify people facing headwinds. It is no coincidence that the groups facing great headwinds in our society are also the

most negatively stereotyped ... Failure to see systemic headwinds and tailwinds in the world around us leads us to blame people facing the headwinds. As a result, we confuse equality and equity. Equality says we treat everyone the same, regardless of headwinds or tailwinds. Equity says we give people what they need to have the same access and opportunities as others, taking into account the headwinds they face which may mean differential treatment for some groups. We see a meritocracy where one does not exist. (pp. 64–66)

When people encounter headwinds or tailwinds, it is easy to chalk up the challenges or opportunities to the individual. Yet, "inequality emerges through unconscious bias ... [and] group advantage of privilege" (Chugh & Bock, 2018, p. 81). Chugh and Bock explained,

These two levels—individual and systemic—are rarely addressed jointly. In fact, the individual perspective dominates our current national dialogue and mental attention. Activist and writer Tim Wise notes that we take greater notice of a single victim of a hate crime than of 1,000,000 victims of systemic injustice. As journalist Greg Howard wrote, "Racism ceased to be a matter of systems and policy and became a referendum on the root of the individual soul." Most Americans think about bias through this individual perspective ... Physician and researcher Kamara Jones argues that we can only understand bias when we consider the three interdependent levels at which it occurs: the systemic level, the individual level, and the internalized level. (p. 81)

It is important to understand the challenges individuals and marginalized groups encounter in their work and careers are not only about the person. Individuals experience systemic trends that marginalize or privilege them in a particular situation or context. Constant racism, sexism, or other injustice wears on a person and becomes internalized oppression or the belief that the negative social messages about one's identity or identities are true. Box 7.2 provides an opportunity to reflect on Chugh and Bock's (2018) message about headwinds and tailwinds in your work and career.

◡ BOX 7.2 REFLECTIVE PRACTICE

Identifying your Headwinds and Tailwinds

Reflect on your headwinds (challenges) and Tailwinds (forward-propelling force) as a career explorer, sustainer, or changer. Remember that some may be invisible to others. List them in Table 7.1. Take a moment to reflect on whether these headwinds and tailwinds are individual or more systemic based on your identity or intersecting identities.

Table 7.1   Identifying your headwinds and tailwinds

Headwinds	Tailwinds

The next sections describe work and career challenges based on various posi-tionalities of gender; age; race and ethnicity; social class and poverty; lesbian, gay, bisexual, transgender, queer, questioning intersex, asexual+ people; and disability. Although each demographic identity will be described individually, people's identities intersect in complex ways, as described in Chapter 4.

GENDER

Gender equity remains a hot topic, but an elusive reality for most women. Although they make up nearly half of the global workforce, women are underpaid, undervalued, and encounter obstacles to advancement. Coleman (2020) interviewed 60 senior women leaders in the UK to understand how they perceived career challenges, facilitators of career progress, and the changes they had witnessed and anticipated for women leaders. She found that the main obstacles were (a) Masculine organization culture, (b) Discrimination and the glass ceiling, (c) Gender stereotyping, and (d) Balancing life and family with work demands. Women benefited from determination, resilience, mentoring, and networking, although reported little support from their organizations. The women foresaw gradual changes, although expected masculine industries would be more change resistant. A reality of Coleman's (2020) participants and many women leaders is they were unsupportive of feminist stances and accepting of prioritizing the business over equity issues.

Fouad et al. (2019) examined CD literature from the past 20 years, noting that it focused on a narrow population segment and incorrectly assumed people had equal access. Fouad et al. (2023) conducted a systematic review of women's CD literature, contemplating whether a separate theory of women's CD was necessary, concluding more research is needed:

> Women continue to experience barriers to any career path that deviates from the patriarchal status quo. We have known this with some degree of certainty for the past 30 years. The present review has added more voices to this chorus, but overall, we are essentially in the same place we were 25 years ago in terms of methodo-logical and theoretical rigor as well as design approaches used to ask and answer questions on the career development of women. Although we have been pleased to see questions in this area continue to be asked, we ask that they be investigated with

an increasing level of design sophistication that allow us to establish causality and evidenced based practice in our work with, and on behalf of women. (p. 831)

Compounding the problem of gender equity is that women's and men's aware-ness of gender inequity differs, as men broadly think gender inequity is a myth (Piacenza, 2019). Schultheiss (2021) acknowledged that workplaces are challenged by "persistent occupational disparities" (p. 274), including issues of civility, sexual harassment, gender stereotyping, and stereotype threat, and recommended viewing the issues from an intersectional perspective, as discussed in Chapter 4, emphasizing "an intersectional conceptualization of women's and men's identities could minimize the risk of making assumptions that homogenize gendered CD and work experiences" (p. 274). Gender is not the only inequity in the workplace, it intersects with other positionalities and identities, such as race.

Gendered Demographic Issues

Catalyst (2022) reported that women have earned more bachelor's, master's, and doctoral degrees than men for decades across all racial and ethnic groups. Although women represent 47% of the US workforce, they are overrepre-sented in industries that were negatively impacted by the COVID-19 pan-demic, such as residential and home nursing care, childcare, food service, and leisure and hospitality (Fry, 2022; Hegewisch & Mefferd, 2022). During 2021, women held 52% of all management, professional, and related occupations (Bureau of Labor Statistics, 2022b). Yet, women account for only 44, or 8.8%, of CEOs in the Fortune 500 (Catalyst, 2022), and the majority of boards are men-dominated, with women holding 33% of S&P 500 board seats, with 9% being women of color (Stuart, 2023). Chapter 4 also discussed the gender pay gap women face in their careers.

Gendered Occupational Disparities

Although women face barriers and challenges in their work and careers, Hoobler et al. (2018) found convincing evidence that gender-diverse top man-agement teams outperform less diverse teams. Women face difficulty access-ing influential leadership positions, hiring, and promotional opportunities, and being represented by women at all levels of their organization, according to a study that reviewed recurring themes related to the gender pay gap (Bishu & Alkadry, 2017). These issues are intensified by gender bias and gendered job discrimination where women get concentrated in work that is "gender appro-priate" such as education and social services.

Metaphors abound for discussing women's career challenges, such as the glass ceiling (Morrison et al., 1987)—invisible barriers that block women from advancing, the glass cliff—when women are hired when organization performance is trending downward and if the women fail, they tend to do so publicly and swiftly as if they represent the failings of women in general (Ryan & Haslam, 2005), the "leaky" pipeline (Zeng, 2011) —the assumption women "leak" out of contention for career advancement due to barriers and disadvantages. Leaks are often due to inequity and injustice, not individual women's issues or challenges, or the concrete ceiling, coined by Jasmine Babers to describe barriers faced by women of color that make advancing more impermeable than breaking the glass ceiling (Helms & Roussos, 2021). Sexual harassment has also been reported by 60% of all women over their career lifespan (Lean In, 2023).

Gedro (2017) critiqued human resource development and related fields for producing little scholarship on the nexus of gender and age, particularly for older women. She conducted a literature review examining older women's CD. Gedro found three themes in her analysis. First, the literature is masculinized, assuming homogeneity and linear career trajectories, and existing career theory is inadequate to consider intersections of age and gender. Second, women have intersecting identities, for example how caretaking and working entwine to create complexities as women negotiate life balance. These complexities are more "punishing" for women as they face ageism, unrealistic standards of beauty, invisibility as they age, and double standards of how women are expected to behave at work—be firm, but not too firm; be direct but not bossy. The third theme in Gedro's (2017) analysis painted a more positive picture of older women's experience in the wisdom they amassed from experience that gives them perspective, strength, and a sense of authenticity.

AGE

Age discrimination is prohibited by law in many countries, and the workforce is predicted to become more age-diverse, healthier, and better educated (OECD, n.d.). By 2050, the OECD predicts that the number of people aged 50 and older will increase from 37% (in 2020) to 45%. These population trends mean that multigenerational workplaces will become the norm, as discussed in Chapter 2. Despite the larger numbers of older workers, Hirschi and Pang (2021) critiqued CD theory for historically neglecting older workers and retirees, noting, "there is no clear-cut criterion or age … to determine when someone is an 'older worker'" (p. 438). Box 7.3 summarizes generational differences represented in the workforce.

ⅠⅠ BOX 7.3 ADULT CAREER DEVELOPMENT BY THE NUMBERS

Multiple Generations at Work

The workforce is multigenerational. Rather than assuming it causes conflict, it is important to also regard multiple generations as opportunities to learn and consider workplace issues and challenges differently. The generations actively employed include:

- Baby Boomers (1946–1964)
- Generation X (1965–1980)
- Generation Y (Millennials) (1981–1996)
- Generation Z (1997–2015)

The descriptions in Table 7.2 offer nuanced differences between the generations. How can you make the best of multiple generations in your own experience as a career explorer, sustainer, or changer?

Table 7.2   Multiple generations at work

Experiences and values	Baby Boomers	Generation X	Millennial	Generation Z
Experienced:	Television, moon landing, Watergate, Vietnam War	MTV, Nintendo, PCs	Natural disasters, diversity, and mobile technology	Economic downturn, global warming
Work is:	Expected	A difficult challenge	A means to an end	Constantly evolving
Career aspiration:	Job security	Work-life balance, independence	Freedom and flexibility	Structure and stability
Changing jobs:	Loyal to employer; connecting to values	If necessary for compensation	Is expected	Frequently
Career paths:	Upward mobility	Need to know options now	Switch frequently and fast	Career "multitaskers"

Source: Adapted from OECD Forum (2017).

Age-related Career Challenges

Given the age diversity in the workforce and the benefits older workers bring to organizations, being mindful of how to support effective aging at work is an essential consideration for individuals, leaders, organizations, and society. Despite the benefits older workers bring to the workforce, they face ageist stereotypes about their job performance with erroneous beliefs they are less productive, less interested in or able to learn, and have lower commitment and motivation (Hirschi & Pang, 2021), even though such assumptions about older workers are not empirically sound (Dordoni & Argentero, 2015; Ng & Feldman, 2012). Ageism is stereotypes, prejudice, or age-based discrimination that negatively affects older workers in hiring, employability assessment, and performance evaluation (Cebola et al., 2023). The age stereotypes Ng and Feldman (2012) refuted included that older workers are less motivated, more resistant to change and less willing to change, less trusting, less healthy, and more vulnerable to life balance challenges than their younger co-workers. The only stereotype with some empirical evidence is that older workers are less willing to participate in learning and development activities. This is likely due to the perceived lack of relevance that the learning opportunity is worthwhile.

The most noticeable shift in older workers is their level of job satisfaction. Although job satisfaction tends to decline until people are in their thirties and forties, it begins to rise with age (Hirschi & Pang, 2021). Ng and Feldman (2010) found that although satisfaction tends to rise with age, older workers are less pleased with promotions as they age. Part of this dissatisfaction may correspond with reaching a career plateau or a stalling of upward career progression (Ference et al., 1977). Career plateaus are not solely age-related, although correspond with older workers slowing down career progress and shifting interests elsewhere. Hirschi and Pang (2021) argued that human resource policies and organization practices are ill-prepared to manage an aging workforce and should be developing flexible work schedules, voluntary scaled retirement or demotions, reduced workloads, recognition programs, and engagement to accommodate all workers, particularly older ones.

Although older workers are diverse in how they perceive and participate in work, the transition to retirement is a significant process that impacts a person's sense of identity and generativity. Retirement is difficult to define because many workers take on new work or pick up part-time work when they retire. Lytle et al. (2015) explained that retirement incorporates decreasing work hours, collecting retirement benefits, self-identifying as "retired," or withdrawing entirely from paid work. Retirement can be explored from three different theoretical stances: (a) Decision-making—factors influence the decision to retire such as motivation, attitudes, health, finances, meanings attached to retirement, and other interests; (b) Adjustment—level of well-being and capacity to adjust to retirement that depends on personality, finances, and skills; and (c) A career development phase—how variables affect how a person moves toward ending a career and also factors in health, work experience, work characteristics, organization culture and climate, and stressors (Wang & Shi, 2014).

Adult Development for Older Workers

Ackerman and Kanfer (2020) reviewed theoretical and empirical frameworks of adult development over 30 years to gain insights into aging and work in the 21st century to propose broad themes for theory and research. They advocated for more research to develop an empirical account of work experience, expertise, and aging. They recommended that older workers be assessed for their repertoire of foundational knowledge and expertise, especially in high-tech work contexts, instead of chronological age. Although aging makes it more challenging to do cognitively demanding jobs that require handling new information and problem-solving, such as an air traffic controller, they concluded that aging effects on the cognitive abilities of older workers have fewer adverse effects on performance than multitasking, distractions, or other shared work conditions. Ackerman and Kanfer (2020) also proposed more relevant adult knowledge and skill assessments and the creation of whole-person assessments that consider adult knowledge, skills, abilities, interests, attitudes, and motivation. How they change over time could assist older workers in career planning and adjustment. Adult learning and CD in a world where technology is constantly evolving needs consideration and better matching of tacit knowledge and experience of older workers and leveraging their existing knowledge and skills for new learning. They urged, "The key to successful use of psychological theory and empirical research in the context of the future work is to optimize organizational goals and societal needs by maximizing adult development and worker well-being across the lifespan and socioeconomic circumstances" (Ackerman & Kanfer, 2020, p. 496).

RACE AND ETHNICITY

The 2020 US Census Bureau (Shrider et al., 2021) measured the population as more racially and ethnically diverse than in 2010, and estimated that by 2050 the share of the "White and not Hispanic" population will drop to under 50% for the first time (Schneider, 2023). Although 54% of White UK respondents indicated their CD had met or exceeded expectations, only 49% of respondents from minority ethnic groups agreed, and the survey also showed that this group viewed access to development and progression opportunities as less equitable (CIPD, 2023). The Chartered Institute of Personnel Development also concluded that the key barriers to progression indicated dissatisfaction due to the overlooking of skills and talent, poor quality line management, and not belonging to the "in" group (CIPD, 2023). The CIPD report also indicated that 20% of respondents from minority ethnic groups desired senior leadership to (a) Question the lack of racial diversity in senior roles, (b) Take firm action on discrimination, and (c) Provide more transparency in pay to highlight and correct inequities.

Populations are projected to continue to diversify. Although organizations may fear revealing data about racial compositions not matching the populations, Apfelbaum and Suh (2024) found that when organizations disclose their lack of progress in reaching racial diversity, they are perceived as more trustworthy and committed to diversity than companies maintaining silence. There is also a higher level of accountability when an organization is public about its quest to become more equitable and diverse.

Racial and ethnic background also affect people's CD through educational and occupational disparities, with clear US data revealing these individuals are more likely to drop out of high school, not graduate from college, and be disproportionately overrepresented in lower-paid, lower-skilled work than White European Americans (Fouad & Kantamneni, 2021). Cultural factors affecting the work and CD of racial and ethnic minorities include cultural values, acculturation, ethnic identity, role models, perceptions of discrimination, perceived barriers and supports, and occupational aspirations and expectations (Fouad & Kantamneni, 2021). Sisco (2020) reported on how racial disparities in career outcomes have been exacerbated by

> The sociopolitical and cultural foundations of race and racism [where] ... Whites have traditionally occupied positions of authority and influence across all job sectors, while Black, Indigenous, and People of color (BIPOC) have mostly worked in entry-level positions and labor-intensive industries. (Collins, 1997; Eby et al., 1998; Vallas, 2003; Sisco, 2020, p. 420)

Race affects employment opportunities, and levels of disparity and incivility are higher for people of color.

Race and Employment Disparities

The Bureau of Labor Statistics (2023a) reported that White people make up 77% of the US workforce, followed by Hispanic or Latino ethnicity representing 18%, Black people and Asian people representing 13% and 7%, respectively, with American Indian and Alaska Native people making up 1%. Native Hawaiians and Other Pacific Islanders account for less than 0.5%. Catalyst (2023) reported women of color are overrepresented in frontline roles, representing 28.8% of the hospitality and leisure sector as compared to 9% of White women, 31.9% of retail as compared to 11.1% of White women, and 19.8% of the manufacturing industry, compared to 6.1% of White women. Women of color also experience the highest rates of unemployment, with 2022 figures showing 5.3% of Black women, 2.2% of Asian women, 3.4% of Hispanic/Latinas, and 2.6% of White women. White men accounted for 2.8% of the unemployed that year. Triana et al. (2021) reviewed 60 years of discrimination and diversity research in human resource management. They noted that the unemployment rate of Black compared to White Americans had changed little over that time, with the rate for Black workers being nearly twice that of White people since the 1950s. Although it is well-documented that racial minorities encounter discrimination throughout their careers, the research foci have shifted away from racial discrimination towards diversity management.

The 2021 weekly median earnings of full-time White workers is US$1,006 compared to US$799 for Black workers, US$1,286 for Asian workers, and US$750 for Hispanic or Latin American workers (Bureau of Labor Statistics, 2023a; Nelson & Vallas, 2021). Wages in occupations where White people are highly represented average approximately US$120,000 (more than twice the national average) in comparison to high representation in jobs at the income of US$31,000 for Black people, US$104,000 for Asian people, and US$32,000 for Hispanic/Latin American people (Fox, 2017).

Race and Incivility

Sisco (2020) detailed how Black professionals experience incivility in their work, using Welbourne et al.'s (2015) definition that "Workplace incivility is a subtle type of deviant work behavior that is low in intensity and violates workplace norms of respect" (p. 205). She explained that uncivil behavior can be racist when it "reinforce[s] the cultural superiority of a dominant group within an organization," and how "Black professionals are consciously working against false perceptions of their racial and professional identity" (p. 422). Further, Black professionals are often stereotyped, subject to being tokens—the only Black professional in their unit, segregated socially from White people in the organization, subject to higher levels of scrutiny in the hiring process, and less likely to have a high-level mentor who supports their CD (Sisco, 2020). Not only is incivility a reality for people of colour in their work and careers, but this treatment also makes them more susceptible to burnout, and the emotional burden of shouldering racism and unjust treatment can even cause some Black professionals to lower career aspirations (Brown & Segrist, 2016; Sisco, 2020).

Sisco (2020) studied Black professionals' resilience to racial bias using phenomenology and found they persisted by engaging in self-preservation and coping strategies. Self-preservation was achieved by safeguarding personal narratives and Blackness by announcing their accomplishments, forging alliances with White colleagues, and educating Black allies about how they could help advance the Black community. Coping strategies involved micro-managing expectations by celebrating achievements but anticipating resistance and by micro-targeting opportunities or seizing ways to gain social capital and minimize social isolation. Box 7.4 provides some strategies for finding a mentor when they seem scarce.

BOX 7.4 TIPS AND TOOLS FOR CAREER DEVELOPMENT

How to Find a Mentor

Mentoring has been shown to yield objective outcomes of promoting career advancement and promotions, elevating earnings, improving performance evaluations, and advancing people into higher positions of power, as well as more subjective outcomes including enhancing organization commitment, job and career satisfaction, career progress expectations, and well-being while reducing turnover, stress and burnout, family-work conflict, and work alienation (Allen et al., 2004; Ivey & Dupré, 2022). With all these benefits, you may wonder, as a career explorer, sustainer, or changer, "How do I get a mentor?"

Phan (2021) explained that although 76% of people believe mentors are important, only 37% have one. She mused that the gap is caused by fear of asking someone to meet with you to discuss becoming your mentor. Here are her tips:
1. Ask for that first meeting—Identify someone you admire and perhaps do not know well and invite them to meet virtually or in person. You can ask in person or send a short email (see Phan, 2021, for examples of recommended communications you can send the mentor).
2. Presuming they say yes, nurture the relationship. Get to know your mentor and send a thank you note after the meeting. Follow up.
Maintain the relationship by providing updates, offering to help them somehow, and expressing gratitude.

SOCIOECONOMIC STATUS AND POVERTY

Career development (CD) is one way to improve an individual's income potential and social standing, yet socioeconomic status (SES) intertwines with CD influencing income, occupation, occupational status, benefits, health care access, social network, cultural privilege, and capacity to influence the local community or context (Juntunen et al., 2021). Hollingshead (1975) defined social class as a combination of a person's income, educational attainment, and work or career. Juntunen et al. (2021) offered that more nuanced definitions attempted to capture the complexity of SES and incorporate a person's class worldview. The American Psychological Association (APA) (2019) resolved these differences by defining SES as:

> Social class is a relative social rank based on income, wealth, education, status and/ or power and can be both objective and subjective ... The objective method of measuring social class assesses variables that are external to the individual such an educational attainment, income, assets, occupational prestige scores, and family size, among others. Any of these variables can be utilized as an indicator of social class, and they can be evaluated individually or collectively ... The subjective method of assessing social class is concerned with an individual's personal understanding of their own social class in comparison to others. This can include an employed behavior and attitude, and an expected consequence, as the individual attempts to navigate within and between classes. (p. 35)

SES affects a person's preparation for work, linking it closely with CD, although connecting the two is neglected (Blustein, 2006, Juntunen et al., 2021). Women and racial and ethnic minorities are often also at an SES disadvantage. Juntunen et al. (2021) noted:

> A full discussion of social class must include groups with sufficient and even significant resources, and there is some evidence that individuals who are identified as privileged (i.e., wealthy, upper, or upper middle class) may also confront important issues that limit their career options (Lapour & Heppner, 2009). However, people with limited resources are both more likely to be in need of vocational resources and less likely to have them. (p. 342)

Due to disparities in income and the impact poverty has on work and career choice and outcomes, I will focus on low-income and economic marginalization in this chapter because this population suffers inequities in education, health care, housing, and occupational attainment. Work and career challenges compounded by poverty include inequality, indecent work, and precarious labor. Women and people from ethnic and racial minorities also tend to suffer disproportionately from poverty and its implications for work and life.

Inequality Based on SES

In 2020, 37.2 million Americans, or 11.4% of the population, lived below the official poverty line, according to the US Census Bureau (Shrider et al., 2021), 6.3 million of whom were among the "working poor"—"people who spent at least 27 weeks in the labor force (that is, working or looking for work) but whose incomes still fell below the official poverty level" (Bureau of Labor Statistics, 2022a, para. 1). According to the Bureau of Labor Statistics (2022a), women who were working poor outnumbered men (3.4 versus 3.0 million, respectively), and Hispanic and Black people represented 7.4% and 6.7% of the working poor, respectively, as compared to 3.7% of White people and 2.6% for Asian people. In 2021, women were a majority (59.1%) of part-time workers—and over two-thirds (67.7%) of part-time workers in low-wage jobs (LePage, 2022). Educational attainment affects the incidence of being impoverished. People with less than a high school diploma represented the largest group of working poor in 2020 who were primarily in service occupations. The average worker is working longer hours, although wages have remained stagnant, as discussed in Chapter 2.

Indecent Work

Not all work provides a good job or decent work. To understand what indecent work is, one must understand the definition of decent work first:

> Decent work sums up the aspirations of people in their working lives. It involves opportunities for work that is productive and delivers a fair income, security in the workplace and social protection for all, better prospects for personal development and social integration, freedom for people to express their concerns, organize and participate in the decisions that affect their lives and equality of opportunity and treatment for all women and men. (International Labour Organization, n.d., para. 1)

Indecent work is characterized by inequity, low pay, few or no benefits, insecurity, lack of support, little or no provision of learning and development, little opportunity for advancement, poor management, and a lack of workplace democracy or avenues to influence decisions. Indecent work is not sustainable and often has negative effects on people's health and well-being. Indecent work is also characterized by workers having little control over their schedule or job security, which causes stress (Christie et al., 2021).

Precarious Work

Precarity is a state of persistent insecurity in employment or income. "Precarious work exhibits uncertainty, instability, vulnerability, and insecurity where employees are required to bear the risks of work" (Hewison, 2016, p. 428). Precarious work is typically contract, temporary, or work that does not provide a living wage (above the poverty level). Precarious positions are unstable and often end in layoffs or outsourcing (Juntunen et al., 2021). Box 7.5 profiles research on social mobility and vocational outcomes.

ıl BOX 7.5 ADULT CAREER DEVELOPMENT BY THE NUMBERS

Social Mobility and Vocational Outcomes from a Psychology of Working Perspective

Perez et al. (2023) developed profiles of social mobility from a sample of 533 working adults and compared profile membership to Psychology of Working Theory (PWT) outcomes of work volition, career adaptability, and decent work. (Note: PWT was discussed in Chapter 5.) Their findings are summarized in Table 7.3.

Perez et al. (2023) explained that people tend to maintain similar economic constraints and experiences with marginalization from childhood to adulthood, buying into the "American Dream" narrative when it is not often true in reality due to systemic inequity and injustice. They also noted that even when people have a good income, they may still identify with the experience of marginalization. Considering these findings, it can be helpful to reflect on how one's identity affects how one views and experiences work. The authors also advocated helping marginalized workers develop critical consciousness to resist and change inequitable systems, which will be discussed in Chapter 8.

Table 7.3   Social mobility and vocational outcomes from a psychology of working perspective

Social mobility profile	Description
1. Sustained privilege	Characterized by low levels of marginalization and economic constraints during childhood and adulthood.
2. Downward mobility	Characterized by low levels of marginalization and economic constraints in childhood and high levels in adulthood.
3. Upward mobility	Characterized by high levels of marginalization and economic constraints in childhood, and low levels in adulthood.
4. Highly marginalized	Characterized by high levels of marginalization at both points.

Social mobility profile	Description
5. Sustained barriers	Characterized by high levels of marginalization and economic constraints in childhood and adulthood.

Work and Career Issues Related to Social Class and Poverty

Social class, SES, and poverty influence people's career trajectories by impacting lifelong CD and intervention opportunities. Career aspirations and career choices are diminished in these situations, especially since children raised in low-income families are at risk of future poverty due to the lack of educational opportunities or financial resources to prepare for the workforce (Juntunen et al., 2021). Children often do not develop a critical consciousness about their circumstances. Juntunen et al. (2021) recommended that people be made aware of their sociopolitical realities and how they create obstacles that might impinge their career prospects.

Job finding and transitions can also be difficult for the impoverished, although job search interventions help attain employment, particularly when they include emotional and skills training (Abel et al., 2018; Liu et al., 2014). Juntunen et al. (2021) suggested work role salience and satisfaction for this population can be enhanced if people reflect on what they value about work (e.g., security, learning, advancement opportunities) and what defines decent work for them (e.g., supportive colleagues, fair wages, flexibility), and then seek work or a career path that fits their personal values and meanings of decent work as a way of broadening the options for the type of work they are seeking.

LGBTQIA+

LGBTQIA+ is an acronym for lesbian, gay, bisexual, transgender, queer and/ or questioning, intersex, asexual/aromantic/agender that recognizes diverse gender and sexual identities that often face marginalization across society (Gold, 2018), also known as gender and sexual minorities (GSM). Although this acronym has variations, it is important to use the most inclusive acronym in one's community. Eighty-one countries prohibit employment discrimination based on sexual orientation, including Australia, Canada, France, Germany, Mexico, Switzerland, the United Kingdom, and the United States (Mendos et al., 2020). Despite the existence of some legal protections, LGBTQIA+ workers experience hostile work climates. Twenty-three percent of US LGBTQIA+ workers reported workplace discrimination, as did 31% of transgender workers (Medina & Mahowald, 2023). A pay gap exists for LGBTQIA+ workers averaging US$.89 for each dollar as compared to a "typical worker," and non-binary, genderqueer, genderfluid, and Two-Spirit workers in the United States earn approximately 70 cents for every dollar that the "typical worker" earns, and transgender women earn approximately 60 cents for every dollar (Tohl, 2023).

Sexual Orientation and Identity Development

Gedro (2017) noted that although models of sexual orientation identity development (e.g., Collins, 2012; Gedro, 2009) provide context and process for how sexual and gender minorities make sense of their identity, there is no corresponding work on identity theory for heterosexual identity since it is assumed to be the "norm." Gedro (2009) critiqued human resource development for its scant exploration of career issues faced by lesbian, gay, bisexual, and transgender (LGBT) people. Gedro (2009) described the workplace as "characterized by heterosexual ubiquitousness" (p. 55). She explained:

> Sexual orientation manifests anytime a worker places a picture of his or her spouse or children on a desk, wears a wedding ring, or brings a spouse to a company function. LGBT people do not have this privilege and must negotiate the heterosexism of their organizational settings to a variety of strategies. (p. 55)

Gedro et al. (2004) identified negotiation strategies of lesbians in corporate manager, director, and executive positions and identified they decided when and how to come out and learned how to advocate for change and educate people about sexual orientation workplace issues. One in ten LGBTQIA+ people in the US reported discrimination in 2020, with half reporting facing employment bias at some point in their careers (Sears et al., 2021).

LGBTQIA+ Representation

LGBTQIA+ workers fear bringing their whole selves to work, with about half not being out to their bosses and about 25% not being out to anyone in their organization (Mallory et al., 2022). This covering of one's authentic self to avoid stigmatization can result in stress and health problems (Sears et al., 2021), and unsupportive culture is a primary factor in LGBTQIA+ workers leaving their jobs (Medina & Mahowald, 2023). Openly LGBTQIA+ leaders are rare, with only 25 or 0.4% holding board seats in the Fortune 500, and with only two of the seats held by people of color (Smith, 2021).

LGBTQIA+ Career Disparities

LGBTQIA+ people experience work and career disparities according to data from the Census Bureau (Medina et al., 2022), such as working more and at higher rates in that they were more likely to report working in the past seven days (65% versus 57%), including overtime. They were more likely to work at grocery and convenience stores and to use unemployment insurance (11% versus 6%), with LGBTQIA+ people of color working in these settings at a rate of 12% and transgender respondents at 14%. Medina et al. (2022) concluded that reliable data are lacking with this population and that better-quality surveys are needed to support LGBTQIA+ workers better. They also advocated for good jobs, health benefits, and fair wages, strengthening anti-discrimination protections, and empowering LGBTQI+ workers to stand up for their rights.

DISABILITY

The World Health Organization (WHO) estimated that 1.3 billion people, or 16% of the world's population, lived with a disability in 2023. People with disability (PWD) die up to 20 years earlier than those without disability, and they have double the risk of developing other health conditions, including depression, asthma, diabetes, stroke, obesity, or poor oral health (WHO, 2023b). Although one in six people live with disability worldwide (WHO, 2023b), they are often viewed as different or deficient by society—socially constructed perceptions that are inaccurate. PWDs represented 21.3% of the US labor force in 2022 (Bureau of Labor Statistics (BLS), 2023a), although their unemployment rate was higher than that of people without disability: 7.6% versus 3.5%, respectively. Additionally, PWDs are less likely to possess a bachelor's degree and more likely to work part time in service occupations or be self-employed (BLS, 2023b).

PWDs desire satisfying work and careers, yet are impeded by discrimination, inadequate access to CD support, and often a lack of accommodations to provide equitable access throughout their career span. According to the WHO (2023b), "Health inequities arise from unfair conditions faced by persons with disabilities, including stigma, discrimination, poverty, exclusion from education and employment, and barriers faced in the health system itself" (para. 1). PWDs also have more difficulty accessing transportation, making finding and sustaining work more challenging.

Disability is often omitted from definitions of diversity, and when it is included the definition tends to refer to physical disability but excludes mental and cognitive disabilities (Procknow & Rocco, 2016). Further, Rocco and Fornes (2010) lamented little critically oriented work about disability has been published outside conference proceedings in adult education. When disability is discussed, it tends to be regarded as a "problem" in one's life and work, following the "medical model" of disability. The medical model looks for deficits in what is "wrong" with PWDs rather than what the person needs or how society has created systemic barriers, including physical, attitudinal, practical, and political obstacles. Alternatively, the "social model" of disability recognizes it is not the individual but the disability that is the challenge, as well as the way society has created barriers in systems, attitudes, beliefs, and practices that detract from how individuals, organizations, and society provides support to PWDs. Table 7.4 contrasts the medical and social models of disability presented by Haegele and Hodge (2016).

Table 7.4   Contrasts between medical and social models of disability

	Medical model	Social model
Disability	A deficiency or abnormality that results from impairments in body functions or structures	A social construct imposed on top of impairments by society; a "difference"
Interventions	Fixing the disability to the greatest extent possible by the professional—"normalizing"	Social or political change in an effort to decrease environmental barriers and increase levels of understanding
Outcome	Normalized function, functioning members of existing society	Social inclusion, changes in environment and understanding

Source: Adapted from Haegele and Hodge (2016).

Work and Career Challenges Associated with Disability

"Long-standing traditions of disablism, against people labeled *disabled*, have divested them of normative citizenship and employment" (Procknow & Rocco, 2016, p. 381). Disablism is "discriminatory, oppressive or abusive behaviour arising from the belief that disabled people are inferior to others" (Miller et al., 2004, p. 9). Prockow and Rocco (2016) explained that PWDs are denied access to meaningful work, and their career prospects have been diminished with the assumption they are not as productive, reliable, or as expensive as non-disabled people. They reviewed disability-related publications in the Academy of Human Resource Development Proceedings and sponsored journals and identified issues for PWDs in work and career as (a) Organizational entry barriers, (b) Organizational post-entry barriers, (c) Career development and advancement, (d) Workplace training for diversity inclusiveness and disabled workers, and (e) Harassment discrimination, and allegations of discharge-related discrimination.

Organizational entry barriers

Organizational barriers (access bias) to entry for PWDs prevent access to work and careers due to attitudes, institutional, and self-imposed obstacles. Attitudes are the prejudices and biases that cause people to stigmatize disabled candidates. For example, a hiring manager's attitudes toward PWDs might cause them to make unfair assumptions about a disabled worker's skills, productivity, or safety. Institutional barriers might be embedded in hiring procedures that require applicant testing or skills demonstration that are not necessary to do the work or fully accessible to PWDs, creating unfair hiring conditions. PWDs may also suffer from self-imposed barriers of self-doubt that may prevent them from pursuing employment they are qualified to perform due to anxiety, guilt, or fears of self-disclosure of disability (Prockow & Rocco, 2016).

Organizational post-entry barriers

Post-entry barriers (treatment bias) occur once a PWD is employed, and they encounter obstacles related to equitable pay, benefits, access to learning and development, career advancement, and attitudes of supervisors and other colleagues. Although legislation exists to protect PWDs, improvements in the mindsets and practices of employers toward this population have been modest (Houtenville & Kalargyrou, 2015). Fabian and Morris (2021) observed that barriers are even more pronounced for people with emotional and mental disabilities and also chronic diseases such as AIDS. Further, employers exhibit a disconnect between their favorable attitudes toward recruiting, hiring, and advancing PWDs and their worries about legal issues, safety, effects on co-workers, and insurance costs (Burke et al., 2013). Appropriate job accommodations require disclosure and, once disclosed, may be denied, making it difficult or impossible for a PWD to complete their work. Further, inadequate or nonexistent accommodation hurts PWDs' ability to achieve job retention and career advancement (Prockow & Rocco, 2016). The US Department of Labor (n.d.a) has several recommendations to make organizations more accessible and equitable for PWDs, such as policy recommendations, employee resource groups, training, and mentoring.

Career development and advancement

Although CD activities may be less accessible to PWDs, Prockow and Rocco (2016) surmised that they could mitigate the barriers disabled workers face by making workplaces more socially inclusive and providing more effective training to help PWDs advance in their work and careers. Creating cultures where PWDs feel they belong and are valued helps them build networks and social support that are important for learning and advancement. Helpful career interventions include career planning, flexible and supportive work environments, and improved training. The US Department of Labor (n.d.b) offered strategies for advancing disability inclusion that promote CD, including creating disability employee resource groups and the Hiring Initiative to Reimagine Equity (HIRE) to help organizations establish policies and practices to improve access to employment and help people attain good jobs and identify and remove barriers in hiring.

Workplace training for diversity inclusiveness and disabled workers

Although most organizations offer ample learning and development opportunities, they tend to be less available for PWDs. Diversity inclusiveness training can make organizations more accepting of PWDs while reducing stereotyping and prejudice and changing mindsets about disability, as well as helping managers build capacity for supporting PWDs (Prockow & Rocco, 2016). An organization's commitment to being disability-inclusive is also needed and should be reflected in the organization's values and actions.

Workplace training for PWDs can help promote needed learning and development to help them attain and maintain employment, reinforce a sense of self-efficacy, and connect them with other workers to build a more robust network and sense of belonging. Organizations can also provide needed accommodations to promote learning by providing alternative materials and formats and accurately aligning training with work responsibilities (Prockow & Rocco, 2016).

Harassment discrimination and allegations of discharge-related discrimination

PWDs experience disadvantages such as pay gaps, mistreatment, discrimination, bullying, and sexual harassment but are also unreasonably discharged at a higher rate than other workers, often due to their disability (Prockow & Rocco, 2016). Although it is illegal to dismiss workers based on disability, EEOC lawsuits alleging disability spiked 77% in 2023 as compared to 2022, with hearing impairments being the most common issue, with a trend of more cases for failure to accommodate mental impairments such as autism, depression, anxiety, or post-traumatic stress disorder (O'Malley, 2023).

CHAPTER SUMMARY

Chapter 7 explored work and career challenges connected to people's positionality and intersectionality, specifically gender; age; race and ethnicity; social class and poverty; LGBTQA+ people; and disability. Although the chapter examined specific challenges of each population, it is crucial to recognize that people's work and career experiences are intersectional, meaning they bring gender, race, socioeconomic status, and other identities to their lives and work. The challenges described for each population may also afflict other groups. As Maya Angelou's words at the beginning of the chapter urged, "We all have it, or none of us has it"; it is everyone's job to value and work for equity and justice in the workplace and society.

8. Considering work and career challenges, and making interventions

📖 BOX 8.1 CHAPTER OVERVIEW AND LEARNING OBJECTIVES

Actress Cicely Tyson (2022) said,

> To soar toward what's possible, you must leave behind what's comfortable. (p. 358)

Tyson was an American actress who devoted her career to portraying strong Black women. Chapter 8 focuses on career challenges and interventions to navigate or overcome them. Learning to address a challenge means stepping out of one's comfort zone.

Chapter 8 identifies appropriate interventions for facilitating adult career development (CD) at the individual, team, leadership, organization, and community levels. Adult CD is not solely the individual's responsibility, yet there is individual accountability in the process. Work and CD will only be just and equitable when there is also accountability on group and systems levels for creating the infrastructure and support for adults to experience career learning and development across the lifespan.

As a result of reading this chapter and completing the exercises, you, the reader, should be able to:
1. Classify work and career changes and relate them to your own experience.
2. Define traditional and critical career interventions.
3. Contrast critical career interventions with traditional ones.
4. Learn critical career interventions.

Rethinking Adult Career Development foregrounds issues of social justice and equity. Career development (CD) challenges are not just individual, nor should individuals be expected to navigate them solely. As Chapter 7 illustrated, work and CD are contested; not all people have full access and privilege when choosing and pursuing a career. Despite this disconcerting reality, organizations and society have an ethical responsibility to uphold people's right to equitable, decent work. McWhirter and McWha-Hermann (2021) defined social justice in the context of CD as a process that "addresses inequities and inequalities in peoples' work and life experiences, analyzes injustice within and across multiple ecological levels, and asserts a preferential option for securing basic, non-renounceable human rights over the interests of market, profit, and the maintenance of privilege" (p. 2). Individuals, leaders, organizations, and communities can take action to make work and CD more just by intervening in ways that help people choose and pursue a sustainable work life that has significance for individuals and society as a whole. This chapter begins by classifying career challenges adults face, regardless of their positionality and identity, although those variables will exacerbate some of these challenges. The second part of the chapter focuses on work and career interventions designed to disrupt the status quo and work towards more equity.

CLASSIFYING WORK AND CAREER CHALLENGES

Most career explorers, sustainers, and changers desire to do work that is satisfying, interesting, and valued by others in a context of support and collegiality. Even when people derive satisfaction from their work, they still encounter challenges. Hopson and Adams (1977) characterized career transitions into two categories of voluntary and involuntary. Voluntary career challenges are changes and problems entered willingly, such as planned resignation, job change, retraining, relocation, and other career shifts that can be anticipated and managed. Conversely, involuntary career challenges are changes and problems that are unanticipated and often unwelcome to the career explorer, sustainer, or changer, such as job loss, job change, demotion, need for retraining, relocation, and other career shifts. Table 8.1 summarizes some challenges people face in work and career according to organization and individual levels. Leaders and supervisors also profoundly impact a person's work life, and they are addressed under the organization in this section.

Table 8.1   Career challenges at organization and individual levels

Organization	Individual
• Culture and climate	• Cultural
• Consciousness	• Engagement
• Diversity, equity, and inclusion	• Discrimination
• Genderwashing	• Harassment
• Toxic organization environment	• Support
• Access	• Identity and self-assurance
• Awareness	• Efficacy
• Hiring procedures	• Confidence
• Stereotypes and bias	• Burnout
• Treatment	• Learning and development
• Policies and procedures	• Life circumstances
• Stereotypes and bias	• Career threats
• Support	• Inequity
• Recognition and rewards	• Pet-to-threat
• Leadership and supervision	• Dissatisfaction
	• Career shocks
• Learning and development	• Stress
• Support	• Career plateau
• Employee development	• Job loss
• Recognition and rewards	

Organization-Level Career Challenges

Organizational health is the degree to which an organization promotes economic, environmental, and human sustainability and is an important determinant of career satisfaction for most people. Toxic, stressful, unhealthy environments are taxing and lower workers' willingness to remain in an organization. Pfeffer (2018) explained, "You don't have to work in a coal mine, on an oil rig, in a chemical plant, or in construction to face a passively toxic, health destroying workplace" (p. 1). He emphasized that stress at work has been accepted as an inevitability and continues to worsen for most jobs. Pfeffer (2018) defined human sustainability as "creating workplaces where people can thrive and experience physical and mental health, where they can work for years without facing burnout or illness from management practices in the workplace" (p. 3). Through extensive research, Pfeffer projected that the US workplace is responsible for 120,000 excess deaths per year, making work the fifth leading cause of death and accounting for about US$180 billion in annual health care expenditures. Through his research, Pfeffer (2018) ranked workplace exposures that drive mortality from the most dangerous: unemployment, no insurance, shift work, long hours and job insecurity, work-family conflict, minimal job control, low social support, unfairness, and high job demands. Career challenges created at the organizational level are related to culture and climate, access to jobs, treatment of people, and the quality of leadership and supervision. Beyond the organization level, community and global events can also create career challenges such as economic shifts, environmental crises, a global pandemic, and other dynamics.

Culture and climate
Organization leaders are responsible for developing a culture or a set of values, artifacts, and behaviors expressed in observable actions, artifacts, and the ways an organization functions internally and externally. Chapter 5 discussed the Patagonia company as a culture that values play, the outdoors, and conservation. The company actively seeks people who are the best at their work, use Patagonia products, and love nature (Chouinard, 2016). Climate is a more fluid concept than culture as it is the way work is accomplished and how people feel about the organization at a given point in time. The abrupt firing of OpenAI's CEO Sam Altman in 2023 is an example of how the Board of Directors' seemingly arbitrary action created chaos in the organization as workers threatened to quit unless the board reinstated their CEO. OpenAI values developing AI and serving humanity. Yang (2023) described the culture as characterized by humility, where nearly everyone has the same title of "member of the technical staff." Small integrated teams work with researchers to develop products. Peralta (2023) wrote that the board violated OpenAI's cultural values of openness and collaboration. Due to employee threats to leave and offers from other high-tech firms to hire the entire workforce, the board was forced to reinstate the CEO. The climate shifted overnight from collaboration to quitting in solidarity if the CEO's firing was upheld. The CEO was reinstated, and the climate returned to the openness and collaboration the company was founded to uphold. Culture and climate do not always affect organizations so dramatically, but they constantly impact how workers experience their careers.

Diversity, equity, and inclusion (DEI) were defined in Chapter 2, incorporating efforts organizations use to appreciate workers' intersecting social identities, promote fairness and justice, and ensure people feel a sense of belonging. Alarmingly, DEI efforts are being eroded in the current political environment where organizations are disbanding DEI offices, DEI professionals are quitting twice as fast as those in non-DEI positions, and hiring of diverse workers has declined in companies devaluing DEI (Ayas et al., 2023). Yet, companies with robust DEI infrastructure have better representations of Asian, Black, and Hispanic employees than those without (Ayas et al., 2023).

An alarming consequence of organizations devaluing DEI is genderwashing, "the process whereby organizational rhetoric differs from the affective, embodied experiences of those who work or study in organizations ... [that creates] the myth of gender equity in the workplace" (Gardiner et al., 2024, p. x). Essentially, the leadership's professed value of DEI is contradicted by the organization's actions that discriminate. "Genderwashing is not just the disingenuous advocacy of gender equity, but also denials that equity is necessary, or overt arguments that equity seeking is destructive" (Bierema, 2024, p. 19).

A toxic organization is a work environment that feels unsafe due to behaviors that are injurious, hostile, or harassing that perpetuate an unhealthy atmosphere dominated by conflict and distrust. Toxic environments damage people's health and well-being due to stress, demotivation, dissatisfaction, and attrition. Toxic workplaces are recognizable when there is gossip, cut-throat competition, lack of DEI policy or commitment, bullying, and harassment. Sull et al. (2022) analyzed Glassdoor reviews criticizing company culture. They identified five attributes of toxic culture as (a) Disrespectful—a lack of respect, which was the strongest predictor of employees' overall assessment of the organization culture; (b) Noninclusive—people do not feel they are treated fairly or do not have a sense of belongingness across intersectional variables including gender, race, sexual and gender identity, disability, age, and others; (c) Unethical—a lack of integrity and rampant dishonesty where people lie, deceive, and make false promises; (d) Cut-throat—uncooperative colleagues with a lack of collaboration and a backstabbing culture; and (e) Abusive— sustained hostile behavior of management toward the workforce such as bullying, belittling, shouting, and talking down to people. Toxic cultures are costly, with one estimate of an incremental US$16 billion in US health care costs in 2008 (Goh et al., 2016). Toxicity exposes organizations to lawsuits, high degrees of attrition, higher health care costs, absenteeism, incivility, and injustice.

Access

Access is how workers enter a particular organization and involves recruitment, selection, evaluation, and promotion practices. Access bias refers to the stereotyping and structural inequities embedded in recruitment, selection, evaluation, and promotion practices and policies that exclude women and other historically excluded and marginalized groups (Bertrand & Mullainathan, 2024). If access is not equitable, it will be difficult for some workers to realize employment in the organization or on career paths they seek. The burden is on organizations to ensure their policies and practices relating to access are equitable, which usually requires clear policy language and training of search committees and hiring authorities on how to conduct a fair search. This means that measures need to be taken to reduce the incidence of bias in the selection process. Box 8.2 profiles ways to reduce hiring bias.

BOX 8.2 TIPS AND TOOLS FOR CAREER DEVELOPMENT

Reduce Bias in Hiring

Knight (2017) offered practical steps to reduce unconscious bias in the hiring process. Unconscious bias is sexism, racism, ageism, and other isms that influence hiring decisions and ultimately have a significant impact on organizational culture. These are practices to watch for as a career explorer, sustainer, or changer, or implement if you are an organization leader.

1. Seek to understand: Learn to recognize how bias is created in the hiring process. This might involve awareness training and dialogue about how biases infiltrate the hiring process. This foundation will allow for simplifying and standardizing hiring processes to avoid bias.
2. Rework job descriptions: Remove gendered language such as masculine words like "competitive" or "determined" from job descriptions that might discourage people from applying.
3. Implement anonymous recruiting: Remove names and other demographic information from resumes before review by the search committee. This allows the search committee to focus on the candidate's talents and qualifications, not identities.
4. Give candidates a simple work sample test: This allows candidates to solve work-related problems that provide insights into who is best qualified for the role.
5. Standardize interviews: Create a standard interview process that asks each candidate the same questions, gives them the same amount of interview time, and provides the same access to people in the organization for the interview. Create a scoring rubric that rates how well the candidate fits the position requirements.
6. Rethink "likability": People rank candidates they like higher than others. This practice creates a danger of bias. It is important to consider whether likability matters for the job at hand. In environments where likability matters, it is suggested to rank the characteristic on the same rubric as the other position requirements.
7. Set DEI goals: Organizations should track how well they have achieved diversity goals in hiring. It is also important to have diverse finalist pools. According to Moody (2013, 2015), pools with only one diverse candidate all but guarantee they will not be hired. Thus, ensuring finalist pools are diverse increases the odds of making a hire aligned with DEI goals.

Treatment

Treatment is how an organization regards and respects workers once they are hired. Treatment bias reflects the culture and climate created by access bias (Kanter, 1977; Turco, 2010) as well as implicit stereotypes that impede women and other historically excluded and marginalized groups from establishing career-enhancing developmental relationships and networks necessary for advancement (Castilla, 2008). Similarly to access and access bias, the burden is on organizations to ensure they are creating cultures where workers want to remain. This means developing and cultivating a culture and climate of inclusion and development of people to their highest potential, with no tolerance for behaviors contributing to toxicity. Equity in learning and development, opportunities, and promotions must also be assessed for bias. Providing a culture of support is one of the ten issues that the lack thereof hurts workers. Ensuring that the work culture supports workers, provides flexibility, connects people with mentors and sponsors, and offers equitable pay and recognition is also imperative.

Leadership and supervision

The people who lead the organization and supervise workers also profoundly impact a person's work career experiences. Providing management, supervisory, and leadership development to people in these roles is crucial, as is holding them accountable for upholding levels of fairness and integrity that contribute to a healthy organization. This training is not only on job-related content but also on how to create organizations that value DEI and provide high levels of support to the workforce. Helping leaders learn how to create supportive environments, become allies, and build trusting relationships is crucial to keeping good workers in the organization because it is a good place to work.

Individual-Level Career Challenges

Individual career challenges create both identity capital and cost. Box 8.3 presents Schlossberg's (1984, 2011) characterization of transition in adulthood and also profiles Heppner's (1998) career transitions. Individual career challenges occur due to culture, individual identity and self-assurance, learning and development, life circumstances, and career threats.

☾ BOX 8.3 REFLECTIVE PRACTICE

Making Transitions

Schlossberg's (1984, 2011) transition theory applies to how events of life and work create transitions for adults. Consider whether you have experienced one of the transitions described in Table 8.2 as a career explorer, sustainer, or changer, or have helped someone through these phases as a career coach or counselor.

Table 8.2   Transition theory

Transition	Definition and example
Anticipated:	Changes occurring predictably in the lifespan of most people, such as graduation from college.
Unanticipated:	An unpredictable, unexpected, or unscheduled change or event such as divorce, the sudden death of a loved one, being fired, or being promoted.
Chronic hassles:	Continual life events that cause stress, such as long commutes to work, workplace bullying, conflict within a workgroup, or a difficult boss.
Non-events:	Transitions that are expected but do not occur, such as failure to be admitted to graduate school, a promotion that does not materialize, or a boss that remains in their position long term.

Heppner's (1998) Career Transitions Inventory suggested that the factors in Table 8.3 influence the capacity to make career changes and transitions. How do they align with the transitions you have experienced or observed?

Table 8.3   Career Transitions Inventory

Capacity	Definition and example
Readiness:	Precontemplation, dissatisfaction, or other variables that prompt someone to think about making career changes, such as not enjoying the work, feeling unsupported, or not seeing advancement opportunities.
Confidence:	A sense of self-efficacy toward a career change, or belief you have the knowledge, skills, and ability to do the career well.
Control:	Your ability to influence career outcomes, such as knowing your worth, relationships, or access to other options.
Perceived support:	The degree to which you feel care for and trust toward others who influence your career path.
Decision independence:	The degree to which you can make a career decision versus factoring in other people such as family, friends, and co-workers.

Cultural

Organization culture and climate have a significant impact on a person's work and career experience. Engagement is the degree to which people direct their cognitive, emotional, and behavioral energy toward positive organizational outcomes (Shuck & Rose, 2013). Adults will be more engaged in organizations where they feel a sense of belonging, safety, and support. Shuck and Rose (2013) advocated that organizations should invest in workers' psychological well-being because it creates holistic benefits by contributing to organizational performance and improving the quality of life for workers. They recommended that people should be able to connect meaning and purpose through their work, and making those connections drives engagement, as discussed in Chapter 6.

Workplace culture and engagement are damaged when people are not treated equitably and when the culture is toxic. When certain groups are discriminated against in hiring, promotions, pay, and daily treatment, it takes a toll on both life and work. Sexual, racial, and other identity-based harassment and bullying create toxic, sometimes dangerous working conditions and will be important factors in workers deciding to leave.

Pfeffer (2018) noted the lack of support can lead to negative health consequences and even death for some workers. Yet, support and autonomy (also on Pfeffer's list) are low-cost or free to provide. Rasool et al. (2021) found that employee engagement is negatively affected by toxic work environments but that when workers feel supported, their sense of belongingness is strengthened. Gabriel and Aguinis (2022) reviewed the literature to recommend five strategies for organizations to implement to prevent and combat burnout as: "(1) provide stress management interventions, (2) allow employees to be active crafters of their work, (3) cultivate and encourage social support, (4) engage employees in decision-making, and (5) implement high-quality performance management" (p. 183).

Identity and self-assurance

A strong sense of self and purpose is helpful for effectively navigating one's career. Knowing your value as a career explorer, sustainer, or changer can help you make decisions, cope with stress, and balance life more effectively. Believing in yourself helps you learn, grow, try new things, and approach relationships with support and curiosity. It is also being honest about where you need to grow or what scares you. Career mishaps can sometimes shake or erode self-efficacy and self-confidence may be impacted when this happens. Confidence can also be damaged if your high standards make you doubt yourself or tear down the work of others, you are micro-managed, you fear failure, or you have strained relationships with some of your co-workers. If you lack confidence or self-esteem, identify the specific area and work on it for the next month. Ask your boss or trusted colleagues for feedback. Realize you might make mistakes and celebrate your small wins as they occur. Ultimately, seek mentoring or coaching for a longer-term approach to problem-solving and career advancement.

Learning and development

Learning is lifelong; adults spend time learning and training, and sometimes relearning and retraining for careers. This schooling begins in childhood. Some workers will not seek further education beyond high school. Others will achieve technical and higher education certifications and degrees to prepare for the workforce. Many adults continue learning as they progress in their work through self-direction, organization-sponsored, or formal learning programs. Chapter 5 detailed the theoretical and practical components of lifelong learning. Career explorers, sustainers, and changers seeking a new career or advancement in a current career path will want to continue their learning.

Life circumstances

Gedro (2017) emphasized how life events such as "marriage, divorce, coming out as an LGBT person, financial issues, and recovering from addiction or alcoholism" (p. 89) manifest and impact adults' CD. She explained that these "undiscussables" must be examined to understand how they affect people's work lives. "The ability to empathize with the human condition and the ways that life and circumstances can facilitate a person's success (broadly defined) or lack thereof, is one way that human resource professionals can become both more skilled and more compassionate" (p. 95).

Balancing life is challenging for working adults juggling a job, family, and community activities. Family and work intertwine in complex ways that can have positive or negative influences when work interferes with one's family or vice versa. This is increasingly problematic as the lines between life and work have become blurred (Kinnunen et al., 2014) and the COVID-19 pandemic exacerbated this blurring. Gragnano et al. (2020) found that workers consider health as important as the family in their survey of 318 workers, and a sense of balance also affected job satisfaction. Wood et al. (2020) examined the relationship between work engagement and life-work balance in organizations. They concluded that the direction of causality between work engagement and balance is inconclusive, and more research is needed. From a practical standpoint, the authors recommended considering balance and engagement holistically, sustaining life balance through supportive culture, stress reduction, and efforts to acknowledge that workers have families.

Career threats

Social dynamics pose career threats to individuals. These include inequity, pet-to-threat, dissatisfaction, career shock, career plateauing, and job loss.

Often career threats overlap, making them complex dynamics affecting CD. Although these threats affect individuals, they are usually created by social systems or organizational actions.

According to Tulshyan (2022), equity is the act of "identifying and dismantling systemic barriers to the representation and inclusion of women, people of color, and people from other historically marginalized communities" (p. 6). Inequity is the absence of fairness or justice created by social forces, including poverty, racism, sexism, bias, discrimination, and other dynamics reinforcing prevailing power relations. When people experience inequity, it might be through slights or discrimination in daily work interactions. Pay inequity is a common problem for people other than heterosexual White men. There is also evidence that there is gender variation in experiences that lead to career advancement, including challenging assignments, developmental relationships, coursework or training, hardships, and personal life experiences (Clerkin et al., 2024). Clerkin et al. concluded that women miss out on critical job experiences that prepare them for advancement. Tulshyan (2022) urged that "Inclusion on purpose requires every single one of us" (p. 252), or the imperative that equity is everyone's responsibility.

Thomas et al. (2013) illustrated how women of color go from "Pet-to-threat" as they gain organizational power. This phenomenon is a form of genderwashing that affects women of color in particular when, early in their careers, "pets" are regarded less as professionals and treated more like favored children who are mentored on how to behave in and assimilate into the dominant culture. As women resist their pet status and gain power, colleagues question their capability, commit microaggressions, and sometimes recast them as "threats." This phenomenon was at play with the resignation of Harvard President Claudine Gay.

Another individual challenge is when something positive or negative happens that impacts a person's work life, which is known as career shock.

> A career shock is a disruptive and extraordinary event that is, at least to some degree, caused by factors outside the focal individual's control and that triggers a deliberate thought process about one's career. Examples of career shocks include layoffs, promotions, environmental disaster, accidents, or injustice. The incidence of career shocks can differ in terms of inevitability and can be both negative and positive valenced. (Akkermans et al., 2018, p. 4)

Career shocks can be positive or negative. The COVID-19 pandemic might have been both (Akkermans et al., 2020). The pandemic forced people into remote work overnight, which was shocking. Some workers found it difficult, or if they were essential workers had to face uncertainty and chaos daily at work. Other workers rediscovered balance, reconnected with their families, and re-evaluated their values and goals. Akkermans et al. (2020) summarized the lessons the pandemic career shocks taught: (a) Career shock is impacted by the interplay of contextual and individual factors—how an individual can function within a particular social setting; (b) Career shock can have different impacts over the short versus long term and depend on career stage—often a career shock is negative in the short term (a crisis, or disaster) but over the longer term opens new possibilities that are positive (new career paths, wisdom, advancement opportunities); and (c) Negative career shocks can incur positive outcomes—a job loss becomes an opportunity to return to school or leave a toxic environment.

Work or career satisfaction is how people feel about their jobs; job satisfactoriness is how well a person does their job (Lent & Brown, 2021). Locke (1976) defined job satisfaction as "a pleasurable or positive emotional state resulting from the appraisal of one's job or job experiences" (p. 1300).

> These language conventions in the vocational literature imply that, as in any contract, it is important for both parties to be satisfied—in this case, the worker with the job (and what it offers), and the employer with the worker (and what they contribute to the work organization). (Lent & Brown, 2021, p. 733)

Satisfaction and satisfactoriness are assumed to lead to longevity in one's job. The opposite is also true. If a person is dissatisfied with their job and the organization is dissatisfied with their performance, turnover is to be expected. Brown and Lent (2021) explained that job dissatisfaction is often driven by the absence of desired job attributes such as interesting work, better pay, or friendly colleagues or the presence of something unpleasant such as stress, role conflict, or harassment. Sources of dissatisfaction can come from the work environment itself (e.g., discrimination, incivility, level of support, meaningfulness of work), the person (e.g., affective and personality dispositions, self-efficacy, and goals), and how well the person and environment fit (e.g., are interests, values, and abilities a good match between the person and the environment?).

Work dissatisfaction can be a source of stress for many workers. Stress, according to the World Health Organization (2023a), is:

> A state of worry or mental tension caused by a difficult situation. Stress is a natural human response that prompts us to address challenges and threats in our lives. Everyone experiences stress to some degree. The way we respond to stress, however, makes a big difference to our overall well-being. (para. 1)

Work is a regular source of stress for most people who face deadlines, learn new concepts or skills, navigate relationships, resolve conflict, and adjust to change. McDonald and Hite (2020) suggested that the conservation of resources theory (Hobfoll, 1989) helped explain how people cope with career challenges, shocks, and stressors by building and preserving resources that help them protect their confidence, energy, or working conditions when stress occurs. Of course, resource capacity is not equal across all workers and depends on having resources to draw on to enhance one's resilience to stress.

Another challenge is when someone hits a career plateau or their upward career progression stalls (Ference et al., 1977). Lin and Chen (2021) described a career plateau as an undesirable state when the likelihood of career advancement or promotion is low. There are two types of career plateaus (Bardwick, 1986a, 1986b), known as a hierarchical career plateau, when a person's vertical advancement prospects are limited, and job content plateau, when people no longer feel challenged by their work and correspondingly do not feel valued by their organization. Although career plateaus are predictable by the length of job tenure, it is a more subjective assessment, not necessarily related to age. Hitting a plateau is often a career crisis where a person will question their self-efficacy, life purpose, and whether to remain in their current role.

Job loss occurs when someone resigns, is fired, or is laid off. Although there are several causes of job loss, it usually leaves a person with a sense of loss and perhaps trauma (Falcon & Wiens, 2022). Whatever the cause, Falcon and Weins (2022) urged practicing self-compassion and recognizing it is a difficult time. It is a good time to reconnect with people outside of work who are important. It is also important to attend to unmet needs and focus on what can be controlled. Accepting the loss is important as it helps prepare to move on to new opportunities.

TRADITIONAL WORK AND CAREER INTERVENTIONS

Traditional career interventions are those that are commonly prescribed by career counselors or human resource developers and should be familiar to you as a career explorer, sustainer, or changer. This section focuses on various interventions appropriate for addressing CD challenges at multiple levels, including the individual, group or team, organization, and community or system levels.

Defining and Making Traditional Career Interventions

A work or career intervention is a planned action to address a challenge or goal. Sometimes interventions are facilitated by a career coach or counselor who helps career explorers, sustainers, or changers establish goals and determine structured activities to address the career challenge. Argyris (1970, 2000) advocated three primary intervention tasks that needed to be completed to effectively address problems, amended for career focus: (a) Interventions must be evidence-based; (b) The career explorer, sustainer, or changer maintains discretion and autonomy; and (c) The career explorer, sustainer, or changer commits to learning and change.

The typical assumption is a CD intervention would be aimed at the individual, although that is a narrow view. Table 8.4 outlines types of career interventions according to the multiple levels of organizations and society, and Table 8.5 offers a brief typology of traditional CD interventions.

Table 8.4   Traditional career development interventions by level

Individual	Group-Team	Organization	Community
• Learning & development • Leadership & management development • Performance management • 360-degree feedback • Developmental relationships • Coaching • Career and life planning • Self-awareness and assessment tools • Reflective practice • Action learning	• Action learning • Team learning • DEI interventions • Education & training • Leadership & management development • Coaching & counseling	• Leadership & management development • Survey feedback • Strategic career management & talent development	• Job training programs • Community mentoring • Virtual mentoring

Table 8.5   *Career development intervention descriptions*

Career intervention	Level(s)	Description	Resources
Learning and development (L&D)	Individual Group Organization Community	L&D interventions ensure organization members have the knowledge, skills, and abilities needed to do their jobs effectively and help the organization perform optimally in their current or future positions.	Daffron & Caffarella (2021) Merriam & Bierema (2013)
Reflective practice	Individual Group	Thinking critically about experiences and actions relating to past, current, and future careers.	Schön (1983, 1987)
Action learning	Individual Group	A continuous cycle of learning by doing, followed by reflecting on the doing. For example, exploring or trying a particular career and making meaning about the experience.	Lawrence (1991) Revans (2017)
Leadership development	Individual Group Organization Community	Involves developing people to guide the organization, create a long-term vision, develop strategy, strengthen DEI, staff the organization, communicate, and motivate people toward the vision.	McLean (2005)
Values clarification	Individual Group Organization Community	Exercises that help individuals articulate their key values and incorporate them into their thoughts and actions about career decisions.	Brown (n.d.)
Coaching	Individual Group Organization	"A personal and frequent one-on-one meeting designed to produce specific, positive changes in business behavior within a fixed time frame" (Corbett & Colemon, 2006, p. 1).	Corbett & Colemon (2006)
Assessments	Individual Group	Instruments that measure myriad aspects of individual attributes related to career decisions.	Brown & Lent (2021)
Developmental relationships	Individual	A relationship that helps advance someone's career, such as mentoring, sponsorship, networks, coaching, peer support, and other helping relationships.	Rock & Garavan (2006) Ghosh & Hutchins (2022)

Career intervention	Level(s)	Description	Resources
Dialogue	Group	Invigorating, exciting conversations that privilege inquiry where each participant builds on the points being made, and people are open to questioning their viewpoints, learning from each other, and changing their minds.	Isaacs (2001)
Diversity, equity, and inclusion (DEI)	Individual Group Organization Community	Diversity refers to a heterogeneous group in which members differ in gender, race, age, religion, sexuality, and other attributes. Equity is fairness and justice, for example, in access to CD opportunities. Inclusion is embracing all people and making them feel a sense of belongingness.	Byrd & Scott (2018)
Appreciative inquiry (AI)		AI focuses only on the positive aspects of an issue or culture. It frames questions and future visioning positively, seeking to identify the basic goodness in a person, a situation, or an organization to enhance the organization's capacity for collaboration and change.	Cooperrider et al. (1995)
Career planning	Individual	Completing a written plan for an immediate, midterm, and long-term career, including developmental needs.	Lea & Leibowitz (1992)
SMART goals	Individual Group Organization Community	Goals that are: Specific, Measurable, Attainable, Realistic or Relevant, and Time-bound	Haughey (2014)
Talent management	Individual Group Organization Community	Interventions aimed at developing and optimizing the organization's workforce productivity, especially concerned with recruiting, onboarding, retaining, managing, and developing a high-performing workforce.	Kim & McLean (2012)
Performance management	Individual Organization	The process of aligning organization resources, systems, and people with business goals and strategy. In careers, it would be important to align individual career progress with organizational goals.	Pulakos (2004)

Career intervention	Level(s)	Description	Resources
Succession planning	Organization Community	The process of identifying employees with high potential to assume leadership roles in the organization. Targeted positions typically include top executives and the management levels immediately below that level that will eventually feed the executive pipeline.	Miles (2009)
Environmental scanning	Organization Community	When external and internal factors are scrutinized (e.g., economic, competitive, social, political, and so forth) to yield critical information about the future.	Auster & Choo (1994)

CRITICAL WORK AND CAREER INTERVENTIONS

Bierema's (2010) *Implementing a Critical Approach to Organization Development* offered a critical perspective of OD and created a roadmap for those interested in facilitating organization change that results in structural changes (e.g., addressing sexism or racism in ways that change the culture and create lasting equity and inclusion) and ensuring the organization is healthy and a good citizen. Her definition of a critical intervention has been tweaked to make it appropriate for work and CD:

1. The work or career intervention is practiced with critical consciousness.
2. The intervention is concerned with enhancing well-being (this includes individual, group, organization, social, and system well-being).
3. Interventions are intended to disrupt the status quo and prevailing assumptions.
4. The intervention will create more democratic and equitable work and career outcomes.

Each of these aspects of critical work and career intervention will be described.

Practicing with Critical Consciousness

Chapter 4 described critical consciousness (CC) as acknowledging how structural oppression based on intersecting identities (e.g., race and poverty) affects people's access to sustainable and satisfying work and careers and their capacity to overcome the barriers created by inequitable access to resources and social injustice. A CC is developed through learning and a curiosity for understanding social inequities through what Merriam and Bierema (2013) described as having a critical perspective, engaging in critical thinking and reflection, and taking mindful, critical action. Diemer and Blustein (2006) found a statistically significant relationship from a sample of 220 urban adolescents showing that people with higher levels of CC had increased clarity about their vocational identity and were more committed to future careers and the role work would play in their lives. They recommended helping people maintain their awareness of inequity and situate individual agency within one's assessment of the social context. For example, a Black man grew up in a family that talked about historical social inequity and how it influenced their lives individually and also contributed to sustaining racist educational, economic, and political structures. He used this knowledge to motivate him toward his career goal of becoming a lawyer who would fight for social justice. Not only is it important for individuals to develop CC about their work and careers, but also for people who are helping career explorers, sustainers, and changers make decisions about their work lives. Leaders are also responsible for understanding the dynamics of social inequity and considering them as they make decisions that affect their workforce.

Enhancing Well-being

The concepts of organizational health and human sustainability were discussed in the previous section. Critical interventions privilege these states of being from the individual to community levels. It is a holistic approach to health and wellness. Box 8.4 overviews key aspects of well-being.

BOX 8.4 TIPS AND TOOLS FOR CAREER DEVELOPMENT

Well-being and Career Development

There is no consensus around a single definition of well-being. In general, however, well-being is defined as being comfortable, healthy, or happy. Five elements of well-being interact with each other (Jones & Jones, 2016). Consider these questions as a career explorer, sustainer, or changer:
1. Career well-being: How much do I enjoy what I do each day?
2. Social well-being: How strong are relationships and love in my life?
3. Financial well-being: How effective am I in managing my economic life?

4. Physical well-being: How much health and energy do I have to do what
    I want each day?
5. Community well-being: How engaged am I with my community?

Questions for reflection:

*   How do these aspects of well-being affect each other?
*   What area(s) of well-being needs attention?

Disrupting the Status Quo and Prevailing Assumptions

Although critical interventions might not be the first thought when considering work and CD, it is the ideal space to help all levels of the organization consider equity and inclusion. Making critical interventions might seem a lofty or even risky goal. Yet, many practitioners desire to engage in mindful practice and need a strategy that is grounded in evidence. These interventions do not follow the traditional levels of analysis (individual, group, organization) typical for classifying traditional interventions. Instead, I looked at the strategic intent of the interventions to develop the categories. They are listed in Table 8.6 and defined in Table 8.7.

Table 8.6   Critical interventions

Conversational	Opportunistic	Learning

• Dialogue
• Fierce conversations
• Verbal jujitsu
	• Small wins
	• Variable-term
	  opportunism
		• Reflective practice
		• Critical action
		  technologies

• Coalition building	• Activism	
• Networks • Strategic alliance building	• Tempered radicalism • Disruptive self-expression	

Source: Bierema (2010).

Table 8.7   *Defining critical interventions*

Critical intervention	Definition
Dialogue	Invigorating, exciting conversations that privilege inquiry over discussion where each participant builds on the points being made and people are open to questioning their viewpoints, learning from each other, and changing their minds.
Fierce conversations	Taking chances in conversations that help individuals or groups take large strides toward working on what really matters. Goals of fierce conversations include: interrogating reality, provoking learning, tackling tough challenges, and enriching relationships (Scott, 2004). Although intended to be respectful, fierce conversations do not necessarily use dialogue as a structuring principle.
Verbal jujitsu	Uses the martial arts principle of channeling a force coming toward you and redirecting it to change the situation. In an organization setting, this involves reacting to objectionable, demeaning statements or actions by turning them into change and calling them out, such as when a woman's idea is ignored until suggested by a man and another person points out the discrepancy.
Small wins	Taking advantage of opportunities to make change when they arise (Weick, 1984).
Variable term optimism	Making opportunistic interventions requires spontaneity and keen attention to dynamics in the context so you can jump on serendipitous circumstances and discover "low-hanging fruit."
Reflective practice	Process of thinking critically while engaged in practice and on actions taken during practice.
Critical action technologies	A host of collaborative learning tools, including the best-known action research, action learning, and action science.
Networks	The process of contacting and being contacted by like-minded people in your social network and maintaining these linkages and relationships. A set of relations, linkages, or ties among people for contact, friendship, and support.
Strategic alliance building	A public and collaborative strategy involving banding with other like-minded individuals that offers a sense of legitimacy, access to resources and contacts, technical and task assistance, emotional support, and advice.

Critical intervention	Definition
Tempered radicalism	Tempered radicals, or those Meyerson (2004) refers to as "not quite a full-fledged radical" (p. 14) or "under the radar rebels" (p. 16), act for social change within their organizations. Meyerson explains that tempered radicals: "Engage in small battles, at times operating so quietly that they may not surface on the cultural radar as 'rebels.' By pushing back on conventions, they create opportunities for change within their organizations. They are not heroic leaders of revolutionary action; rather, they are cautious and committed catalysts who slowly make a difference" (p. 16).
Disruptive self-expression	Disruptive self-expression (Meyerson, 2001) includes subtle acts of private, individual acts that defy the expectations of others. Examples include a personal demonstration of values, language, dress, office décor, or behavior that begins to change the work atmosphere. Others notice these disruptions and begin to talk about them. Such disruptions may cause others to incorporate their own into their repertoire.

Critical career interventions disrupt career injustice. For example, Cadenas et al. (2023) found that immigrants benefit from developing a CC about potential work and career barriers. Engaging the support of their family, technology, and community also helps immigrants navigate career choices and experiences. They urged people working in career support to help them build CC through culturally responsive programming.

Tempered radicalism, one of the critical strategies recommended by Bierema (2010) is carried out by tempered radicals, or those Meyerson (2004) referred to as "not quite a full-fledged radical" (p. 14) or "under the radar rebels" (p. 16) who act for social change. Meyerson explained that tempered radicals:

> Engage in small battles, at times operating so quietly that they may not surface on the cultural radar as "rebels." By pushing back on conventions, they create opportunities for change within their organizations. They are not heroic leaders of revolutionary action; rather, they are cautious and committed catalysts who slowly make a difference. (p. 16)

Tempered radicalism is one way people can work for change in work and careers from individual to system levels. Box 8.5 offers some strategies for this approach.

BOX 8.5 TIPS AND TOOLS FOR CAREER DEVELOPMENT

Tempered Radicalism

Tempered radicalism can be used to help career explorers, sustainer, changers, and their helpers to:
1. Raise awareness about inequities and social justice issues.
2. Make inquiries by asking questions to bring attention to inequity such as, "Why are the Black women leaving at a higher rate than any other group?"
3. Engage in outright activism for change.
4. Work on a "fault line" of mitigating their desire to advance their change agenda while simultaneously fitting into the dominant corporate culture (Meyerson & Scully, 1995).
5. Engage in "little acts of self-expression—their dress, language or leadership style" (Meyerson, 2004, p. 17).
6. Find other like-minded individuals.

How can you put tempered radicalism to work for you?

Creating More Democratic, Equitable Work and Career Outcomes

The goal of critical career interventions is to address systems of inequity that prevent equitable access to work and careers. Stable employment should be restored through culturally relevant CD, ongoing and inclusive learning, and development across the career lifespan, helping marginalized individuals critically view their situation and make informed choices about careers as well as resist social forces that are structured to perpetuate inequity (Cinamon et al., 2019). Education of people providing career counseling and coaching is also imperative, particularly given the findings by Vespia et al. (2010), who found a discrepancy between their self-assessed cultural competence and their ability to engage in culturally sensitive practice. Table 8.8 offers additional tools and resources for critical career interventions.

Table 8.8   Tools and resources for critical career interventions

Intervention category	Issue	Intervention	Source(s)
Critical and cross-cultural career assessment	Traditional career assessment is problematic for essentializing gender roles and reproducing the status quo and is not culturally appropriate.	Use assessments that are culturally competent and sensitive to multicultural issues: • Culturally encompassing information gathering • Culturally appropriate: consideration of assessment instruments • Culturally sensitive administration • Culturally appropriate data interpretation	Flores et al. (2003) Osborn (2012)
Cross-cultural career assessment, critical career mentoring, coaching, counseling, and education	Career development theory and practice is based on research with White middle-class men in the Western world.	• Design research using critical consciousness principles • Collaborate with marginalized communities to conduct action research on career consciousness • Engage people in critical consciousness reflection and action across social positions of power and privilege	Cadenas & McWhirter (2022)
Critical consciousness and radical action	A holistic, developmental approach that is centered on the community and aware of context is needed, along with a focus on advocacy and justice-oriented counseling.		Reynolds (2022)
Feminist career mentoring	Women's mentoring programs are often reflective of neoliberal feminism that focuses on "fixing the individual woman" instead of addressing structural patriarchal systems that prevent women's advancement.	• Feminist mentorship focuses on both parties (mentor and mentee) co-mentoring each other in a mutual process of relational mentoring that requires both partners to learn each other's needs and openly address disagreements (Ghosh, 2015) • Feminist mentoring focuses on collective action and organization change to address gender inequality	Harris (2022)

Intervention category	Issue	Intervention	Source(s)
• Femtoring	• Women and men in the military have to follow a masculinity culture to pursue advancement.	eMentoring is helpful for military women due to its boundarylessness, egalitarianism, and trustworthiness, and has the potential to disrupt masculine military culture	Bierema & Yoon (2019)
• Femme-toring	• "Men-toring" can sustain and replicate toxic masculinist norms in academia.	Using frameworks of femme theory and critical femininities using more feminist epistemology and ethics of care unsettles toxic masculinist norms	Hoskin & Whiley (2023)
• Aspects of critical consciousness (CC)	• Applicability of psychology of work theory (PWT) to adults of color	CC buffered the effects of racial marginalization on career adaptability. Recognizing the structural nature of racial inequality may help people self-advocate more effectively. Found support for PWT	Autin et al. (2022)
Multicultural career counseling		Career helpers should follow a metacognitive awareness process: 1. Establish a helping relationship and begin planning for ways to help 2. Identify career issues through assessment, observation, and dialogue 3. Assess the impact of culture on the person's career development 4. Set work and career goals with the client 5. Intervene 6. Make decisions about the efficacy of interventions through evaluation, cultural congruence, and sustainability	Byars-Winston & Fouad (2006)

CHAPTER SUMMARY

Chapter 8 explored a range of approaches and interventions for facilitating adult career development at the individual, team, leadership, organization, and community levels from both traditional and critical perspectives. Although individuals will likely take an interest in and action on their careers, adult career development is not, nor it should be, the sole responsibility of the individual. Educators, leaders, politicians, organizations, and communities must create infrastructure to support people in their work and careers to realize just and equitable career development for all. It may not always be comfortable, but it is just.

9. Introducing a critical, intersectional, feminist model of adult career development theory

⊞ BOX 9.1 CHAPTER OVERVIEW AND LEARNING OBJECTIVES

Gedro (2017) urged that it is imperative to think deeply and compassionately about adults' identities:

> … to see and to consider employees and prospective employees with greater awareness and sensitivity and understanding that humans are complex, and that life can present challenges and opportunities that impact current development. (p. 137)

In her book, Gedro spoke to career explorers, sustainers, changers, and their career counselors, facilitators, and coaches, underscoring how human identity is a source of strength in career development (CD).

Chapter 9 concludes *Rethinking Adult Career Development* by introducing a critical, intersectional, feminist career development model. The chapter begins with a summary of the book's key foci, introduces the model, and discusses implications for CD.

As a result of reading this chapter and completing the exercises, you, the reader, should be able to:
1. Understand how identity cost and capital interact with career headwinds and tailwinds.
2. Connect intersectionality with career experiences.

Rethinking Adult Career Development began with Guillebeau's (2016) quote, "It's better to be at the bottom of the ladder you want to climb than the top of one you don't" (p. 163), underscoring the notion that adults do not want to toil at work that is soul-draining, tedious, and unfulfilling. Yet, finding fulfilling work where there is security and support is difficult for many. People's access to career information, choice, and opportunity is influenced by their intersectional identities that function to marginalize or privilege people depending on race, gender, disability, socioeconomic status, sexual and gender identity, and age.

SUMMARIZING *RETHINKING ADULT CAREER DEVELOPMENT*

Rethinking Adult Career Development views career development (CD) as a contested practice—that is, it is performed in contexts that are often incompatible with individuals' and communities' interests—such as providing stable jobs but polluting the environment, motivating workers while laying people off, or perpetuating inequities by privileging one group and marginalizing others. The book acknowledges the paradoxes of career advancement: when marginalized people advance in their careers, they become part of the same exclusionary system that previously prevented them from progressing. How might career explorers, sustainers, and changers transform rather than replicate exclusionary systems of power that discriminate?

Rethinking Adult Career Development advocates that experiencing a satisfying, affirming career should be the norm and a human right. The book reconsidered adult CD by discussing it as a lifelong learning and development process characterized by the dilemmas and challenges adults face. Adult CD was explored using an intersectional perspective dedicated to creating more equity and justice. The book provided a historical overview and critical terms associated with CD. It investigated the dynamics shaping adults' work and CD atmosphere, including globalization, neoliberalism, technology, the COVID-19 pandemic, and a multigenerational workforce. Although this book was not intended to provide a deep dive into CD theory, it profiled important theories relevant to adult work and CD. A key feature of *Rethinking Adult Career Development* is its focus on ways adults are marginalized and privileged based on intersectionality and its reframing of CD as a lifelong adult learning, development, and change process. The book delved into how adults derive meaning and purpose from their lives and work. It explored intersecting identities to describe people's challenges and privileges with gender, age, race, socioeconomic status, gender identity and sexuality, and disability. The book also examined typical career challenges most people encounter and appropriate interventions that sometimes disrupt the status quo on individual, team, leadership, organization, and community levels. The book ends with a proposal for reframing how work and CD for adults is understood and implemented.

The rethinking begins with a more critical and provocative analysis of adult CD issues and practices. Centering on adult career issues helps build the capacity to (a) Reassess career paths misaligned with values; (b) Cope with job change or loss; (c) Negotiate career exclusion, injustice, and discrimination; and (d) Handle unanticipated career shifts. The book offered strategies for career facilitators, counselors, and coaches to view careers as lifelong learning and development processes, understand how to critically assess CD practices and outcomes, and apply critical alternatives to practice.

INTRODUCING A CRITICAL, INTERSECTIONAL, FEMINIST MODEL OF ADULT CAREER DEVELOPMENT

Chapter 7 introduced the concepts of identity capital, identity cost, and career headwinds and tailwinds. This section expands those concepts as key constructs for a critical, intersectional, feminist model of adult career development.

Identity Capital and Identity Cost

Côté (1996) explained identity capital from a sociological perspective as denoting "what individuals 'invest' in 'who they are'" (p. 425) within the context of social complexity with aspects of identity both socially visible and invisible and serving as "passports" into social and institutional spaces:

> Identity capital represents attributes associated with sets of psychosocial skills, largely cognitive in nature, that appear to be necessary for people to intelligently strategize and make decisions affecting their life courses ... These personal resources involve agentic capacities such as an internal locus of control, self-esteem and a sense of purpose in life, all of which can help people reflect on their life circumstances, and plan courses of action ... Together, these personality strengths enable people to cognitively understand and behaviorally negotiate the various social, occupational and personal obstacles and opportunities that they are likely to encounter throughout an individualized life course. The obstacles can range from outright discrimination through to institutional voids, while the opportunities can range from the emergence of new social norms allowing for diverse lifestyles to new educational prospects among people who previously would not have obtained higher credentials. (Côté, 2005, pp. 225–226)

Côté (2005) also explained that the environment influences identity capital and can "enable people to reflexively *resist and/or act back upon* certain social forces impinging upon them" (p. 226, italics in original), such as discrimination or marginalization.

Gedro (2017) introduced identity capital as a career development construct and defined it as positionalities that confer privilege in a career. Gedro originated the shadow side of identity capital, or identity cost, "the loss, or marginalization that occurs as the result of having a stigmatized identity that is known to or suspected by others. This is an area that warrants further exploration" (p. 132). For example, a young Black lesbian who belongs to a community mentoring program has visible identities of gender and race that can bring her both identity capital and cost, depending on the setting. If her sexuality is closeted but suspected, it can also serve as both identity capital and cost. She has automatic identity capital with other people in the mentoring organization because they are bonded around the cause of mentoring local youth.

Career Headwinds and Tailwinds

The intersection of identity cost or capital with career headwinds or tailwinds creates challenges and opportunities for career explorers, sustainers, and changers. Irving (2016) explained these forces:

> … the manifestation of cradle-to-grave headwinds and tailwinds touch nearly every aspect of Americans' lives creating divergent outcomes that ultimately get misinterpreted as an ability to achieve or lack of an ability in schools, the pattern is referred to as the "achievement gap." The countrywide phenomenon in which Black and Latino students exhibit lower standardized test scores, lower grade point averages, and higher dropout rates than their White and Asian peers is explained by socioeconomic factors, including poor nutrition and limited access to health care, as well as cultural barriers involving language, early exposure to books, and parental involvement. In recognition of this connection between opportunity and achievement, some have begun using the term "opportunity gap" instead of achievement gap. Either way it's a pervasive issue with which American educators are grappling. (pp. 180–181)

Headwinds and tailwinds are metaphors for systemic racism in Irving's (2016) work, and I am using them here to illustrate how systems of oppression and privilege function to hurt or help people based on intersecting identities such as race, age, gender, disability, sexual and gender identity, and other positionalities. Identity cost and capital are individual dynamics of identity within social context, and headwinds and tailwinds are social structures that influence CD.

A Critical, Intersectional, Feminist Model of Adult Career Development

Rethinking Adult Career Development concludes by offering a critical, intersectional, and feminist model of understanding adult career development. The model is critical because it challenges the efficacy of traditional CD theory and practice, as discussed in Chapter 4, to make the career lifespan more equitable, just, and accessible to everyone while also developing more inclusive and fair work environments. It is intersectional in recognizing how people's identities intertwine to create privilege and disadvantage within social contexts. It is feminist due to concern with addressing the injustices created by patriarchy for not only women but also any people who are marginalized and discriminated against in society—headwinds and tailwinds.

This model of adult CD addresses individual factors and systemic structures to understand what occurs when adults face opportunities and challenges in their careers and to develop better responses to help people more effectively diagnose and address the challenge. The model also recognizes individuals interacting with their network or support (career helpers), organizations, and social context. The interactions of these dynamics are illustrated in Figure 9.1 that depicts how identity cost and capital intersect with career headwinds and tailwinds at the individual, support, organization, and social levels. These intersections are summarized in Table 9.1, described in this section, and written to you as a career explorer, sustainer, or changer, or as a helping professional such as a career coach, counselor, or facilitator.

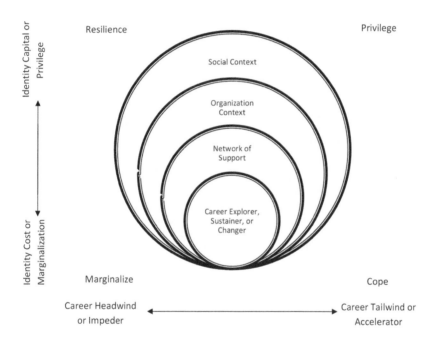

Figure 9.1   Model of critical, intersectional, feminist career development

*Table 9.1   Career identity cost and capital plotted with career
               headwinds and tailwinds*

	Identity Privilege and Career Challenge = Identity Capital + Career Headwinds	Identity and Career Privilege = Identity Capital + Career Tailwinds
Identity Capital	• Draw on resilience and stay positive. • Lean on strong self-efficacy to navigate the career challenge. • Reflect on the challenge from various perspectives. • Remain flexible to options. • Recognize identity privilege. • Seek or provide support to address the challenge. • Learn from the experience. • Reprioritize goals. • Seek or be an ally.	• Discuss how privilege works in your favor. • Help others experiencing identity cost and headwinds. • Advocate for change. • Be an ally and a mentor.
	Identity and Career Challenge = Identity Cost + Career Headwinds	Identity Challenge and Career Advantage = Identity Cost + Career Tailwinds
Identity Cost	• Name the discrimination or marginalization. • Name the identity(ies) creating cost and the headwind. • Seek support by enlisting the help of a career coach, counselor, or mentor. • Use it to reprioritize goals or reassess commitment to the organization or work. • Seek or be an ally.	• Name the identity(ies) creating cost. • Cope with discrimination or marginalization. • Seek support. • Enlist the help of a career coach, counselor, or mentor. • Use the career tailwind to gain an advantage. • Seek or be an ally.

Career Headwinds ⟵⟶ Career Tailwinds

Identity and career challenge: marginalized status
When a person experiences identity cost, they are likely experiencing low levels of self-esteem and self-efficacy as a result of being discriminated against or mistreated. Campbell et al. (2020) found that over 20 years, adults with a history of adverse childhood experiences (e.g., discrimination, inequality, poverty) reported significantly higher levels of inequity across the domains of home, work, and family relationships with perceived daily discriminatory experiences. A marginalized status affects a person at work by creating stress, dissatisfaction, burnout, and less access to advancement opportunities. Individuals in this situation can benefit by seeking out others experiencing similar marginalization and discussing occupational barriers and aspirations.

Finding role models and mentors can mitigate these dynamics. Garnering the support of others can allow the career explorer, sustainer, or changer to name the issues and engage in narrative meaning-making and learning about the situation. Career supporters (e.g., mentors, coaches, counselors) must learn how systemic discrimination affects individual self-efficacy and intervene with appropriate recommendations (e.g., counseling) and coaching. Organizations and communities should develop policies that reduce or eliminate bias and give more equitable access to CD and opportunities. Box 9.2 offers some resources for countering these challenges.

BOX 9.2 TIPS AND TOOLS FOR CAREER DEVELOPMENT

Countering Discrimination and Marginalization in Employment

What can be done if you find yourself or someone you are helping in a marginalized employment position? Table 9.2 highlights some resources for addressing inequity and bolstering self-esteem.

Table 9.2   Countering discrimination and marginalization in employment

Addressing discrimination and marginalization	Boosting self-esteem

• US EEOC (Equal Employment Opportunity Commission), https://www.eeoc.gov/outreach-education-technical-assistance:
• Provides no-cost outreach and education programs
• Supports veterans with disabilities
 	
• Organization-sponsored recruiting initiatives, mentoring programs, and DEI task forces (Dobbin & Kalev, 2016).
	• Focus on strengths and goals.
	• Seek or give support.
	• Engage in self-care and respond to the infraction slowly.
	• Find a free mentoring program that suits your needs:
	  • Tap friends and family
	  • Identify co-workers
	  • Join LinkedIn and search for a mentoring group in your area of interest
	• Free Mentoring Platforms:
	  • The Mentoring Club https://www.mentoring-club.com/
	  • Women Who Create: Mentoring for Women of Color By Women of Color https://www.womenwhocreate.org/
	  • RE:Create: Mentoring for Creatives https://www.re-create.com/
	  • MENTOR: Find or Be a Mentor https://www.mentoring.org/

Addressing discrimination and marginalization	Boosting self-esteem
• Mentors and coaches should effectively broach issues of discrimination and marginalization (Bierema, 2022; Bierema et al., 2022). • Implement innovative human resource development practices (Bierema et al., 2024).	• Veterans Business Outreach Center https://www.sba.gov/local-assistance/resource-partners/veterans-business-outreach-center-vboc-program • Minority Business and Development Agency https://www.mbda.gov/mbda-programs#3/43.44/-111.95 • Join a professional or community network. • Seek professional help using the APA Psychologist Locator Service https://locator.apa.org/

Identity challenge and career advantage: coping status

Sometimes a person's identity, for example, a Latina, causes marginalizing and discriminatory treatment, but they also experience career advantages such as a promotion, recognition, or developmental opportunity. Although the tailwind in this situation can be esteem and career-boosting, it does not negate or change the inequitable treatment. It becomes a situation of needing to cope with inequity, which is physically, mentally, and emotionally draining. Individuals in these situations need to seek out the same support as recommended for addressing marginalized statuses but also recognize that the career tailwind will provide more power and opportunity to pursue one's desired work or career. Community and organization leaders are accountable for guarding against discrimination and inequity. They can begin taking steps toward valuing mutual respect and diversity immediately, with zero tolerance for bias or harassment. Policies and practices can also be revised to combat inequity and bias. Box 9.3 offers strategies for promoting workplace equity.

◊ BOX 9.3 TIPS AND TOOLS FOR CAREER DEVELOPMENT

Promoting Workplace Equity

What can be done if you find yourself or someone you are helping in the position of coping with identity cost and marginalization? This box highlights some steps for addressing inequity based on the work of Livingston (2020). Livingston noted, "Workplace discrimination often comes from well-educated, well-intentioned, open-minded, kindhearted people who are just floating along, severely underestimating the tug of the prevailing current on their actions, positions, and outcomes" (para. 18).

 Livingston (2020) advocated a five-stage process called PRESS for addressing equity at work:

1. **P**roblem awareness: Helping people understand the problems caused by inequity. This data can exemplify a lack of awareness: 57% of White people and 66% of working-class White people think discrimination against White people is as much of a problem as discrimination against Black people and other people of color (Livingston, 2020); men tend to believe gender inequity is a myth (Piacenza, 2019); and CD literature has tended to focus narrowly on the population and assume equal access is a reality (Fouad et al., 2019).
2. **R**oot-case analysis: Understanding what is creating the problem (cognitive biases, personality characteristics, insecurities, worldviews, perceived threat, or power and ego needs), with an eye toward the structural dynamics that create inequity.
3. **E**mpathy and concern about the problem and the people developed through exposure and education.
4. **S**trategies for addressing the problem by getting employee buy-in and co-creating policy and practice.
5. **S**acrifice: Willingness to invest the time, energy, and resources needed to address the problem.

"The real challenge for organizations is not figuring out 'What can we do?' But rather 'Are we willing to do it?'" (Livingston, 2020, para. 27).

Identity privilege and career challenge: resiliency status

Chapters 7 and 8 detailed the challenges adults face due to the interactions of identities, career headwinds, and tailwinds. Even when someone is privileged by identity capital, they will encounter career challenges and can usually navigate them with personal resiliency. Although challenges or career shocks can be positive, negative, or perhaps a combination, they are learning opportunities and deserve time and reflection for someone to absorb and plot the next steps. They can present good opportunities to reflect on one's current role and future prospects and reprioritize as appropriate. Box 9.4 offers some tips on learning from career mistakes.

⚓ BOX 9.4 TIPS AND TOOLS FOR CAREER DEVELOPMENT

Learning from Career Challenges and Mistakes

As a career explorer, sustainer, or changer, or a career coach or counselor, you may have made or observed career mistakes in your lifetime. Table 9.3 identifies strategies for learning from the challenges and missteps that inevitably get made in a career.

Table 9.3   Learning from career challenges and mistakes

Mistake	Key learning
Not developing a career plan: If you do not have a short-, mid-, and long-term career plan, it will be impossible to reach your goals.	Establish goals by consulting with your family, friends, peers, boss, mentors, and people in the role you aspire to, and write them down. Consider creating a Personal "Board of Directors" and share your career plan with them and ask for their advice.
Failing to network and build collaborative and professional ties: When you are busy with your work or career, it may seem like you don't have time to develop trusting relationships.	Make time to build trusting, solid relationships—it is through relationships that work gets accomplished. You can do this by communicating regularly, inviting collaborators and offering to collaborate, being appreciative and caring, and asking for feedback.
Letting experience get in the way of learning: When you have a lot of experience, it can become a barrier to learning, as discussed in Chapter 5.	Be open to learning from your mistakes and other people. Question your assumptions and thinking regularly and seek new opportunities to learn.
Not keeping up to date: Knowledge and technology are accelerating in a VUCA context, as discussed in Chapter 2.	Identify new knowledge or skills you want to develop and then seek out the learning. Pay attention to trends in your field and seek learning to address them.
Forgetting that people get hired for their skills and fired for their behavior: No one wants to work with a jerk or bully.	Know when you have crossed the line in some way. Apologize and assume accountability for your behavior. Learn how to apologize appropriately.

Identity and career privilege: privileged status

When you have identity capital and a tailwind as a career explorer, sustainer, or changer, it is an exciting and gratifying experience. It is also a privileged position. Recognizing privilege is important, and the status is fluid because it will depend on the social context. As Jourdan (2021) explained,

> Privilege does not mean that you were born with a silver spoon in your mouth and never had to work hard or that you achieved success with no struggle. It simply means that you are likely to have enjoyed certain *tailwinds* because, based on parts of your demographic makeup, you are in the majority. (para. 6, italics added for emphasis)

Jourdan (2021) emphasized that acknowledging your privilege lowers defenses, shows vulnerability, and sets the tone for building inclusivity. It can be helpful to think about where you experience privilege and openly discuss the concept with family and colleagues, and when you have it, use it to help others who may be experiencing identity cost or a career headwind.

CHAPTER SUMMARY

Rethinking Adult Career Development interrogated traditional, unquestioned assumptions about CD, raised critical questions, and offered strategies for individuals grappling with CD, coaches, and mentors providing career guidance, and leaders and policymakers seeking to build inclusive, equitable cultures that engage people in meeting their career aspirations. Chapter 9 provided a summary of the book and introduced a critical, intersectional, feminist model of adult career development theory as a step toward creating more work and career justice and equity for adults to confidently choose the career ladder they want to climb.

References

Abel, J. R., Florida, R., & Gabe, T. M. (2018). Can low-wage workers find better jobs? *FRB of New York Staff Report* No. 846. https://doi.org/10.2139/ssrn.3164963

Acker, J. (1990). Hierarchies, jobs, bodies: A theory of gendered organizations. *Gender & Society, 4*(2), 139–158. https://doi.org/10.1177/089124390004002002

Ackerman, P. L., & Kanfer, R. (2020). Work in the 21st century: New directions for aging and adult development. *American Psychologist, 75*(4), 486–498. https://doi.org/10.1037/amp0000615

Adichie, C. (2009). The danger of a single story [Video]. *Ted Conferences.* https://www.ted.com/talks/chimamanda_ngozi_adichie_the_danger_of_a_single_story

Afifi, T. D., & Coveleski, S. (2015). Relational competence. In A. F. Hannawa & B. H. Spitzberg (Eds.), *Communication competence* (pp. 317–340). De Gruyter Mouton. https://doi.org/10.1515/9783110317459-014

AHRD Board of Directors. (2020). *Black lives matter: Living, learning, and unlearning into an AHRD pandemic of antiracism, learning, and change.* AHRD. https://www.ahrd.org/page/Black-Lives-Matter

Akkermans, J., Richardson, J., & Kraimer, M. L. (2020). The Covid-19 crisis as a career shock: Implications for careers and vocational behavior. *Journal of Vocational Behavior, 119*, 103434. https://doi.org/10.1016/j.jvb.2020.103434

Akkermans, J., Seibert, S. E., & Mol, S. T. (2018). Tales of the unexpected: Integrating career shocks in the contemporary careers literature. *SA Journal of Industrial Psychology, 44*(1), 1–10. https://hdl.handle.net/10520/EJC-ee9643e8c

Allan, B. A., & Duffy, R. D. (2014). Calling, goals, and life satisfaction: A moderated mediation model. *Journal of Career Assessment, 22*(3), 451–464. https://doi.org/10.1177/1069072713498574

Allen, T. D., Eby, L. T., Poteet, M. L., Lentz, E., & Lima, L. (2004). Career benefits associated with mentoring for protégés: A meta-analysis. *Journal of Applied Psychology, 89*(1), 127. https://doi.org/10.1037/0021-9010.89.1.127

Alvesson, M. (2010). Self-doubters, strugglers, storytellers, surfers and others: Images of self-identities in organization studies. *Human Relations, 63*(2), 193–217. https://doi.org/10.1177/0018726709350372

Alvesson, M., & Willmott, H. (1997). Making sense of management: A critical introduction. *Journal of the Operational Research Society, 48*(7), 762–763. https://doi.org/10.1057/palgrave.jors.2600827

Amann, T. (2003). Creating space for somatic ways of knowing within transformative learning theory. In *Proceedings of the fifth international conference on transformative learning* (pp. 26–32). https://www.yogafit.com/research/transformative.doc

American Psychological Association [APA] (2019). *APA guidelines for psychological practice for people with low-income and economic marginalization.* APA. https://www.apa.org/about/policy/guidelines-lowincome.pdf

Amis, J. M., Mair, J., & Munir, K. A. (2020). The organizational reproduction of inequality. *Academy of Management Annals, 14*(1), 195–230. https://doi.org/10.5465/annals.2017.0033

Anonymous (1973). The burger that conquered the country. *Time*, 102, 84–92.

Apfelbaum, E. P., & Suh, E. Y. (2024). Transparency about lagging diversity numbers signals genuine progress. *Journal of Experimental Psychology: General*, *153*(1), 255–267. https://doi.org/10.1037/xge0001489

Argyris, C. (1970). *Intervention theory & method: A behavioral science view*. Addison-Wesley.

Argyris, C. (2000). *Flawed advice and the management trap: How managers can know when they're getting good advice and when they're not*. Oxford University Press.

Arthur, M. B., & Rousseau, D. M. (1996). The boundaryless career as a new employment principle. In M. B. Arthur & D. M. Rousseau (Eds.), *The boundaryless career* (pp. 3–20). Oxford University Press.

Arunprasad, P., Dey, C., Jebli, F., Manimuthu, A., & El Hathat, Z. (2022). Exploring the remote work challenges in the era of COVID-19 pandemic: Review and application model. *Benchmarking: An International Journal*, *29*(10), 3333–3355. https://doi.org/10.1108/BIJ-07–2021–0421

Auster, E., & Choo, C. W. (1994). How senior managers acquire and use information in environmental scanning. *Information Processing & Management*, *30*(5), 607–618. https://doi.org/10.1016/0306–4573(94)90073–6

Autin, K. L., Williams, T. R., Allan, B. A., & Herdt, M. E. (2022). Decent work among people of color: The moderating role of critical consciousness. *Journal of Career Assessment*, *30*(3), 455–473. https://doi.org/10.1177/10690727211039811

Ayas, R., Tilly, P., & Rawlings, D. (2023). *Cutting costs at the expense of diversity*. Revilo Labs. https://www.reveliolabs.com/news/social/cutting-costs-at-the-expense-of-diversity/

Bailyn, L. (1991). The hybrid career: An exploratory study of career routes in R&D. *Journal of Engineering and Technology Management*, *8*(1), 1–14. https://doi.org/10.1016/0923-4748(91)90002-9

Bainbridge, H. T., & Townsend, K. (2020). The effects of offering flexible work practices to employees with unpaid caregiving responsibilities for elderly or disabled family members. *Human Resource Management*, *59*(5), 483–495. https://doi.org/10.1002/hrm.22007

Bandura, A. (1977). *Social learning theory*. General Learning Press.

Bandura, A. (1986). The explanatory and predictive scope of self-efficacy theory. *Journal of Social and Clinical Psychology*, *4*(3), 359–373. https://doi.org/10.1521/jscp.1986.4.3.359

Bardwick, J. M. (1986a). The plateauing trap, part 1: Getting caught. *Personnel*, *63*(10), 46–51. https://eric.ed.gov/?id=EJ346541

Bardwick, J. M. (1986b). The plateauing trap, part 2: Setting employees free. *Personnel*, *63*(11), 35–40. https://eric.ed.gov/?id=EJ346543

Baruch, Y. (2004). Transforming careers: From linear to multidirectional career paths: Organizational and individual perspectives. *Career Development International*, *9*(1), 58–73. https://doi.org/10.1108/13620430410518147

Baruch, Y. (2015). Organizational and labor markets as career ecosystem. In A. De Vos & B. I. J. M. Van der Heijden (Eds.), *Handbook of Research on Sustainable Careers* (pp. 364–380). Cheltenham, UK and Northampton, MA, USA: Edward Elgar Publishing.

Baruch, Y., & Sullivan, S. E. (2022). The why, what, and how of career research: A review and recommendations for future study. *Career Development International*, *27*(1), 135–159. https://doi.org/10.1108/CDI-10–2021–0251

Baumeister, R. F., & Wilson, B. (1996). Life stories and the four needs for meaning. *Psychological Inquiry*, *7*(4), 322–325. https://doi.org/10.1207/s15327965pli0704_2

Beatty, J. E., & Torbert, W. R. (2003). The false duality of work and leisure. *Journal of Management Inquiry*, *12*(3), 239–252. https://doi.org/10.1177/1056492603256340

Bellah, R. N. (1985). *Habits of the heart: Individualism and commitment in American life.* University of California Press.

Belli, G. (2018). *Here's how many years you'll spend at work in your lifetime.* Payscale. https://www.payscale.com/career-news/2018/10/heres-how-many-years-youll-spend-work-in-your-lifetime

Berger, B. (1963). The sociology of leisure. In E. O. Smigel (Ed.), *Work and leisure: A contemporary social problem* (pp. 21–40). College and University Press.

Bermúdez, J. M., Muruthi, B. A., & Jordan, L. S. (2016). Decolonizing research methods for family science: Creating space at the center. *Journal of Family Theory & Review*, *8*(2), 192–206. https://doi.org/10.1111/jftr.12139

Bertrand, M., & Mullainathan, S. (2004). Are Emily and Greg more employable than Lakisha and Jamal? A field experiment on labor market discrimination. *The American Economic Review*, *94*(4), 991–1013. https://doi.org/10.1257/0002828042002561

Betzler, M., & Löschke, J. (2021). Collegial relationships. *Ethical Theory and Moral Practice*, *24*, 213–229. https://doi.org/10.1007/s10677-021-10165-9

Bierema, L. L. (2009). Critiquing human resource development's dominant masculine rationality and evaluating its impact. *Human Resource Development Review*, *8*(1), 68–96. https://doi.org/10.1177/1534484308330020

Bierema, L. L. (2010). *Implementing a critical approach to organization development.* Krieger.

Bierema, L. L. (2019). Adult learning theories and practices. In M. Fedeli & L. L. Bierema (Eds.), *Connecting adult learning and knowledge management: Strategies for learning and change in higher education and organizations* (pp. 3–26). Springer.

Bierema, L. L. (2020a). HRD research and practice after "The Great COVID-19 Pause": The time is now for bold, critical, research. *Human Resource Development International*, *23*(4), 347–360. https://doi.org/10.1080/13678868.2020.1779912

Bierema, L. L. (2020b). Ladies and gentlemen, your implicit bias is showing: Gender hegemony and its impact on HRD research and practice. *Human Resource Development International*, *23*(5), 473–490. https://doi.org/10.1080/13678868.2020.1809254

Bierema, L. L. (2022). "Can You Hear Me Now?" Technical and human factors in virtual developmental relationships. In R. Ghosh & H. Hutchins (Eds.), *HRD perspectives on developmental relationships: Connecting and relating at work* (pp. 241–272). Springer Nature.

Bierema, L. L. (2024). Foreword. In R. A. Gardiner, W. Fox-Kirk, C. J. Elliott, & V. Stead (Eds.), *Genderwashing in Leadership: Policies, practices, and politics* [Manuscript submitted for publication]. Emerald Publishing, UK.

Bierema, L. L., He, W., & Sim, E. (2022). Applying critical, feminist perspectives to developmental relationships in HRD. In J. C. Collins & J. L. Callahan (Eds.), *The Palgrave handbook of critical human resource development* (pp. 257–280). Springer International Publishing.

Bierema, L. L., & Yoon, H. (2019). *Mentoring as a counter to gendered organizations: A case study of the military* [Paper presentation]. Academy of Human Resource Development Conference, Richmond, VA.

Bierema, L. L., Callahan, J. L., Elliott, C. J., Greer, T. W., & Collins, J. C. (2024). *Human resource development: Critical perspectives and practices.* Routledge.

Bilash, O. (2019). Study abroad, transformation, and ikigai: A case study. *FIRE: Forum for International Research in Education, 5*(2), 245–260. https://doi.org/10.32865/fire201952170

Bishu, S. G., & Alkadry, M. G. (2017). A systematic review of the gender pay gap and factors that predict it. *Administration & Society, 49*(1), 65–104. https://doi.org/10.1177/0095399716636928

Blackman, A. (2019). *How to make your workplace more LGBT friendly (& why you should).* Envatotuts. https://business.tutsplus.com/tutorials/make-your-workplace-lgbt-friendly--cms-32756

Blanchard, C. A., & Lichtenberg, J. W. (2003). Compromise in career decision making: A test of Gottfredson's theory. *Journal of Vocational Behavior, 62*(2), 250–271. https://doi.org/10.1016/S0001-8791(02)00026-X

Blustein, D. L. (2001). Extending the reach of vocational psychology: Toward an inclusive and integrative psychology of working. *Journal of Vocational Behavior, 59*(2), 171–182. https://doi.org/10.1006/jvbe.2001.1823

Blustein, D. L. (2006). *The psychology of working: Exploring the inner world of dreams and disappointments.* Lawrence Erlbaum.

Blustein, D. L., & Duffy, R. D. (2021). Psychology of working theory. In S. D. Brown & R. W. Lent (Eds.), *Career development and counseling: Putting theory and research to work* (pp. 201–236). John Wiley & Sons.

Blustein, D. L., Kenny, M. E., Di Fabio, A., & Guichard, J. (2019). Expanding the impact of the psychology of working: Engaging psychology in the struggle for decent work and human rights. *Journal of Career Assessment, 27*(1), 3–28. https://doi.org/10.1177/1069072718774002

Bohonos, J. W., & James-Gallaway, A. (2022). Enslavement and the foundations of human resource development: Covert learning, consciousness raising, and resisting antiBlack organizational goals. *Human Resource Development Review, 21*(2), 160–179. https://doi.org/10.1177/15344843221076292

Bolisani, E., Fedeli, M., De Marchi, V., & Bierema, L. (2020). Together we win: Communities of practice to face the COVID crisis in higher education. In *Proceedings of the 17th international conference on intellectual capital, knowledge management & organisational learning ICICKM* (pp. 72–80). https://www.researchgate.net/profile/Evangelia-Maritsa/publication/345177788_Leadership_Readiness_in_Crisis_Context_Health_Preservation_through_Shared_Knowledge/links/5fa02bce299bf1b53e5a2430/Leadership-Readiness-in-Crisis-Context-Health-Preservation-through-Shared-Knowledge.pdf#page=91

Boud, D., & Walker, D. (1991). Experience and learning: Reflection at work. EAE600 adults learning in the workplace: Part A. Adult and Workplace Education, Faculty of Education, Deakin University, Geelong, Victoria, Australia 3217. https://eric.ed.gov/?id=ED384696

Bowleg, L. (2008). When Black+ lesbian+ woman≠ Black lesbian woman: The methodological challenges of qualitative and quantitative intersectionality research. *Sex Roles, 59*(5), 312–325. https://doi.org/10.1007/s11199-008-9400-z

Boyatzis, R. E., Kolb, D. A., Arthur, M., Goffee, R., & Morris, T. (2000). Performance, learning, and development as modes of growth and adaptation throughout our lives and careers. In M. B. Arthur, M. A. Peiperl, R. Goffee, & T. Morris (Eds.), *Career frontiers: New conceptions of working lives* (pp. 76–98), Oxford University Press.

Briscoe, J. P., & Hall, D. T. (2006). The interplay of boundaryless and protean careers: Combinations and implications. *Journal of Vocational Behavior, 69*, 4–18. https://doi.org/10.1016/j.jvb.2005.09.002

Brockett, R. G., & Hiemstra, R. (1991). *Self-direction in adult learning: Perspectives on theory, research and practice.* Routledge.

Brookfield, S. (2012). A critical theory of adult and community education. *International Journal of Adult Vocational Education and Technology, 3*(3), 1–15. https://doi.org/ 10.4018/JAVET.2012070101

Bronk, K. C., & McLean, D. C. (2016). The role of passion and purpose in leader developmental readiness. *New Directions for Student Leadership, 149*, 27–36. https://doi .org/10.1002/yd.20159

Brown, B. (n.d.). *Living into our values.* Brené Brown. https:// brenebrown .com/ resources/living-into-our-values/

Brown, B. (2024). *Operationalizing Your Organization's Values.* Brené Brown. https:// brenebrown.com/operationalizing-your-orgs-values/

Brown, D. (1996). Brown's values-based, holistic model of career and life-role choices and satisfaction [Special section]. In D. Brown, L. Brooks, & 8c Associates (Eds.), *Career choice and development* (pp. 337–338). Jossey-Bass.

Brown, D. (Ed.) (2002). *Career choice and development.* John Wiley & Sons.

Brown, D. (2016). *Career information, career counseling, and career development* (11th ed.). Pearson.

Brown, D. L., & Segrist, D. (2016). African American career aspirations: Examining the relative influence of internalized racism. *Journal of Career Development, 43*(2), 177–189. https://doi.org/10.1177/0894845315586256

Brown, S. D., & Lent, R. W. (Eds.). (2021). *Career development and counseling: Putting theory and research to work.* Wiley & Sons.

Budig, M. J., & Lim, M. (2016). Cohort differences and the marriage premium: Emergence of gender-neutral household specialization effects. *Journal of Marriage and Family, 78*(5), 1352–1370. https://doi.org/10.1111/jomf.12326

Bureau of Labor Statistics (2022a). *A profile of the working poor, 2020.* US Bureau of Labor Statistics. https://www.bls.gov/opub/reports/working-poor/2020/home.htm #_edn1

Bureau of Labor Statistics (2022b). Table 11: Employed persons by detailed occupation, sex, race, and Hispanic or Latino ethnicity [Data set]. *Current population survey.* https://www.bls.gov/cps/cpsaat11.htm

Bureau of Labor Statistics (2023a). *Labor force characteristics by race and ethnicity, 2021.* US Bureau of Labor Statistics. https:// www .bls .gov/ opub/ reports/ race -and -ethnicity/2021/home.htm#:~:text=of%20any%20race.-,%E2%80%8B%20Source %3A%20U .S . %20Bureau%20of%20Labor%20Statistics ,Current %20Population %20Survey%20(CPS).&text=Survey%20(CPS).-,Among%20adult%20men%20(20 %20years %20and %20older) %20in %20the %20largest ,percent)%20were%20 the%20least%20likely

Bureau of Labor Statistics (2023b). *Persons with a disability: Labor force characteristics—2022.* US Bureau of Labor Statistics. https://www.bls.gov/news.release/ pdf/disabl.pdf

Burke, J., Bezyak, J., Fraser, R. T., Pete, J., Ditchman, N., & Chan, F. (2013). Employers' attitudes towards hiring and retaining people with disabilities: A review of the literature. *The Australian Journal of Rehabilitation Counselling, 19*(1), 21–38. https://doi.org/10.1017/jrc.2013.2

Byars-Winston, A. M., & Fouad, N. A. (2006). Metacognition and multicultural competence: Expanding the culturally appropriate career counseling model. *The Career Development Quarterly, 54*(3), 187–201. https://doi.org/10.1002/j.2161–0045.2006 .tb00151.x

Byrd, M. Y. (2018a). Diversity branding strategy: Concealing implicit stereotypes and biased behaviors. *Advances in Developing Human Resources, 20*(3), 299–312. https://doi.org/10.1177/1523422318778006

Byrd, M. Y. (2018b). Does HRD have a moral duty to respond to matters of social injustice? *Human Resource Development International, 21*(1), 3–11. https://doi.org/10.1177/1523422318778006 https://doi.org/10.1080/13678868.2017.1344419

Byrd, M. Y. (2022). Creating a culture of inclusion and belongingness in remote work environments that sustains meaningful work. *Human Resource Development International, 25*(2), 145–162. https://doi.org/10.1080/13678868.2022.2047252

Byrd, M. Y., & Scott, C. L. (Eds.) (2018). *Diversity in the workforce: Current issues and emerging trends* (2nd ed.). Routledge.

Byrd, M. Y., & Sparkman, T. E. (2022). Reconciling the business case and the social justice case for diversity: A model of human relations. *Human Resource Development Review, 21*(1), 75–100. https://doi.org/10.1177/15344843211072356

Cadenas, G. A., & McWhirter, E. H. (2022). Critical consciousness in vocational psychology: A vision for the next decade and beyond. *Journal of Career Assessment, 30*(3), 411–435. https://doi.org/10.1177/10690727221086553

Cadenas, G. A., Cantú, E. A., Sosa, R., Carroll, S., Lynn, N., Suro, B., & Ruth, A. (2023). An educational program affirming immigrant entrepreneurship, critical consciousness, and cultural strengths. *The Career Development Quarterly, 71*(4), 284–299. https://doi.org/10.1002/cdq.12335

Callahan, J. L., & McCollum, E. E. (2002). Obscured variability: The distinction between emotion work and emotional labor. In J. L. Callahan & E. E. McCollum (Eds.), *Managing emotions in the workplace* (pp. 219–231). Routledge.

Campbell, E. T. (1973). *Give ye them to eat.* Internet archive. https://archive.org/details/sermongiveyethem00camp/page/8/mode/2up

Campbell, J. (2003). *The hero's journey: Joseph Campbell on his life and work* (Vol. 7). New World Library.

Campbell, J. A., Walker, R. J., Garacci, E., Dawson, A. Z., Williams, J. S., & Egede, L. E. (2020). Relationship between adverse childhood experiences and perceived discrimination in adulthood. *Journal of Affective Disorders, 277*, 999–1004. https://doi.org/10.1016/j.jad.2020.09.023

Campbell, L. (2017). We've broken down your entire life into years spent doing tasks. *Huffpost.* https://www.huffpost.com/entry/weve-broken-down-your-entire-life-into-years-spent-doing-tasks_n_61087617e4b0999d2084fec5

Canzittu, D. (2022). A framework to think of school and career guidance in a VUCA world. *British Journal of Guidance & Counselling, 50*(2), 248–259. https://doi.org/10.1080/03069885.2020.1825619

Castilla, E. J. (2008). Gender, race, and meritocracy in organizational careers. *American Journal of Sociology, 113*(6), 1479–1526. https://doi.org/10.1086/588738

Catalyst. (2022). *Women in the workforce: United States (Quick take).* Catalyst. https://www.catalyst.org/research/women-in-the-workforce-united-states/

Catalyst. (2023). *Women of color in the United States (Quick take).* Catalyst. https://www.catalyst.org/research/women-of-color-in-the-united-states/

Cebola, M. M. J., dos Santos, N. R., & Dionísio, A. (2023). Worker-related ageism: A systematic review of empirical research. *Ageing & Society, 43*(8), 1882–1914. https://doi.org/10.1017/S0144686X21001380

Centeno, M. A., & Cohen, J. N. (2013). *Global capitalism: A sociological perspective.* John Wiley & Sons.

Chalofsky, N. (2003). An emerging construct for meaningful work. *Human Resource Development International, 6*(1), 69–83. https://doi.org/10.1080/1367886022000016785

Chloupek, J. (2023). *How to ID your internal driver and why it matters: Awareness, behaviors, and connections.* DocUmeant Publishing.

Cho, S., Crenshaw, K. W., & McCall, L. (2013). Toward a field of intersectionality studies: Theory, applications, and praxis. *Signs: Journal of Women in Culture and Society, 38*(4), 785–810. https://doi.org/10.1086/669608

Chouinard, Y. (2016). *Let my people go surfing: The education of a reluctant businessman—including 10 more years of business unusual.* Penguin.

Chugh, D., & Bock, L. (2018). *The person you mean to be: How good people fight bias.* HarperBusiness.

Cinamon, R. G., Hardin, E. E., & Flum, H. (2019). Introduction to special issue on career education. *Journal of Career Development, 46*(6), 603–607. https://doi.org/10.1177/0894845319873728

CIPD (2023). *Race inclusion report: Equality of career progression.* Chartered Institute of Personnel Development. https://www.cipd.org/en/knowledge/reports/race-inclusion-career-progression/

Clark, M. C. (1993). Transformational learning. *New Directions for Adult and Continuing Education, 1996*(57), 47–56. https://doi.org/10.1002/ace.36719935707

Clark, M. C. (2010). Narrative learning: Its contours and its possibilities. *New Directions for Adult and Continuing Education, 126*(3), 3–11. https://doi.org/10.1002/ace.367

Clerkin, C., Bergeron, D. M., & Wilson, M. S. (2024). Gender differences in developmental experiences. In S. Madsen (Ed.), *Handbook of Research on Gender and Leadership* (pp. 392–409). Cheltenham, UK and Northampton, MA, USA: Edward Elgar Publishing.

Cohen, R., Bavishi, C., & Rozanski, A. (2016). Purpose in life and its relationship to all-cause mortality and cardiovascular events. *Psychosomatic Medicine, 78*(2), 122–133. https://doi.org/10.1097/psy.0000000000000274

Cole, N. L. (2023). *The critical view on global capitalism.* ThoughtCo. https://www.thoughtco.com/why-is-global-capitalism-bad-3026085

Coleman, M. (2020). Women leaders in the workplace: Perceptions of career barriers, facilitators and change. *Irish Educational Studies, 39*(2), 233–253. https://doi.org/10.1080/03323315.2019.1697952

Collins, J. C. (2012). Identity matters: A critical exploration of lesbian, gay, and bisexual identity and leadership in HRD. *Human Resource Development Review, 11*(3), 349–379. http://doi.org/10.1177/1534484312446810

Collins, J. C. (2017). Leveraging three lessons learned from teaching an HRD undergraduate diversity and inclusion course: An autoethnography of one professor's perceptions. *Advances in Developing Human Resources, 19*(2), 157–175. https://doi.org/10.1177/1523422317695227

Collins, P. H. (1990). *Black feminist thought: Knowledge, consciousness, and the politics of empowerment.* Unwin Hyman.

Collins, P. H. (2022). *Black feminist thought: Knowledge, consciousness, and the politics of empowerment.* Routledge.

Collins, P. H., & Bilge, S. (2020). *Intersectionality* (2nd ed.). Polity.

Collins, S. (1997). *Black corporate executives: The making and breaking of a black middle class.* Temple University Press.

Collinson, C., &. Hodin, M. (2023). Best practices for engaging a multigenerational workforce. *Harvard Business Review.* https://hbr.org/2023/10/best-practices-for-engaging-a-multigenerational-workforce

Cooperrider, D. L., Barrett, F., & Srivastva, S. (1995). Social construction and appreciative inquiry: A journey in organizational theory. In D. Hosking, H. P. Dachler, & K. Gergen (Eds.), *Management and organization: Relational alternatives to individualism* (pp. 157–200). Ashgate Publishing.

Corbett, B., & Chloupek, J. (2019). *Why it matters: The Sherpa guide to what you are looking for.* Sasha Corporation.

Corbett, B., & Colemon, J. (2006). *The Sherpa guide: Process-driven executive coaching.* South-Western Publishing.

Cornileus, T. H. (2013). "I'm a Black man and I'm doing this job very well": How African American professional men negotiate the impact of racism on their career development. *Journal of African American Studies, 17,* 444–460. https://doi.org/10.1007/s12111-012-9225-2

Côté, J. E. (1996). Sociological perspectives on identity formation: The culture–identity link and identity capital. *Journal of Adolescence, 19*(5), 417–428. https://doi.org/10.1006/jado.1996.0040

Côté, J. E. (2005). Identity capital, social capital and the wider benefits of learning: Generating resources facilitative of social cohesion. *London Review of Education, 3*(3), 221–237. DOI: 10.1080/14748460500372382

Craig, N., & Snook, S. (2014). From purpose to impact. *Harvard Business Review, 92*(5), 104–111. https://hbr.org/2014/05/from-purpose-to-impact

Cranton, P. (2016). *Understanding and promoting transformative learning: A guide to theory and practice.* Routledge.

Crenshaw, K. (1989). Demarginalizing the intersection of race and sex: Black feminist critique of antidiscrimination doctrine, feminist theory and antiracist politics. *University of Chicago Legal Forum, 1989,* 139–168.

Cronen, S., McQuiggan, M., & Isenberg, E. (2017). *Adult training and education: Results from the national household education surveys program of 2016* (NCES 2017–103rev), National Center for Education Statistics, Institute of Education Sciences, US Department of Education. Washington, http://nces.ed.gov/pubsearch

Crumbaugh, J. C., & Maholick, L. T. (1964). An Experimental study in existentialism: The psychometric approach to Frankl's concept of noogenic neurosis. *Journal of Clinical Psychology, 20,* 200–207. https://doi.org/10.1002/1097-4679(196404)20:2<200::AID-JCLP2270200203>3.0.CO;2-U

Czekierda, K., Banik, A., Park, C. L., & Luszczynska, A. (2017). Meaning in life and physical health: Systematic review and meta-analysis. *Health Psychology Review, 11*(4), 387–418. https://doi.org/10.1080/17437199.2017.132732 5

Daffron, S. R., & Caffarella, R. S. (2021). *Planning programs for adult learners: A practical guide.* John Wiley & Sons.

Daly, N. (2020). 17 reasons why remote work is the future. Wrike. https://www.wrike.com/blog/remote-work-stats-infographic/

Damon, W., Menon, J., & Bronk, K. C. (2003). The development of purpose during adolescence. *Applied Developmental Science, 7,* 119–128. https://doi.org/10.1207/S1532480XADS0703_2

Datareportal (n.d.). *Digital around the world.* Datareportal. https://datareportal.com/global-digital-overview

Davis, T. J., Greer, T. W., Sisco, S., & Collins, J. C. (2020). "Reclaiming my time" amid organizational change: A dialectical approach to support the thriving and career development for faculty at the margins. *Advances in Developing Human Resources, 22*(1), 23–40. https://doi.org/10.1177/1523422319885115

De Silver, D. (2017). *Access to paid family leave varies widely across employers, industries*. United States of America. https://policycommons.net/artifacts/617977/ access-to-paid-family-leave-varies-widely-across-employers-industries/1598870/

De Smet, A., Mysore, M., Reich, A., & Sternfels, B. (2021). *Return as a muscle: How lessons from COVID-19 can shape a robust operating model for hybrid and beyond*. McKinsey Quarterly. https://www.mckinsey.com/business-functions/people-and -organizational-performance/our-insights/return-as-a-muscle-how-lessons-from -covid-19-can-shape-a-robust-operating-model-for-hybrid-and-beyond

De Vos, A., Van der Heijden, B. I., & Akkermans, J. (2020). Sustainable careers: Towards a conceptual model. *Journal of Vocational Behavior*, *117*, 103196. https:// doi.org/10.1016/j.jvb.2018.06.011

Dewey, H. (1938). *Experience and education*. Collier Books.

Dhingra, N., Samo, A., Schaninger, B., & Schrimper, M. (2021). *Help your employees find purpose—or watch them leave*. McKinsey & Company. https://www.mckinsey .com/capabilities/people-and-organizational-performance/our-insights/help-your -employees-find-purpose-or-watch-them-leave

Diemer, M. A., & Blustein, D. L. (2006). Critical consciousness and career development among urban youth. *Journal of Vocational Behavior*, *68*(2), 220–232. https:// doi.org/10.1016/j.jvb.2005.07.001

Dik, B. J., & Duffy, R. D. (2009). Calling and vocation at work definitions and prospects for research and practice. *The Counseling Psychologist*, *37*(3), 424–450. https://doi.org/10.1177/0011000008316430

Dik, B. J., Steger, M. F., & Autin, K. L. (2021). Emerging perspectives: Calling, meaning, and volition. In S. D. Brown & R. W. Lent (Eds.), *Career development and counseling: Putting theory and research to work* (pp. 201–236). John Wiley & Sons.

Dillard, A. (2013). *The writing life*. Harper Perennial.

Diversity Intelligence (2021). *The world's first diversity intelligence® (DQ) Assessment: Reimagining diversity begins here*. Diversity Intelligence. https://www.dive rsityintelligencellc.com/

Dobbin, F., & Kalev, A. (2016). Why diversity programs fail. *Harvard Business Review*. https://hbr.org/2016/07/why-diversity-programs-fail

Dobrow, S. R., & Tosti-Kharas, J. (2011). Calling: The development of a scale measure. *Personnel Psychology*, *64*, 1001–1049. https://doi.org/10.1111/j.1744-6570.2011 .01234.x

Dordoni, P., & Argentero, P. (2015). When age stereotypes are employment barriers: A conceptual analysis and a literature review on older workers stereotypes. *Ageing International*, *40*, 393–412. https://doi.org/10.1007/s12126-015-9222-6

Doyle, A. (2020). *How often do people change jobs in a lifetime?* The balance. https:// www.thebalancemoney.com/how-often-do-people-change-jobs-2060467

Driver, M. J. (1985). Demographic and societal factors affecting the linear career crisis. *Canadian Journal of Administrative Sciences/Revue Canadienne des Sciences de l'Administration*, *2*(2), 245–263. https://doi.org/10.1111/j.1936-4490.1985.tb00405 .x

Duckworth, A. (2016). *Grit: The power of passion and perseverance*. Scribner/Simon & Schuster.

Duffy, R. D., & Dik, B. J. (2013). Research on calling: What have we learned and where are we going? *Journal of Vocational Behavior*, *83*, 428–436. https://doi.org/ 10.1016/j.jvb.2013.06.006

Duffy, R. D., Diemer, M. A., & Jadidian, A. (2012). The development and initial validation of the Work Volition Scale–Student Version. *The Counseling Psychologist*, *40*(2), 291–319. https://doi.org/10.1177/0011000011417147

Duffy, R. D., Allan, B. A., Autin, K. L., & Douglass, R. P. (2014). Living a calling and work well-being: A longitudinal study. *Journal of Counseling Psychology*, *61*(4), 605. https://psycnet.apa.org/record/2014–36321–001#:~:text=https%3A//doi.org/10 .1037/cou0000042

Duffy, R. D., Blustein, D. L., Diemer, M. A., & Autin, K. L. (2016). The psychology of working theory. *Journal of Counseling Psychology*, *63*(2), 127. https://doi.org/10 .1037/cou0000140

Eby, L. T., Johnson, C. D., & Russell, J. E. (1998). A psychometric review of career assessment tools for use with diverse individuals. *Journal of Career Assessment*, *6*(3), 269–310. https://doi.org/10.1177/106907279800600302

Emerson, J. (2017). Colorblind diversity efforts don't work. *Harvard Business Review*. https://hbr.org/2017/09/colorblind-diversity-efforts-dont-work

England, P., Bearak, J., Budig, M. J., & Hodges, M. J. (2016). Do highly paid, highly skilled women experience the largest motherhood penalty? *American Sociological Review*, *81*(6), 1161–1189. https://doi.org/10.1177/0003122416673598

English, L. M., & Tisdell, E. J. (2010). Spirituality and adult education. In C. E. Kasworm, A. D. Rose, & J. M Ross-Gordon (Eds.), *Handbook of adult and continuing education* (pp. 285–293). Sage.

English, L. M., Fenwick, T. J., & Parsons, J. (2003). *Spirituality of adult education and training. Professional practices in adult education and human resource development series.* Krieger Publishing.

Erikson, E. H. (2001). *The Erik Erikson reader*. WW Norton & Company.

Ewuoso, C. (2023). Decolonization projects. *Voices in Bioethics*, *9*, 1–7. https://phil papers.org/rec/EWUDPW

Fabian, E. S., & Morris, T. R. (2021). The career development of youth and young adult s with disabilities. In S. D. Brown & R. W. Lent (Eds.), *Career development and counseling: Putting theory and research to work* (pp. 405–436). John Wiley & Sons.

Falcon, S., & Wiens, K. (2022). Reeling from a sudden job loss? Here's how to start healing. *Harvard Business Review*. https://hbr.org/2022/07/reeling-from-a-sudden -job-loss-heres-how-to-start-healing

FastCompany (2021). *Is now a good time to change careers? More workers are feeling good about it*. FastCompany. https://www.fastcompany.com/90607167/is-now-a -good-time-to-change-careers-more-workers-are-feeling-good-about-it

Feltman, C. (2021). *The thin book of trust: An essential primer for building trust at work* (2nd ed.). Thin Book Publishing Co.

Fenwick, T. (2003). Reclaiming and re-embodying experiential learning through complexity science. *Studies in the Education of Adults*, *35*(2), 123–141. https://doi.org/ 10.1080/02660830.2003.11661478

Ference, T. P., Stoner, J. A., & Warren, E. K. (1977). Managing the career plateau. *The Academy of Management Review*, *2*(4), 602–612. https://doi.org/10.2307/257512

Flores, L. Y., Spanierman, L. B., & Obasi, E. M. (2003). Ethical and professional issues in career assessment with diverse racial and ethnic groups. *Journal of Career Assessment*, *11*(1), 76–95. https://doi.org/10.1177/106907202237461

Fouad, N. A., & Kantamneni, N. (2021). The role of race and ethnicity in career choice, development, and adjustment. In S. D. Brown & R. W. Lent (Eds.), *Career development and counseling: Putting theory and research to work* (pp. 309–340). John Wiley & Sons.

Fouad, N. A., Diaz Tapia, W. A., Kozlowski, M., Weber, K., & Schams, S. (2019). (Chair) Why aren't we there yet? The current state of the research on the career development of women. Symposium conducted at the Annual meeting of the American Psychological Association. Chicago, IL.

Fouad, N. A., Kozlowski, M. B., Schams, S. S., Weber, K. N., Tapia, W. D., & Burrows, S. G. (2023). Why aren't we there yet? The status of research in women's career development. *The Counseling Psychologist*, Advance Online Publication. https://doi.org/10.1177/00110000231178539

Fox, J. (2017). *The jobs most segregated by gender and race*. Bloomberg View. https://www.bloomberg.com/view/articles/2017–08–16/the-jobs-most-segregated -by-gender-and-race

Fox, M. (2022). *The Great Reshuffle: Companies are reinventing rules as employees seek remote work, flexible hours and life beyond work*. CNBC. https://www.cnbc .com/2022/02/04/companies-are-reinventing-rules-as-employees-seek-remote-work -and-flexible-hours.html

Frankl, V. E. (1946). From death-camp to existentialism: A psychiatrist's path to a new therapy. *The Posen Library of Jewish culture and civilization; Volume 9: Catastrophe and rebirth*, 468–468.

Frankl, V. E. (1955). *The doctor and the soul. An introduction to logotherapy*. A. A. Knopf.

Frankl, V. E. (1958). On logotherapy and existential analysis. *American Journal of Psychoanalysis*, *18*(1), 28.

Frankl, V. (1959). *Man's search for meaning*. Beacon Press.

Frankl, V. E. (1985). *Man's search for meaning*. Simon and Schuster.

Freifeld, L. (2023). *2023 Training industry report*. Training. https://trainingmag.com/ 2023-training-industry-report/

Freire, P. (1973a). *Pedagogy of the oppressed: Ethnics, democracy and civic courage*. Seabury Press.

Freire, P. (1973b). *Education for critical consciousness* (Vol. 1). Bloomsbury Publishing.

Fry, R. (2022). *Some gender disparities widened in the U.S. workforce during the pandemic*. Pew Research Center. https://www.pewresearch.org/fact-tank/2022/01/14/ some-gender-disparities-widened-in-the-u-s-workforce-during-the-pandemic/

Gabriel, K. P., & Aguinis, H. (2022). How to prevent and combat employee burnout and create healthier workplaces during crises and beyond. *Business Horizons*, *65*(2), 183–192. https://doi.org/10.1016/j.bushor.2021.02.037

Gambuto, J. V. (2020). *Prepare for the ultimate gaslighting*. Forge Medium. https:// forge.medium.com/prepare-for-the-ultimate-gaslighting-6a8ce3f0a0e0

Gander, M. (2021). The hybrid career concept: Creating hybrid career pathways. *Career Development International*, *26*(7), 853–868. https://doi.org/10.1108/CDI-07–2020–0189

Garcia, H., & Miralles, F. (2016). *Ikigai: The Japanese secret to a long and happy life* (H. Cleary Trans.). Penguin.

Gardiner, R. A., Fox-Kirk, W., Elliott, C. J., & Stead, V. (2024). *Genderwashing in leadership: Policies, practices, and politics* [Manuscript submitted for publication]. Emerald Publishing, UK.

Garrison, D. R. (1997). Self-directed learning: Toward a comprehensive model. *Adult Education Quarterly*, *48*(1), 18–33. https://doi.org/10.1177/074171369704800103

Gedro, J. (2009). LGBT career development. *Advances in Developing Human Resources*, *11*(1), 54–66. https://doi.org/10.1177/1523422308328396

Gedro, J. (2017). *Identity, meaning, and subjectivity in career development: Evolving perspectives in human resources*. Springer.

Gedro, J. A., Cervero, R. M., & Johnson-Bailey, J. (2004). How lesbians learn to negotiate the heterosexism of corporate America. *Human Resource Development International, 7*(2), 181–195. https://doi.org/10.1080/1367886042000243790

Gedro, J. Allain, N., M., De-Souza, D., Dodson, L., & Mawn, M. V. (2020). Flattening the learning curve of leadership development: Reflections of five women higher education leaders during the Coronavirus pandemic of 2020. *Human Resource Development International, 23*(4), 395–405. https://doi.org/10.1080/13678868.2020.1779911

George, L., & Park, C. L. (2016). Meaning in life as comprehension, purpose, and mattering: Toward integration and new research questions. *Review of General Psychology, 20,* 205–220. https://doi.org/10.1037%2Fgpr0000077

George, T. J., Atwater, L. E., Maneethai, D., & Madera, J. M. (2022). Supporting the productivity and wellbeing of remote workers: Lessons from COVID-19. *Organizational Dynamics, 51*(2), 100869. https://doi.org/10.1016/j.orgdyn.2021.100869

Gerhardt, M., Nachemson-Ekwall, J., & Fogel, B. (2021). *Gentelligence: The revolutionary approach to leading an intergenerational workforce.* Rowman & Littlefield.

Ghosh, R. (2015). Mentoring – Is it failing women? *New Horizons in Adult Education and Human Resource Development, 27*(4), 70–74. https://doi.org/10.1002/nha3.20126

Ghosh, R., & Chaudhuri, S. (2023). Immigrant academic mothers negotiating ideal worker and mother norms during the COVID-19 pandemic: Duoethnography as a co-mentoring tool for transformative learning. *Management Learning, 54*(2), 152–176. https://doi.org/10.1177/13505076211062900

Ghosh, R., & Hutchins, H. M. (2022). *HRD perspectives on developmental relationships.* Springer International Publishing.

Gillet, R. (2015). Facebook is at the forefront of a radical workplace shift—And every business in America should take notice. *Business Insider.* https://www.businessinsider.com/facebook-parental-leave-policy-2015-8

Giroux, H. (2006). *America on the edge: Henry Giroux on politics, culture, and education.* Springer.

Glavin, K. W., & Savickas, M. L. (2010). Vocopher: The career collaboratory. *Journal of Career Assessment, 18*(4), 345–354. https://doi.org/10.1177/1069072710374568

Goasduff, L. (2021). *Gartner forecasts 51% of global knowledge workers will be remote by the end of 2021.* Gartner. https://www.gartner.com/en/newsroom/press-releases/2021-06-22-gartner-forecasts-51-percent-of-global-knowledge-workers-will-be-remote-by-2021

Goh, J., Pfeffer, J., & Zenios, S. A. (2016). The relationship between workplace stressors and mortality and health costs in the United States. *Management Science, 62*(2), 608–628. https://doi.org/10.1287/mnsc.2014.2115

Gold, M. (2018). The ABCs of L.G.B.T.Q.I.A.+. *The New York Times.* https://www.nytimes.com/2018/06/21/style/lgbtq-gender-language.html

Goldsmith, M. (2010). *What got you here won't get you there: How successful people become even more successful.* Profile Books.

Goodale, J. G., & Hall, D. T. (1976). Inheriting a career: The influence of sex, values, and parents. *Journal of Vocational Behavior, 8*(1), 19–30. https://doi.org/10.1016/0001-8791(76)90029-4/

Gottfredson, L. S. (2002). Gottfredson's theory of circumscription, compromise, and self-creation. In D. Brown (Ed.), *Career choice and development* (4th ed.) (pp. 85–148). Jossey-Bass.

Gragnano, A., Simbula, S., & Miglioretti, M. (2020). Work–life balance: Weighing the importance of work–family and work–health balance. *International Journal of Environmental Research and Public Health, 17*(3), 907. https://doi.org/10.3390/ijerph 17030907

Grant, P., & McGhee, P. (2021). Hedonic versus (true) eudaimonic well-being in organizations. In S. Dhiman (Ed.), *The Palgrave handbook of workplace well-being* (pp. 925–943). Palgrave Macmillan.

Grant, P., Arjoon, S., & McGhee, P. (2018). In pursuit of Eudaimonia: How virtue ethics captures the self-understandings and roles of corporate directors. *Journal of Business Ethics, 153*(2), 389–406. https://doi.org/10.1007/s10551-016-3432-z

Graves, R. L. (1977). Grace, in pedagogy. In R. P. Foehr & S. A. Schiller (Eds.), *The spiritual side of writing* (pp. 15–25). Boynton/Cook.

Green, L., & Burke, G. (2007). Beyond self-actualization. *Journal of Health and Human Services Administration, 30*(2), 116–128. https://www.jstor.org/stable/41288077

Greenberg, J., Pyszczynski, T., & Solomon, S. (1986). The causes and consequences of a need for self-esteem: A terror management theory. In R. F. Baumeister (Ed.), *Public self and private self* (pp. 189–212). Springer-Verlag.

Greer, T., Bierema, L. L., He, W., & Sim, E. (2023). Rebooting feminist research in HRD: Shifting from gender binary to gender diversity. *The International Journal of Human Resource Development: Practice, Policy and Research, 7*(2023), 69–82. https://www.calameo.com/read/0064269856f9b55896c30

Grier-Reed, T. L., & Conkel-Ziebell, J. L. (2009). Orientation to self and career: Constructivist theory and practice in the classroom. *Learning Assistance Review, 14*(1), 23–36. https://eric.ed.gov/?id=EJ839148

Grow, G. O. (1991). Teaching learners to be self-directed. *Adult Education Quarterly, 41*(3), 125–149. https://doi.org/10.1177/0001848191041003001

Guillebeau, C. (2016). *The happiness of pursuit: Finding the Quest that will bring purpose to your life.* Harmony.

Gulati, R. (2022). The great resignation or the great rethink? *Harvard Business Review.* https://hbr.org/2022/03/the-great-resignation-or-the-great-rethink

Gunz, H. (2009). The two solitudes: The vocational psychological/organisational gap, as seen from the organisational perspective. In A. Collin & W. Patton (Eds.), *Vocational psychological and organisational perspectives on career* (pp. 19–27). Sense.

Gupta, N. D., Smith, N., & Verner, M. (2008). The impact of Nordic countries' family friendly policies on employment, wages, and children. *Review of Economics of the Household, 6*(1), 65–89. https://doi.org/10.1007/s11150–007–9023–0

Haan, K. (2023). Remote work statistics and trends in 2023. *Forbes Advisor.* https://www.forbes.com/advisor/business/remote-work-statistics/

Haegele, J. A., & Hodge, S. (2016). Disability discourse: Overview and critiques of the medical and social models. *Quest, 68*(2), 193–206. https:// doi .org/ 10 .1080/ 00336297.2016.1143849

Hall, D. T. (1976). *Careers in organizations.* Goodyear.

Hall, D. T. (1996). Protean careers of the 21st century. *The Academy of Management Executive, 10*(4), 8–16. https://doi.org/10.5465/ame.1996.3145315

Hall, D. T. (2002). The protean career identity and attitudes. In D. T. Hall (Ed.), *Careers in and out of organizations* (pp. 169–204). Sage.

Hall, D. T., & Moss, J. E. (1998). The new protean career contract: Helping organizations and employees adapt. *Organizational Dynamics, 26*(1), 22–37. https://doi.org/ 10.1016/S0090–2616(98)90012–2

Hammer, E. (2021). HRD interventions that offer a solution to work-life conflict. *Advances in Developing Human Resources, 23*(2), 142–152. https://doi.org/10.1177/1523422321991192

Hansen, J. C. (2013). A person-environment fit approach to cultivating meaning. In B. Dik, Z. Byrne, & M. Steger (Eds.), *Purpose and meaning in the workplace* (pp. 37–56). APA.

Hardy, L. (1990). *The fabric of this world: Inquiries into calling, career choice, and the design of human work*. Eerdmans.

Harris, D. A. (2022). Women, work, and opportunities: From neoliberal to feminist mentoring. *Sociology Compass, 16*(3), e12966. https://doi.org/10.1111/soc4.12966

Hartung, P. (2021). Life-span, life-space career theory and counseling. In S. D. Brown & R. W. Lent (Eds.), *Career development and counseling: Putting theory and research to work* (pp. 95–127). John Wiley & Sons.

Hartung, P. J., & Taber, B. J. (2013). Career construction: Heeding the call of the heart. In B. Dik, Z. Byrne, & M. Steger (Eds.), *Purpose and meaning in the workplace* (pp. 17–36). APA.

Harwood, M., & Heydemann, S. (2019). *By the numbers: Where do pregnant women work*. National Women's Law Center. https://nwlc.org/wp-content/uploads/2019/08/Pregnant-Workers-by-the-Numbers-v3–1.pdf

Hastwell, C. (2023). *Engaging and managing a multigenerational workforce*. Great Place To Work. https://www.greatplacetowork.com/resources/blog/engaging-and-managing-multigenerational-workforce

Haughey, D. (2014). *A brief history of SMART goals*. Project Smart website. https://www.projectsmart.co.uk/smart-goals/brief-history-of-smart-goals.php

Headlee, C. (2020). *Do nothing: How to break away from overworking, overdoing, and underliving*. Harmony.

Hegewisch, A., & Mefferd, E. (2022). *Women make gains in men-dominated jobs, but still lag behind in COVID-19 recovery*. Institute for Women's Policy Research. https://iwpr.org/iwpr-publications/quick-figure/women-make-gains-in-men-dominated-jobs-but-still-lag-behind-in-covid-19-recovery/

Helgesen, S., & Goldsmith, M. (2018). *How women rise: Break the 12 habits holding you back*. Random House.

Helms, B., & Roussos, P. (2021). *How social entrepreneurship can advance women's economic empowerment: Toward a more inclusive and equitable economic system*. Miller Center for Social Entrepreneurship. https://www.millersocent.org/wp-content/uploads/2021/10/WEE_Whitepaper_Final.pdf

Henderson, S. J. (2000a). Career happiness: More fundamental than job satisfaction. *Career Planning and Adult Development Journal, 15*(4), 5–10.

Henderson, S. J. (2000b). Follow your bliss: A process for career happiness. *Journal of Counseling and Development, 78*(3), 305–315. https://doi.org/10.1002/j.1556-6676.2000.tb01912.x

Henry, A. (2013). *Learn to manage up to keep your boss happy and off your back*. LifeHacker. https://lifehacker.com/learn-to-manage-up-to-keep-your-boss-happy-and-off-your-5988523

Henry, A. (2019). How to succeed when you're marginalized or discriminated against at work. *The New York Times*. https://www.nytimes.com/2019/10/01/smarter-living/productivity-without-privilege-discrimination-work.html

Heppner, M. J. (1998). The career transitions inventory: Measuring internal resources in adulthood. *Journal of Career Assessment, 6*(2), 135–145. https://doi.org/10.1177/106907279800600202

Heppner, M. J., & Scott, A. B. (2004). From whence we came: The role of social class in our families of origin. *The Counseling Psychologist 32*(4), 596–602. https://doi .org/10.1177/0011000004265670

Herr, E. L. (2001). Career development and its practice: A historical perspective. *The Career Development Quarterly, 49*(3), 196–211. https://doi.org/10.1002/j.2161–0045 .2001.tb00562.x

Herr, E. L., & Cramer, S. H. (1998). *Career guidance and counselling through the lifespan* (2nd ed.). Scott, Foresman & Co.

Hesketh, B., Elmslie, S., & Kaldor, W. (1990). Career compromise: An alternative account to Gottfredson's theory. *Journal of Counseling Psychology, 37*(1), 49–56. https://psycnet.apa.org/doi/10.1037/0022–0167.37.1.49

Hewison, K. (2016). Precarious work. In S. Edgell, H. Gottfried, & E. Granter (Eds.), *The SAGE handbook of the sociology of work and employment* (pp. 428–443). Sage Publications.

Hikmawan, R., Suherman, A., Fauzi, A., & Mubarak, I. (2020). Ikigai as student high order literacy skills intrinsic motivation learning template. *Journal of Education Research and Evaluation, 4*(1), 98–102. https://doi.org/10.23887/jere.v4i1.22449

Hill, P. L., & Turiano, N. A. (2014). Purpose in life as a predictor of mortality across adulthood. *Psychological Science, 25*, 1482–1486. https://doi.org/10.1177/09567 97614 531799.

Hirschi, A., & Pang, D. (2021). Career development of older workers and retirees. In S. D. Brown & R. W. Lent (Eds.), *Career development and counseling: Putting theory and research to work* (pp. 437–469). John Wiley & Sons.

Hite, L. M., & McDonald, K. S. (2020). Careers after COVID-19: Challenges and changes. *Human Resource Development International, 23*(4), 427–437. https://doi .org/10.1080/13678868.2020.1779576

Hobfoll, S. E. (1989). Conservation of resources: A new attempt at conceptualizing stress. *American Psychologist, 44*(3), 513–524. https://doi.org/10.1037/0003–066X .44.3.513

Holland, J. L. (1959). A theory of vocational choice. *Journal of Counseling Psychology, 6*(1), 35–45. https://doi.org/10.1037/h0040767

Holland, J. L. (1985). *Manual for the vocational preference inventory.* Psychological Assessment Resources, Inc.

Holland, J. L. (1997). *Making vocational choices: A theory of vocational personalities and work environments* (3rd ed.). Prentice-Hall.

Holland, J. L., & Messer, M. A. (2013). *Self-directed search form R* (5th ed.). PAR.

Hollingshead, A. A. (1975). *Four-factor index of social status* [Unpublished manuscript]. Yale University. https://sociology.yale.edu/sites/default/files/files/yjs_fall _2011.pdf#page=21

Hoobler, J. M., Masterson, C. R., Nkomo, S. M., & Michel, E. J. (2018). The business case for women leaders: Meta-analysis, research critique, and path forward. *Journal of Management, 44*(6), 2473–2499. https://doi.org/10.1177/0149206316628643

hooks, b. (1994). *Teaching to transgress: Education as the practice of freedom.* Routledge.

Hopson, B., & Adams, J. (1977). Toward an understanding of transition: Defining some boundaries of transition. In N. J. Adams, J. Hayes, & B. Hopson (Eds.), *Transition: Understanding and managing personal change* (pp. 57–69). Allenhold and Osmund.

Hoskin, R. A., & Whiley, L. A. (2023). Femme-toring: Leveraging critical femininities and femme theory to cultivate alternative approaches to mentoring. *Gender, Work & Organization, 30*(4), 1317–1333. https://doi.org/10.1111/gwao.12984

Houle, C. O. (1961). *The inquiring mind.* University of Wisconsin Press.

Houtenville, A., & Kalargyrou, V. (2015). Employers' perspectives about employing people with disabilities: A comparative study across industries. *Cornell Hospitality Quarterly, 56*(2), 168–179. https://doi.org/10.1177/1938965514551633

Howarth, J. (2023). *How many people own smartphones? (2023–2028).* Exploding Topics. https://explodingtopics.com/blog/smartphone-stats

Hughes, C. (2018). Conclusion: Diversity intelligence as a core of diversity training and leadership development. *Advances in Developing Human Resources, 20*(3), 370–378.

Hutchins, H. M., & Ghosh, R. (2022). Situating developmental relationships within HRD research and practice. In R. Ghosh & H. M. Hutchins (Eds.), *HRD perspectives on developmental relationships: Connecting and relating at work* (pp. 1–11). Palgrave Macmillan.

Ibarra, H. (1995). Race, opportunity, and diversity of social circles in managerial networks. *Academy of Management Journal, 38*(3), 673–703. https://doi.org/10.5465/256742

Inkson, K. (2002). Thinking creatively about careers: The use of metaphor. In M. Peiperl, M. B. Arthur, R. Goffee, & N. Anand (Eds.), *Career creativity: Explorations in the re-making of work* (pp. 15–34). Oxford University Press.

Inkson, K. (2004). Images of career: Nine key metaphors. *Journal of Vocational Behavior, 65*(1), 96–111. https://doi.org/10.1016/S0001–8791(03)00053–8

Inkson, K., & Arthur, M. B. (2001). How to be a successful career capitalist. *Organizational dynamics, 30*(1), 48–61. https://doi.org/10.1016/S0090–2616(01)00040–7

International Labour Organization. (n.d.). *Decent work.* International Labour Organization. https://www.ilo.org/global/topics/decent-work/lang--en/index.htm

Irving, D. (2016). *Waking up white: And finding myself in the story of race.* Novel Audio.

Isaacs, W. N. (2001). Toward an action theory of dialogue. *International Journal of Public Administration, 24*(7–8), 709–748. https://doi.org/10.1081/PAD-100104771

Ivey, G. W., & Dupré, K. E. (2022). Workplace mentorship: A critical review. *Journal of Career Development, 49*(3), 714–729. https://doi.org/10.1177/08948453209577

Jaffe, S. (2021). *Work won't love you back: How devotion to our jobs keeps us exploited, exhausted, and alone.* Bold Type Books.

Jarr, K., & Hunderman, J. (2021). *Storytelling: Connecting culture, creativity, and career development in the classroom.* National Career Development Association (NCDA). https://www.ncda.org/aws/NCDA/pt/sd/news_article/401424/_PARENT/CC_layout_details/false

Jobvite. (2018). *2018 Job seeker nation study: Researching the candidate-recruiter relationship.* Jobvite. https://www.jobvite.com/wp-content/uploads/2018/04/2018_Job_Seeker_Nation_Study.pdf

Johnson, L. (2015). *Wall-Mart put me through hell: Inside the retailers pregnancy discrimination horror.* Salon. https://www.salon.com/2015/04/06/walmart_put_me_through_hell_inside_the_retailers_pregnancy_discrimination_horror/

Jones, L. K., & Jones, J. W. (2016). *Career well-being: Defined and strengthened.* NCDA. https://www.ncda.org/aws/NCDA/pt/sd/news_article/118635/_PARENT/CC_layout_details/false

Jourdan, L. (2021). Talk about privilege at work. *Harvard Business Review.* https://hbr.org/2021/08/talk-about-privilege-at-work

Juntunen, C. L., Ali, S. R., & Pietrantonio, K. P. (2021). Social class and poverty: A renewed focus in career development. In S. D. Brown & R. W. Lent (Eds.), *Career* development and counseling: Putting theory and research to work* (pp. 341–373). John Wiley & Sons.

Jyrkinen, M. (2014). Women managers, careers and gendered ageism. *Scandinavian Journal of Management, 30*, 175–185. https://doi.org/10.1016/j.scaman.2013.07.002

Kalleberg, A. L. (2012). Job quality and precarious work: Clarifications, controversies, and challenges. *Work and Occupations, 39*(4), 427–448. https://doi.org/10.1177/0730888412460533

Kamiya, M. (1966). Ikigai ni tsuite. Misuzu Shobō.

Kanter, R. M. (1977). *Men and women of the corporation.* Basic Books.

Kelly, E. L., Moen, P., Oakes, J. M., Fan, W., Okechukwu, C., Davis, K. D., Hammer, L., Kossek, E., King, R. B., Hanson, G., Mierzwa, F., & Casper, L. M. (2014). Changing work and work-family conflict: Evidence from the work, family, and health network. *American Sociological Review, 79*(3), 485–516. https://doi.org/10.1177/0003122414531435

Ketkar, S., Puri, R., & Chowdhury, S. R. (2021). Bridging the gender pay gap. *Empirical Economics, 61*(2021), 2237–2263. https://doi.org/10.1007/s00181–020–01950-z

Kim, S., & McLean, G. N. (2012). Global talent management: Necessity, challenges, and the roles of HRD. *Advances in Developing Human Resources, 14*(4), 566–585. https://doi.org/10.1177/1523422312455610

Kinnunen, U., Rantanen, J., Mauno, S., & Peeters, M. (2014). Work-family interaction. In M. Peeters, J. de Jonge, & T. Taris (Eds.), *An introduction to contemporary work psychology* (pp. 267–290). Wiley-Blackwell.

Klotz, A. (2022). *The great resignation is still here, but whether it stays is up to leaders.* The Forum Network. https://www.oecd-forum.org/posts/the-great-resignation-is-still-here-but-whether-it-stays-is-up-to-leaders

Knight, R. (2017). 7 practical ways to reduce bias in your hiring process. *Harvard Business Review.* https://hbr.org/2017/06/7-practical-ways-to-reduce-bias-in-your-hiring-process

Knowles, M. S. (1975). *Self-directed learning: A guide for learners and teachers.* Association Press.

Knowles, M. S. (1980). *The modern practice of adult education: From pedagogy to andragogy* (2nd ed.). Cambridge Books.

Knowles, M. S. (1984). *Andragogy in action: Applying modern principles of adult learning.* Jossey-Bass.

Kolb, D. A. (1984). *Experiential learning.* Eaglewood Cliffs.

Korten, D. (2020). Why coronavirus is humanity's wakeup call. *YES! Magazine.* https://www.indianz.com/News/2020/03/19/david-korten-why-coronavirus-is-humanity.asp

Kossek, E., Gettings, P., & Misra, K. (2021). The future of flexibility at work. *Harvard Business Review.* https://hbr.org/2021/09/the-future-of-flexibility-at-work

Kramer, K. Z., Pak, S., & Park, S. Y. (2023). The effect of parental leave duration on early-career wage growth. *Human Resource Management Journal, 33*(1), 203–223. https://doi.org/10.1111/1748–8583.12428

Krishnamurti, J. (1992). *On right livelihood.* Harper San Francisco.

Kudo, A. (2018). *My little ikigai journal: Journey into the Japanese secret to living a long, happy, purpose-filled life.* Castle Point Books.

Kumano, M. (2006). The structure of ikigai and similar concepts. *Japanese Journal of Health Psychology, 19*(1), 56–66. https://doi.org/10.11560/jahp.19.1_56

Kumano, M. (2012). *Ikigai-keisei-no-shinrigaku* [A psychology of ikigai development]. Kazamashobo.

Law, B. (1981). Community interaction: A "mid-range" focus for theories of career development in young adults. *British Journal of Guidance and Counselling*, *9*(2), 142–158. https://doi.org/10.1080/03069888108258210

Lawrence, J. (1991). Action learning-a questioning approach. In A. Mumford (Ed.), *Gower handbook of management development* (pp. 214–247). Gower.

Lawrence, R. L. (Ed.) (2012). *Bodies of knowledge: Embodied learning in adult education.* John Wiley & Sons.

Lea, H. D., & Leibowitz, Z. B. (1992). *Adult career development: Concepts, issues, and practices.* National Career Development Association, 5999 Stevenson Avenue, Alexandria, VA 22304.

Lean In (2020). *The state of Black women in corporate America.* Lean In. https://leanin .org/research/state-of-black-women-in-corporate-america

Lean In (2023). *Dealing with sexual harassment.* Lean In. https:// leanin .org/ sexual -harassment

Lee, M. Y., & Johnson-Bailey, J. (2004). Challenges to the classroom authority of women of color. *New Directions for Adult and Continuing Education*, *102*(2004), 55–64. https://doi.org/10.1002/ace.138

Lekas, H. M., Pahl, K., & Fuller Lewis, C. (2020). Rethinking cultural competence: Shifting to cultural humility. *Health Services Insights*, *13*, 1178632920970580. https://doi.org/10.1177/1178632920970580

Lent, R. W. (2013). Promoting meaning and purpose at work: A social-cognitive perspective. In B. Dik, Z. Byrne, & M. Steger (Eds.), *Purpose and meaning in the workplace* (pp. 151–170). APA.

Lent, R. W. (2021). Career development and counseling: A social cognitive framework. In S. D. Brown & R. W. Lent (Eds.), *Career development and counseling: Putting theory and research to work* (pp. 129–163). John Wiley & Sons.

Lent, R. W., & Brown, S. D. (1996). Applying social cognitive theory to career counseling: An introduction. *The Career Development Quarterly*, *44*(4), 307. https:// www .proquest .com/ scholarly -journals/ applying -social -cognitive -theory -career/ docview/219540302/se-2

Lent, R. W., & Brown, S. D. (2013). Understanding and facilitating career development in the 21st century. In S. D. Brown & R. W. Lent (Eds.), *Career development and counseling: Putting theory and research to work* (pp. 1–26). Wiley.

Lent, R. W., & Brown, S. D. (2021). Promoting satisfaction and effective performance at work. In S. D. Brown & R. W. Lent (Eds.), *Career development and counseling: Putting theory and research to work* (pp. 733–767). John Wiley & Sons.

Lent, R. W., Brown, S. D., & Hackett, G. (1994). Toward a unifying social cognitive theory of career and academic interest, choice, and performance. *Journal of Vocational Behavior*, *45*(1), 79–122. https://doi.org/10.1006/jvbe.1994.1027

Lent, R. W., Brown, S. D., & Hackett, G. (2002). Social cognitive career theory. In D. Brown and Associates (Eds.), *Career choice and development* (4th ed.), (pp. 255–311). Jossey-Bass.

LePage, B. (2022). *Part-time workers are facing heightened uncertainty during COVID—and most are women.* National Women's Law Center. https:// nwlc .org/ resource/part-time-workers-factsheet/

Levinson, D. J. (1978). *The seasons of a man's life.* Random House Digital.

Levinson, D. J., Darrow, C. M., Klein, E. B., Levinson, M. H., & McKee, B. (1974). The psychosocial development of men in early adulthood and the mid-life transition. *Life History Research in Psychopathology*, *3*(1), 243–248.

Lewin, K. (1947). Frontiers in group dynamics. In D. Cartwright (Ed.), *Field theory in social science*. London: Social Science Paperbacks.

Lewis, C. S. (1947). *The abolition of man*. Oxford University Press.

Lewis, S., & Cooper, C. (2005). *Work-life integration: Case studies of organisational change*. John Wiley & Sons.

Lin, Y. C., & Chen, A. S. Y. (2021). Experiencing career plateau on a committed career journey: A boundary condition of career stages. *Personnel Review*, *50*(9), 1797–1819. https://doi.org/10.1108/PR-03–2020–0192

Lindeman, E. C. (1961). *The meaning of adult education in the United States*. Harvest House.

Liu, S., Huang, J. L., & Wang, M. (2014). Effectiveness of job search interventions: A meta-analytic review. *Psychological Bulletin*, *140*(4), 1009. https:// doi .org/ 10 .1037/a0035923

Livelihood (n.d.). *The Buddha's advice to laypeople*. Livelihood. https://buddhasadvice .wordpress.com/livelihood/

Livingston, R. (2020). How to promote racial equity in the workplace. *Harvard Business Review*. https://hbr.org/2020/09/how-to-promote-racial-equity-in-the-workplace

Locke, E. A. (1976). The nature and causes of job satisfaction. In M. D. Dunnette & L. M. Hough (Eds.), *Handbook of industrial and organizational psychology* (2nd ed., Vol. 2) (pp. 1297–1349). Consulting Psychologists.

Logan, A. C., D'Adamo, C. R., & Prescott, S. L. (2023). The founder: Dispositional greed, showbiz, and the commercial determinants of health. *International Journal of Environmental Research and Public Health*, *20*(9), 5616. https://doi.org/10.3390/ ijerph20095616

Luceno, J. (2012). *Star wars: Darth plagueis*. Blanvalet.

Lysova, E., Fletcher, L., & Barpido, S. E. (2023). What makes work meaningful? *Harvard Business Review*. https://hbr.org/2023/07/what-makes-work-meaningful

Lytle, M. C., Clancy, M. E., Foley, P. F., & Cotter, E. W. (2015). Current trends in retirement: Implications for career counseling and vocational psychology. *Journal of Career Development*, *42*, 170–184. https://doi.org/10.1177/0894845314545785

Mainiero, L. A., & Sullivan, S. E. (2005). Kaleidoscope careers: An alternate explanation for the "opt-out" revolution. *Academy of Management Perspectives*, *19*(1), 106–123. https://doi.org/10.5465/ame.2005.15841962

Mallory, C., Sears, B., & Flores, A. R. (2022). *The role of sexual orientation and gender in workplace experiences of cisgender LGB employees*. UCLA Williams Institute School of Law. https://williamsinstitute.law.ucla.edu/wp-content/uploads/Bisexual-Workplace -Discrimination-Sep-2022.pdf

Marcroft, D. (2021). *A silenced workforce: Four in five employees feel colleagues aren't heard equally says research from the workforce institute at UKG*. UKG. https://www.ukg.com/about-us/newsroom/silenced-workforce-four-five-employees -feel-colleagues-arent-heard-equally-says

Marks, A. (2023). The Great Resignation in the UK–reality, fake news or something in between? *Personnel Review*, *52*(2), 408–414. https://doi.org/10.1108/PR-09–2022–0608

Marsick, V., & Watkins, K. (1990). *Informal and incidental learning: A new challenge for human resource developers*. Routledge & Kegan Paul.

Martin, W. (2004). *The best liberal quotes ever: Why the left is right*. Perseus Books Group.

Maslow, A. H. (1943). A theory of human motivation. *Psychological Review*, *50*, 370–396. https://doi.org/10.1037/h0054346

Maslow, A. H. (1971). *The farther reaches of human nature*. Viking Press.

McAdams, D. P. (1996). The stories we live by: Personal myths and the making of the self (5., 6. print. ed.). Guilford Press.

McCoy, D. L., Winkle-Wagner, R., & Luedke, C. L. (2015). Colorblind mentoring? Exploring white faculty mentoring of students of color. *Journal of Diversity in Higher Education, 8*(4), 225–242. https://doi.org/10.1037/a0038676

McDonald, K., & Hite, L. (2016). *Career development: A human resource development perspective* (1st ed.). Routledge.

McDonald, K., & Hite, L. (2020). *Career development: A human resource development perspective* (2nd ed.). Routledge.

McDonald, K. S., & Hite, L. M. (2023). *Career development: A human resource development perspective* (3rd ed.). Routledge.

McFadden, C. (2022). Implicit bias training is dead, long live implicit bias training: The evolving role of human resource development in combatting implicit bias within organisations. In P. Holland, T. Bartram, T. Garavan, & K. Grant (Eds.), *The Emerald handbook of work, workplaces and disruptive issues in HRM* (pp. 381–396). Emerald Publishing. https://doi.org/10.1108/978-1-80071-779-420221037

McLean, G. (2005). *Organization development: Principles, processes, performance.* Berrett-Koehler Publishers.

McMahon, M., & Arthur, N. (2018). Career development theory: Origins and history. In N. Arthur & M. McMahon (Eds.), *Contemporary theories of career development: International perspectives* (pp. 3–19). Routledge.

McNicholas, P., & Humphries, M. (2005). Decolonisation through critical career research and action: Maori women and accountancy. *Australian Journal of Career Development, 14*(1), 30–40. https://doi.org/10.1177/103841620501400106

McWhirter, E. H., & McWha-Hermann, I. (2021). Social justice and career development: Progress, problems, and possibilities. *Journal of Vocational Behavior, 126*, 103492. https://doi.org/10.1016/j.jvb.2020.103492

Medina, C., & Mahowald, L. (2023). *Discrimination and barriers to well-being: The state of the LGBTQI+ community in 2022.* Center For American Progress. https://www.americanprogress.org/article/discrimination-and-barriers-to-well-being-the-state-of-the-lgbtqi-community-in-2022/

Medina, C., Mahowald, L., & Khattar, R. (2022). *Fact sheet: LGBT workers in the labor market.* CAP 20. https://www.americanprogress.org/article/fact-sheet-lgbt-workers-in-the-labor-market/

Mendos, L. R., Botha, K., Lelis, R. C., López de la Peña, E., Savelev, I., & Tan, D. (2020). *State-sponsored homophobia report: Global legislation overview update.* ILGA World. https://ilga.org/state-sponsored-homophobia-report

Merriam, S. B., & Baumgartner, L. M. (2020). *Learning in adulthood: A comprehensive guide.* John Wiley & Sons.

Merriam, S. B., & Bierema, L. L. (2013). *Adult learning: Linking theory and practice.* John Wiley & Sons.

Meyerson, D. (2001). *Tempered radicals: How people use difference to inspire change at work.* Harvard Business School Press.

Meyerson, D. E. (2004). The tempered radicals: How employees push their companies—little by little—to be more socially responsible. *Stanford Social Innovation Review*, 14–23.

Meyerson, D. E., & Scully, M. A. (1995). Tempered radicalism and the politics of ambivalence and change. *Organization Science, 6*(5), 585–600. https://doi.org/10.1287/orsc.6.5.585

Mezirow, J. (1978). *Education for perspective transformation: Women's re-entry programs in community colleges.* Teachers College, Columbia University.

Mezirow, J. (1991). *Transformative dimensions of adult learning.* Jossey-Bass.

Miles, S. A. (2009). Succession planning: How everyone does it wrong. *Forbes.* https://www.forbes.com/2009/07/30/succession-planning-failures-leadership-governance-ceos.html

Miller, P., Parker, S., & Gillinson, S. (2004). *Disablism: How to tackle the last prejudice.* Demos.

Mitchell, K. E., Al Levin, S., & Krumboltz, J. D. (1999). Planned happenstance: Constructing unexpected career opportunities. *Journal of Counseling & Development, 77*(2), 115–124. https://doi.org/10.1002/j.1556–6676.1999.tb02431.x

Monaghan, C. H., & Isaac-Savage, E. P. (2022). Community, intersectionality, and social justice in critical HRD. In J. C. Collins & J. L. Callahan (Eds.), *The Palgrave handbook of critical human resource development* (pp. 307–323). Springer International Publishing.

Moody, J. (2013). *Faculty diversity: Removing the barriers.* Routledge.

Moody, J. (2015). *Rising above cognitive errors: Improving searches, evaluations, and decision making.* CreateSpace Independent Publishing Platform.

Moore, C., Gunz, H., & Hall, D. T. (2007). Tracing the historical roots of career theory in management and organization studies. In H. Gunz & M. Peiperl (Eds.), *Handbook of career studies* (pp. 13–38). Sage.

Morrison, A. M., White, R. P., & Van Velsor, E. (1987). *Breaking the glass ceiling: Can women reach the top of America's largest corporations?* Pearson Education.

Mulyo, I. A. (2023). Value chain analysis of McDonald. *Jurnal Ekonomi, 12*(02), 908–913. https://ejournal.seaninstitute.or.id/index.php/Ekonomi/article/view/1815

Murdock, M. (2020). *The heroine's journey workbook: A map for every woman's quest.* Shambhala Publications.

My Work Choice & Workplace Intelligence (2020). *The expansion of workplace flexibility: Building a better hourly workforce through benefits that matter.* Myworkchoice. https://myworkchoice.com/research2021/

Nakanishi, N. (1999). "Ikigai" in older Japanese people. *Age and Ageing, 28*(3), 323–324. https://doi.org/10.1093/ageing/28.3.323

National Center for Education Statistics [NCES] (n.d.). *Table 507.40: Participation rate of persons, 17 years old and over, in adult education during the previous 12 months by selected characteristics of participants: Selected years 1991–2005.* National Center for Educational Statistics: Digest of Education Statistics. https://nces.ed.gov/programs/digest/d19/tables/dt19_507.40.asp

National Center for Education Statistics [NCES] (2017). *Adult training and education: results from the National Household Education Surveys Program of 2016.* https://nces.ed.gov/pubsearch/pubsinfo.asp?pubid=2017103rev

National Women's Law Center (2023). *The lifetime wage gap, state by state.* National Women's Law Center. https://nwlc.org/resource/the-lifetime-wage-gap-state-by-state/

Nauta, M. M. (2021). Holland's theory of vocational choice and adjustment. In S. D. Brown & R. W. Lent (Eds.), *Career development and counseling: Putting theory and research to work* (pp. 55–82). John Wiley & Sons.

Nelson, J. L., & Vallas, S. P. (2021). Race and inequality at work: An occupational perspective. *Sociology Compass, 15*(10), e12926. https://doi.org/10.1111/soc4.12926

Ng, E., & Stanton, P. (2023). The great resignation: Managing people in a post COVID-19 pandemic world. *Personnel Review, 52*(2), 401–407. https://doi.org/10.1108/PR-03–2023–914

Ng, T. W. H., & Feldman, D. C. (2010). The relationships of age with job attitudes: A meta-analysis. *Personnel Psychology, 63*, 677–718. https://doi.org/10.1111/j.1744-6570.2010.01184.x

Ng, T. W. H., & Feldman, D. C. (2012). Evaluating six common stereotypes about older workers with meta-analytical data. *Personnel Psychology, 65*, 821–858. https://doi.org/10.1111/peps.12003

Nice, R. (2023). How to practice reflective thinking. *Harvard Business Review.* https://hbr.org/2023/08/how-to-practice-reflective-thinking#:~:text=Finding%20time%20for%20personal%20reflection,Give%20it%20a%20try

Nicolaides, A. (2023). *Generative knowing: Principles, methods, and dispositions of an emerging adult learning theory*. Stylus Publishing, LLC.

Nilles, J. (1975). Telecommunications and organizational decentralization. *IEEE Transactions on Communications, 23*(10), 1142–1147. https://doi.org/10.1109/TCOM.1975.1092687

Oates, W. E. (1971). *Confessions of a workaholic: The facts about work addiction*. World Publishing Company.

OECD (n.d.). *Key trends: The future workforce is more age divers and offers large potential*. OECD iLibrary. https://www.oecd-ilibrary.org/sites/237dd702-en/index.html?itemId=/content/component/237dd702-en

OECD (2020). *Promoting an age-inclusive workforce: Living, learning and earning longer*. OECD Publishing. https://doi.org/10.1787/59752153-en

OECD Forum (2017). *Five-generation workplace, from Baby Boomers to Generation Z: A look back at the OECD Forum 2017 session*. OCED. https://www.oecd-forum.org/posts/20444-five-generation-workplace-from-baby-boomers-to-generation-z

Olson, M. H. (1983). Remote office work: Changing work patterns in space and time. *Communications of the ACM, 26*(3), 182–187. https://doi.org/10.1145/358061.358068

O'Malley, C. (2023). *EEOC lawsuits alleging disability discrimination spiked 77% in just-completed fiscal year*. ALM Law.com. https://www.law.com/corpcounsel/2023/10/16/eeoc-lawsuits-alleging-disability-discrimination-spiked-77-in-just-completed-fiscal-year/?slreturn=20240026181953

O*Net OnLine (n.d.). Browse by work values. https://www.onetonline.org/find/descriptor/browse/1.B.2/

Osborn, D. S. (2012). An international discussion about cross-cultural career assessment. *International Journal for Educational and Vocational Guidance, 12*, 5–16. https://doi.org/10.1007/s10775-012-9220-0

Ozimek, A. (2021). *Future workforce report 2021: How remote work is changing businesses forever*. Upwork. https://www.upwork.com/research/future-workforce-report

Parris, T. (2021). *White men are not the enemy ... Diversity is not about replacing one power with another*. Inventum Group. https://www.inventum-group.com/blog/2021/11/white-men-are-not-the-enemy-dot-dot-dot-diversity-is-not-about-replacing-one-power-with-another?source=google.com

Parsons, F. (1909). *Choosing a vocation*. Houghton-Mifflin.

Parviainen, J., Koski, A., & Torkkola, S. (2021). "Building a ship while sailing it." Epistemic humility and the temporality of non-knowledge in political decision-making on COVID-19. *Social Epistemology, 35*(3), 232–244. https://doi.org/10.1080/02691728.2021.1882610

Patton, W. (2000). Changing career: The role of values. In A. Collin & R. A. Young (Eds.), *The future of career* (pp. 69–82). Cambridge University Press.

Patton, W. (2019). *Career development as a partner in nation building Australia: Origins, history and foundations for the future.* Brill.

Payscale (2023). *2023 Gender pay gap report.* Payscale. https://www.payscale.com/research-and-insights/gender-pay-gap/

Peavy, R. V. (1998). *Sociodynamic counseling: A constructivist perspective.* Trafford.

Peiperl, M., & Baruch, Y. (1997). Back to square zero: The post-corporate career. *Organizational Dynamics, 25*(4), 7–22. https://doi.org/10.1016/S0090–2616(97)90033–4

Peralta, P. (2023). *What the OpenAI saga says about employee power in the workplace.* Ebn. https://www.benefitnews.com/news/openai-sam-altman-and-the-power-of-employees

Perez, G., Duffy, R. D., Kim, H. J., & Kim, T. (2023). Social mobility and vocational outcomes: A psychology of working perspective. *Journal of Career Assessment, 31*(4), 794–811. https://doi.org/10.1177/10690727231161380

Perry, E. (2021). *What is ikigai and how can it change my life?* BetterUp. https://www.betterup.com/blog/what-is-ikigai

Pfeffer, J. (2018). *Dying for a paycheck: How modern management harms employee health and company performance—and what we can do about it.* HarperCollins.

Phan, J. T. (2021). What's the right way to find a mentor? *Harvard Business Review.* https://hbr.org/2021/03/whats-the-right-way-to-find-a-mentor

Piacenza, J. (2019). *On gender workplace imbalances, man's myth is woman's reality.* Morning Consult. https://pro.morningconsult.com/articles/on-gender-workplace-imbalances-mans-myth-is-womans-reality

Pillay, A. L. (2020). Prioritising career guidance and development services in post-apartheid South Africa. *African Journal of Career Development, 2*(1), 1–5. https://hdl.handle.net/10520/EJC-2092f9c9b3

Pillen, H., McNaughton, D., & Ward, P. R. (2020). Critical consciousness development: A systematic review of empirical studies. *Health Promotion International, 35*(6), 1519–1530. https://doi.org/10.1093/heapro/daz125

Plaut, V. C., Thomas, K. M., Hurd, K., & Romano, C. A. (2018). Do color blindness and multiculturalism remedy or foster discrimination and racism? *Current Directions in Psychological Science, 27*(3), 200–206. https://doi.org/10.1177/0963721418766068

Plimmer, G., Smith, M., Duggan, M., & Englert, P. (2000). Career adaptability, well-being, and possible selves. *Career Planning and Adult Development Journal, 15*(4), 83–92. https://eric.ed.gov/?id=EJ606061

Pope, M. (2000). A brief history of career counseling in the United States. *The Career Development Quarterly, 48*(3), 194–211. https://doi.org/10.1002/j.2161-0045.2000.tb00286.x

Procknow, G., & Rocco, T. S. (2016). The unheard, unseen, and often forgotten: An examination of disability in the human resource development literature. *Human Resource Development Review, 15*(4), 379–403. https://doi.org/10.1177/1534484316671194

Project Implicit (n.d.). *Preliminary information.* Harvard University. https://implicit.harvard.edu/implicit/takeatest.html

Pulakos, E. D. (2004). *Performance management: A roadmap for developing, implementing and evaluating performance management systems* (pp. 1–42). SHRM Foundation.

Purdie-Vaughns, V., & Eibach, R. P. (2008). Intersectional invisibility: The distinctive advantages and disadvantages of multiple subordinate-group identities. *Sex Roles, 59*(5–6), 377–391. https://doi.org/10.1007/s11199–008–9424–4

PwC (2021). *PwC pulse survey: Next in work.* PwC. https://www.pwc.com/us/en/library/pulse-survey/future-of-work.html

Quinn, R. E., & Thakor, A. V. (2018). Creating a purpose-driven organization. *Harvard Business Review.* https://hbr.org/2018/07/creating-a-purpose-driven-organization

Ramdeo, J. (2023). Black women educators' stories of intersectional invisibility: Experiences of hindered careers and workplace psychological harm in school environments. *Educational Review*, Advance Online Publication. https://doi.org/10.1080/00131911.2023.2217358

Rasool, S. F., Wang, M., Tang, M., Saeed, A., & Iqbal, J. (2021). How toxic workplace environment effects the employee engagement: The mediating role of organizational support and employee wellbeing. *International Journal of Environmental Research and Public Health, 18*(5), 2294. https://doi.org/10.3390/ijerph18052294

Rasul, T., Nair, S., Kalendra, D., Robin, M., de Oliveira Santini, F., Ladeira, W. J., Sun, M., Day, I., Rather, R. A., & Heathcote, L. (2023). The role of ChatGPT in higher education: Benefits, challenges, and future research directions. *Journal of Applied Learning and Teaching, 6*(1). https://doi.org/10.37074/jalt.2023.6.1.35

Revans, R. (2017). *ABC of action learning.* Routledge.

Reynolds, A. L. (2022). Grasping at the root: Transforming counseling psychology. *The Counseling Psychologist, 50*(8), 1126–1149. https://doi.org/10.1177/00110000221125419

Richardson, M. S. (1993). Work in people's lives: A location for counseling psychologists. *Journal of Counseling Psychology, 40*(4), 425. https://doi.org/10.1037/0022-0167.40.4.425

Rifkin, J. (1995). *The end of work: The decline of the global labor force and the dawn on the post-market era.* Putnam Publishing Group.

Rittel, H. W. J., & Webber, M. M. (1973). Dilemmas in a general theory of planning. *Policy Sciences, 4*(2), 155–169. https://doi.org/10.1007/BF01405730

Roberts, K. (2009). Opportunity structures then and now. *Journal of Education and Work, 22*(5), 355–368. https://doi.org/10.1080/13639080903453987

Robertson, P. J., Hooley, T., & McCash, P. (Eds.) (2021). *The Oxford handbook of career development.* Oxford University Press.

Rocco, T. S., & Fornes, S. (2010). Perspectives on disability in adult and continuing education. In A. Rose, C. Kasworm, & J. Ross-Gordon (Eds.), *Handbook of adult and continuing education* (pp. 379–388). Sage.

Rock, A. D., & Garavan, T. N. (2006). Reconceptualizing developmental relationships. *Human Resource Development Review, 5*(3), 330–354. https://doi.org/10.1177/1534484306290227

Rolfes, E. (2014). *Maya Angelou, renaissance woman, dies at 86.* PBS. https://www.pbs.org/newshour/arts/maya-angelou-renaissance-woman-dies-86

Rosen, H. E., & Kuehlwein, K. T. (1996). *Constructing realities: Meaning-making perspectives for psychotherapists.* Jossey-Bass/Wiley.

Rosenberg, J. (2022). *Workers got fed up. Bosses got scared. This is how the Big Quit happened.* Mother Jones. https://www.motherjones.com/politics/2022/01/record-quits-great-resignation-labor-workers-pandemic/

Rosenfield, J., Oswalt, M. M., & Denice, P. (2023). The law vs. salary secrecy. *Business Insider.* https://www.businessinsider.com/pay-transparency-laws-fail-salary-wages-sharing-taboo-income-employees-2023-5?r=US&IR=T

Rossiter, M., & Clark, M. C. (2007). *Narrative and the practice of adult education.* Krieger Publishing Company.

Ryan, M. K., & Haslam, S. A. (2005). The glass cliff: Evidence that women are over-represented in precarious leadership positions. *British Journal of Management, 16*(2), 81–90. https://doi.org/10.1111/j.1467–8551.2005.00433.x

Saad, L. (2020). *Me and white supremacy: Combat racism, change the world, and become a good ancestor.* Sourcebooks.

Sartore, M., Buisine, S., Ocnarescu, I., & Joly, L. R. (2023). An integrated cognitive-motivational model of Ikigai (Purpose in Life) in the workplace. *Europe's Journal of Psychology, 19*(4), 387–400. https://doi.org/10.5964/ejop.9943

Savickas, M. L. (1993). Career counseling in the postmodern era. *Journal of Cognitive Psychotherapy, 7*(3), 205–215. https://doi.org/10.1891/0889–8391.7.3.205

Savickas, M. L. (1997). Career adaptability: An integrative construct for life-span, life-space theory. *The Career Development Quarterly, 45*(3), 247–259. https://doi.org/10.1002/j.2161–0045.1997.tb00469.x

Savickas, M. L. (2000). Renovating the psychology of careers for the twenty-first century. In A. Collin & R. A. Young (Eds.), *The future of career* (pp. 53–68). Cambridge University Press.

Savickas, M. L. (2021). Career construction theory and counseling model. In S. D. Brown & R. W. Lent (Eds.), *Career development and counseling: Putting theory and research to work* (pp. 165–199). John Wiley & Sons.

Savickas, M. L., & Porfeli, E. J. (2012). Career adapt-abilities scale: Construction, reliability, and measurement equivalence across 13 countries. *Journal of Vocational Behavior, 80*(3), 661–673. https://doi.org/10.1016/j.jvb.2012.01.011

Savickas, M., & Walsh, W. B. (1996). *Handbook of career counseling theory and practice.* Davies-Black Publishing.

Savickas, M. L., Nota, L., Rossier, J., Dauwalder, J. P., Duarte, M. E., Guichard, J., Soresi, S., Van Esbroeck, R., & Van Vianen, A. E. (2009). Life designing: A paradigm for career construction in the 21st century. *Journal of vocational behavior, 75*(3), 239–250. https://doi.org/10.1016/j.jvb.2009.04.004

Scherger, S. (2021). Flexibilizing the retirement transition: Why, how and for whom? Conceptual clarifications, institutional arrangements and potential consequences. *Frontiers in Sociology, 6*, 734985. https://doi.org/10.3389/fsoc.2021.734985

Schlossberg, N. K. (1984). The midlife woman as student. In G. Baruch & J. Brooks-Gunn (Eds.), *Women in midlife* (pp. 315–339). Springer.

Schlossberg, N. K. (2011). The challenge of change: The transition model and its applications. *Journal of Employment Counseling, 48*(4), 159–162. https://doi.org/10.1002/j.2161–1920.2011.tb01102.x

Schneider, M. (2023). *The Census Bureau sees an older, more diverse America in 2100 in three immigration scenarios.* AP. https://apnews.com/article/growth-population-demographics-race-hispanic-f563ebc4537f83792f3f91ba5d7cdade

Schön, D. A. (1983). *The reflective practitioner: How professionals think in action.* Temple Smith.

Schön, D. A. (1987). *Educating the reflective practitioner: Toward a new design for teaching and learning in the professions.* Jossey-Bass.

Schultheiss, D. E. P. (2007). The emergence of a relational cultural paradigm for vocational psychology. *International Journal for Educational and Vocational Guidance, 7*, 191–201. https://doi.org/10.1007/s10775–007–9123–7

Schultheiss, D. E. (2021). The role of gender in career development. In S. D. Brown & R. W. Lent (Eds.), *Career development and counseling: Putting theory and research to work* (pp. 201–307). John Wiley & Sons.

Schulz, R., & Eden, J. (Eds.) (2016). *Families caring for an aging America.* National Academies of Sciences, Engineering and Medicine. The National Academies Press. https://doi.org/10.17226/23606

SCORE (2021). *The great resignation.* SCORE. https://www.score.org/infographic-great-resignation

Scott, S. (2004). *Fierce conversations (revised and updated): Achieving success at work and in life one conversation at a time.* Penguin.

Sealy, R. H., & Singh, V. (2010). The importance of role models and demographic context for senior women's work identity development. *International Journal of Management Reviews, 12*(3), 284–300. https://doi.org/10.1111/j.1468–2370.2009.00262.x

Sears, B., Mallory, C., Flores, A. R., & Conron, K. J. (2021). LGBT people's experiences of workplace discrimination and harassment. The Williams Institute. https://williamsinstitute.law.ucla.edu/publications/lgbt-workplace-discrimination/

Sheehy, G. (1995). *New passages: Mapping your life across time.* Random House.

Shoukry, H. (2016). Coaching for social change. In T. Bachkirova, G. Spence, & D. Drake (Eds.), *The SAGE handbook of coaching* (pp. 176–194). Sage.

Shrider, E. A., Kollar, M., Chen, F., & Semega, J. (2021). *Income and poverty in the United States: 2020: Current population reports.* US Census Bureau. https://www.census.gov/content/dam/Census/library/publications/2021/demo/p60–273.pdf

Shuck, B., & Rose, K. (2013). Reframing employee engagement within the context of meaning and purpose: Implications for HRD. *Advances in Developing Human Resources, 15*(4), 341–355. https://doi.org/10.1177/1523422313503235

Sim, E., & Bierema, L. L. (2023a). Infusing intersectional pedagogy into adult education and human resource development graduate education. *Adult Education Quarterly,* Advance Online Publication. https://doi.org/10.1177/07417136231198049

Sim, E., & Bierema, L. L. (2023b). Intersectional leadership in the organization: A systematic literature review and conceptual model. *Academy of Management Proceedings, 2023*(1), 16161. https://doi.org/10.5465/AMPROC.2023.16161abstract

Sim, E., & Jeong, S. (2023). Mapping the future of intersectional research in human resource development: An integrated literature review. *Human Resource Development Review, 22*(4), 554–581. https://doi.org/10.1177/15344843231205066

Sim, E., Nicolaides, A., & Bierema, L. L. (2023). Intersectional research in adult education: A diffractive gaze. *New Directions for Adult and Continuing Education, 2023*(180), 11–23. https://doi.org/10.1002/ace.20508

Sinek, S. (2017). *Find your why: A practical guide for discovering your purpose for you and your team.* Portfolio-Penguin.

Singh, A. A. (2019). *The racial healing handbook: Practical activities to help you challenge privilege, confront systemic racism, and engage in collective healing.* New Harbinger Publications.

Singh, A. A., & Moss, L. (2016). Using relational-cultural theory in LGBTQQ counseling: Addressing heterosexism and enhancing relational competencies. *Journal of Counseling & Development, 94*(4), 398–404. https://doi.org/10.1002/jcad.12098

Sisco, S. (2020). Race-conscious career development: Exploring self-preservation and coping strategies of Black professionals in corporate America. *Advances in Developing Human Resources, 22*(4), 419–436. https://doi.org/10.1177/1523422320948885

Sklair, L. (2001). Capitalism: Global. *International encyclopedia of the social and behavioral sciences, 2001,* 1459–1463. https://doi.org/10.1016/B0–08–043076–7/01831–3

Skromme Granrose, C., & Baccili, P. A. (2006). Do psychological contracts include boundaryless or protean careers? *Career Development International, 11*(2), 163–182. https://doi.org/10.1108/13620430610651903

Smith, A. N., Watkins, M. B., Ladge, J. J., & Carlton, P. (2019). Making the invisible visible: Paradoxical effects of intersectional invisibility on the career experiences of executive Black women. *Academy of Management Journal, 62*(6), 1705–1734. https://doi.org/10.5465/amj.2017.1513

Smith, S. (2021). *Visibility counts: The LGBTQ+ board opportunity*. Out Leadership. https://outleadership.com/news/visibility-counts-the-lgbtq-board-opportunity/

Snyder, C. D. (1994). *The psychology of hope: You can get here from there*. The Free Press.

Snyder, C. R. (2002). Hope theory: Rainbows in the mind. *Psychological Inquiry, 13*(4), 249–275.

Sone, T., Nakaya, N., Ohmori, K., Shimazu, T., Higashiguchi, M., Kakizaki, M., Kikuchi, N., Kuriyama, S., & Tsuji, I. (2008). Sense of life worth living (ikigai) and mortality in Japan: Ohsaki Study. *Psychosomatic medicine, 70*(6), 709–715. https://doi.org/10.1097/PSY.0b013e31817e7e64

Spoon, K., LaBerge, N., Wapman, K. H., Zhang, S., Morgan, A. C., Galesic, M., Fosdick, B. K., Larremore, D. B., & Clauset, A. (2023). Gender and retention patterns among US faculty. *Science Advances, 9*(42), eadi2205. https://doi.org/10.1126/sciadv.adi2205

Statista Research Department (2023). *Difference between the inflation rate and growth of wages in the United States from January 2020 to August 2023*. Statista. https://www.statista.com/statistics/1351276/wage-growth-vs-inflation-us/#:~:text=In%20August%202023%2C%20inflation%20amounted,wages%20grew%20by%205.3%20percent

Steger, M. F., Frazier, P., Oishi, S., & Kaler, M. (2006). The meaning in life questionnaire: Assessing the presence of and search for meaning in life. *Journal of Counseling Psychology, 53*, 80–93.

Steger, M. F., Kashdan, T. B., Sullivan, B. A., & Lorentz, D. (2008). Understanding the search for meaning in life: Personality, cognitive style, and the dynamic between seeking and experiencing meaning. *Journal of Personality, 76*, 199–228. https://doi.org/10.1111/j.1467-6494.2007.00484.x

Stelter, S. (2022). Want to advance in your career? Build your own board of directors. *Harvard Business Review*. https://hbr.org/2022/05/want-to-advance-in-your-career-build-your-own-board-of-directors

Stolarski, M., Fieulaine, N., & Van Beek, W. (2015). Time perspective theory: The introduction. In M. Stolarski, N. Fieulaine, & W. Van Beek (Eds.), *Time perspective theory: Review, research and application* (pp. 1–13). Springer International Publishing.

Stuart, S. (2023). *2023 U.S. Spencer Stuart Board Index*. SpencerStuart. https://www.spencerstuart.com/research-and-insight/us-board-index

Sull, D., Sull, C., & Zweig, B. (2022). Toxic culture is driving the great resignation. *MIT Sloan Management Review, 63*(2), 1–9. https://sloanreview.mit.edu/article/toxic-culture-is-driving-the-great-resignation/

Sullivan, S. E., & Arthur, M. B. (2006). The evolution of the boundaryless career concept: Examining physical and psychological mobility. *Journal of Vocational Behavior, 69*(1), 19–29. https://doi.org/10.1016/j.jvb.2005.09.001

Sullivan, S. E., & Baruch, Y. (2009). Advances in career theory and research: A critical review and agenda for future exploration. *Journal of Management, 35*(6), 1542–1571. https://doi.org/10.1177/0149206309350082

Sullivan, S. E., & Mainiero, L. (2007). Women's kaleidoscope careers: A new framework for examining women's stress across the lifespan. In *Exploring the work and non-work interface* (pp. 205–238). Emerald Publishing. https://doi.org/10.1016/S1479–3555(06)06006–9

Sumner, E., Burrow, A. L., & Hill, P. L. (2018). The development of purpose in life among adolescents who experience marginalization: Potential opportunities and obstacles. *American Psychologist, 73*(6), 740–752. http://dx.doi.org/10.1037/amp0000249

Super, D. E. (1957). *The psychology of careers: An introduction to vocational development.* Harper & Bros.

Super, D. E. (1975). Career education and career guidance for the life span and for life roles. *Journal of Career education, 2*(2), 27–42. https://journals.sagepub.com/doi/pdf/10.1177/089484537500200204?casa_token=XJtXic6dnHAAAAAA:0w GUCZqE4PtN qAaUa3bNWU _dQXySWCQBA0fVj0Mi _NGDHyBnR -3XJoC4ME6b2W32UUDfHSrZEStgpQ

Super, D. E. (1980). A life-span, life-space approach to career development. *Journal of Vocational Behavior, 16*(3), 282–298. https://doi.org/10.1016/0001–8791(80)90056–1

Super, D. E. (1990). A lifespan, life-span approach to career development. In D. Brown & L. Brooks (Eds.), *Career choice and development: Applying contemporary theories to practice* (pp. 197–261). Jossey-Bass.

Super, D. E., & Šverko, B. E. (1995). *Life roles, values, and careers: International findings of the Work Importance Study.* Jossey-Bass.

Super, D. E., & Thompson, A. S. (1979). A six-scale, two-factor measure of adolescent career or vocational maturity. *Vocational Guidance Quarterly, 28*(1), 6–15. https://doi.org/10.1002/j.2164–585X.1979.tb00078.x

Swanson, J. L., & Schneider, M. (2021). The theory of work adjustment. In S. D. Brown & R. W. Lent (Eds.), *Career development and counseling: Putting theory and research to work* (pp. 33–38). John Wiley & Sons.

Taherdoost, H. (2023). An overview of trends in information systems: Emerging technologies that transform the information technology industry. *Cloud Computing and Data Science,* 1–16. https://doi.org/10.37256/ccds.4120231653

Tan, M. (2022). How many years do you spend working in your lifetime? *Medium.* https://medium.com/illumination/how-many-years-do-you-spend-working-in-your-lifetime-f5bfd4c7e5f0

Taylor, E. W., & Cranton, P. (2012). *The handbook of transformative learning: Theory, research, and practice.* John Wiley & Sons.

Taylor, P. (2021). The good news about labor shortages. *POLITICO.* https://www.politico.eu/article/good-news-labor-shortages-coronavirus-economic-recovery/

Tefera, A. A., Powers, J. M., & Fischman, G. E. (2018). Intersectionality in education: A conceptual aspiration and research imperative. *Review of Research in Education, 42*(1), vii–xvii. https://doi.org/10.3102/0091732X18768504

Thomas, K. M., Johnson-Bailey, J., Phelps, R. E., Tran, N. M., & Johnson, L. (2013). Women of color at midcareer: Going from pet to threat. In L. Comas-Diaz & B. Greene (Eds.), *Psychological health of women of color: Intersections, challenges, and opportunities* (pp. 275–286). Santa Barbara.

Tims, M., Twemlow, M., & Fong, C. Y. M. (2022). A state-of-the-art overview of job-crafting research: Current trends and future research directions. *Career Development International, 27*(1), 54–78. https://doi.org/10.1108/CDI-08–2021–0216

Tisdell, E. J. (1995). *Creating inclusive adult learning environments: Insights from multicultural education and feminist pedagogy* (No. 361). DIANE Publishing.

Tisdell, E. J. (2001). Spirituality in adult and higher education. ERIC Digest. https://files.eric.ed.gov/fulltext/ED459370.pdf

Tisdell, E. J. (2003). *Exploring spirituality and culture in adult and higher education.* John Wiley & Sons.

Tohl, S. (2023). *There's so much we don't know about the LGBTQI+ wage gap.* National Women's Law Center. https:// nwlc .org/ theres -so -much -we -dont -know -about -the -lgbtqi-wage-gap/

Tong, S., & Hagan, A. (2021). *Patagonia CEO on aligning company values and taking activist stances—No matter the cost.* WBUR Here&Now. https:// www .wbur .org/ hereandnow/2021/09/24/patagonia-politics-activism

Tough, A. (1989). Self-directed learning: Concepts and practice. In C. J. Titmus (Ed.), *Lifelong education for adults: An international handbook* (pp. 256–259). Pergamon Press.

Triana, M. D. C., Gu, P., Chapa, O., Richard, O., & Colella, A. (2021). Sixty years of discrimination and diversity research in human resource management: A review with suggestions for future research directions. *Human Resource Management, 60*(1), 145–204. https://doi.org/10.1002/hrm.22052

Trusty, J., Ward, D. A., Good-Perry Ward, M., & He, M. (2023). Hair bias in the workplace: A critical human resource development perspective. *Advances in Developing Human Resources, 25*(1), 5–26. https://doi.org/10.1177/15234223221135557

Tulshyan, R. (2018). Women of color get asked to do more "office housework." Here's how they can say no. *Harvard Business Review.* https://hbr.org/2018/04/women-of -color-get-asked-to-do-more-office-housework-heres-how-they-can-say-no

Tulshyan, R. (2022). *Inclusion on purpose: An intersectional approach to creating a culture of belonging at work.* The MIT Press.

Turco, C. J. (2010). Cultural foundations of tokenism evidence from the leveraged buyout industry. *American Sociological Review, 75*(6), 894–913. https://doi.org/10 .1177/000312241038849

Tyson, C. (2022). *Just as I am.* Amistad.

United States Bureau of Labor Statistics (2016). Table 1. Employment status of the civilian noninstitutional population by disability status and selected characteristics. *2014 annual averages.* http://www.bls.gov/news.release/disabl.t01.htm

Universitat Oberta de Catalunya eLearning Innovation Center (n.d.). *Technology and education trends for 2023.* Despacho 42. https://blogs.uoc.edu/elearning-innovation -center/wp-content/uploads/sites/114/2023/04/despacho-42_eng.jpg

University of Georgia Career Center (n.d.). *Class of 2022 career outcomes.* https:// career.uga.edu/outcomes

University of Minnesota (n.d.). Theory of work adjustment. https://vpr.psych.umn.edu/ theory-work-adjustment

US Army Heritage and Education Center (2018). *Who first originated the term VUCA (Volatility, Uncertainty, Complexity and Ambiguity)?* USAHEC Ask Us a Question. The United States Army War College. https://usawc.libanswers.com/faq/84869

US Department of Labor (n.d.c.). *FMLA frequently asked questions.* US Department of Labor: Wage and Hour Division. https://www.dol.gov/agencies/whd/fmla/faq#:~:text =The%20Family%20and%20Medical%20Leave%20Act%20(FMLA)%20provides %20eligible%20employees,work%20instead%20of%20taking%20leave

US Department of Labor (n.d.b). *HIRE initiative.* US Department of Labor. https:// www.dol.gov/agencies/ofccp/Hire-Initiative

US Department of Labor (n.d.a). *National disability employment awareness month (NDEAM).* US Department of Labor. https://www.dol.gov/agencies/odep/initiatives/ ndeam

Valentin, C. (2013). Employee engagement interventions: HRD, groups and teams. In C. Valentin & J. Walton (Eds.), *Human resource development: Practices and orthodoxies* (pp. 305–327). Palgrave Macmillan.

Vallas, S. P. (2003). Rediscovering the color line within work organizations: The knitting of racial groups revisited. *Work and Occupations, 30*(4), 379–400. https://doi .org/10.1177/0730888403256454

Van der Steege, M. (2017). Introduction. In R. Elkington, M. v. d. Steege, J. Glick-Smith & J. Moss Breen (eds.), *Visionary leadership in a turbulent world: Thriving in the new VUCA context.* Emerald Publishing.

Van Dijk, H., Kooij, D., Karanika-Murray, M., De Vos, A., & Meyer, B. (2020). Meritocracy a myth? A multilevel perspective of how social inequality accumulates through work. *Organizational Psychology Review, 10*(3–4), 240–269. https:// doi .org/10.1177/2041386620930063

Vanderheiden, E., & Mayer, C. (2021). Ikigai as a resource in transformative processes in adult education. In Y. Kotera & D. Fido (Eds.), *Ikigai: Towards a psychological understanding of a life worth living* (pp. 30–39). CDS Press.

Ventegodt, S., Anderson, N. J., & Merrick, J. (2003). The life mission theory II. The structure of the life purpose and ego. *The Scientific World Journal, 3*, 1227–1285. https://doi.org/10.1100/tsw.2003.114

Vespia, K. M., Fitzpatrick, M. E., Fouad, N. A., Kantamneni, N., & Chen, Y. L. (2010). Multicultural career counseling: A national survey of competencies and practices. *The Career Development Quarterly, 59*(1), 54–71. https://doi.org/10.1002/j .2161–0045.2010.tb00130.x

Volmer, J., & Spurk, D. (2011). Protean and boundaryless career attitudes: Relationships with subjective and objective career success. *Zeitschrift für ArbeitsmarktForschung, 43*(3), 207–218. https://doi.org/10.1007/s12651–010–0037–3

Walker, W. J. (2013). The new work contract: Mitigating the negative effects on work attitudes. *Journal of Organizational Culture, Communications and Conflict, 17*(2), 121–137. https://www.proquest.com/scholarly-journals/new-work-contract -mitigating-negative-effects-on/docview/1465544291/se-2

Wallerstein, I. (1974). Dependence in an interdependent world: The limited possibilities of transformation within the capitalist world economy. *African Studies Review, 17*(1), 1–26. https://doi.org/10.2307/523574

Wang, D., Liu, X., & Deng, H. (2022). The perspectives of social cognitive career theory approach in current times. *Frontiers in Psychology, 13*, 1023994. https://doi .org/10.3389/fpsyg.2022.1023994

Wang, M., & Shi, J. (2014). Psychological research on retirement. *Annual Review of Psychology, 65*, 209–233. https://doi.org/10.1146/annurev-psych-010213–115131

Webber, A. M. (1998). Is your job your calling? *FAST COMPANY* No. 13, 108+. https:// www.fastcompany.com/91025986/19-ceos-died-on-the-job-leaders-work-life-balance

Weick, K. E. (1984). Small wins: Redefining the scale of social problems. *American Psychologist, 39*(1), 40. https://psycnet.apa.org/doi/10.1037/0003–066X.39.1.40

Welbourne, J. L., Gangadharan, A., & Sariol, A. M. (2015). Ethnicity and cultural values as predictors of the occurrence and impact of experienced workplace incivility. *Journal of Occupational Health Psychology, 20*(2), 205–217. https://doi.org/10 .1037/a0038277

Weldon-Caron, R. (2022). HRD: What can we do to create a more just society for African Americans in the workplace? *New Horizons in Adult Education and Human Resource Development, 34*(4), 44–49. https://doi.org/10.1002/nha3.20369

WeWork (2021). *The future of work is hybrid—here's what that will look like*. WeWork Ideas. https://www.wework.com/ideas/research-insights/research-studies/the-future-of-work-is-hybrid#full-report

Whiteman, W. E. (1998). *Training and educating army officers for the 21st century: Implications for the United States Military Academy* (Vol. 32). US Army War College.

Whitmyer, C. (1994a). *Mindfulness and meaningful work: Explorations in right livelihood*. Parallax Press.

Whitmyer, C. (1994b). Doing well by doing good. In C. Whitmyer (Ed.), *Mindfulness and meaningful work: Explorations in right livelihood* (pp. 3–22). Parallax Press.

Wicker, C. J. (2021). The trenches and valleys of corporate America: A Black male human resource leader's autoethnographic account. *Advances in Developing Human Resources, 23*(4), 335–353. https://doi.org/10.1177/15234223211037762

Williams J. C., Phillips, K. W., & Hall, E. V. (2014). *Double jeopardy? Gender bias against women of color in science*. National Science Foundation No. 1106411. http://www.uchastings.edu/news/articles/2015/01/double-jeopardy-report.pdf

Williams, T. R., Autin, K. L., Pugh, J., Herdt, M. E., Garcia, R. G., Jennings, D., & Roberts, T. (2023). Predicting decent work among US black workers: Examining psychology of working theory. *Journal of Career Assessment, 31*(4), 756–772. https://doi.org/10.1177/10690727221149456

Winn, M. (2014). *What is your ikigai?* The View Inside. https://theviewinside.me/what-is-your-ikigai/

Wong, P. T. P. (2012). Toward a dual-systems model what makes a life worth living. In P. T. P. Wong (Ed.), *The human quest for meaning: Theories, research, and applications* (2nd ed.). Routledge.

Wood, J., Oh, J., Park, J., & Kim, W. (2020). The relationship between work engagement and work–life balance in organizations: A review of the empirical research. *Human Resource Development Review, 19*(3), 240–262. https://doi.org/10.1177/1534484320917560

World Economic Forum (2023). *Global gender gap report 2023*. https://www.weforum.org/ publications/ global -gender -gap -report -2023/ in -full/ benchmarking -gender-gaps-2023#:~:text=The%20Global%20Gender%20Gap%20score,compared%20to%20last%20year's%20edition

World Health Organization (2023a). *Stress*. https:// www .who .int/ news -room/ questions -and-answers/item/stress#:~:text=Stress%20can%20be%20defined%20as,experiences%20stress%20to%20some%20degree

World Health Organization (2023b). *Disability*. https://www.who.int/news-room/fact-sheets/detail/disability-and-health#:~:text=Key%20facts,earlier%20than%20those%20without%20disabilities

Yang, P. (2023). *OpenAI: A look at its unique culture that helped it survive a crisis.* Creator Economy by Peter Yang. https:// creatoreconomy .so/ p/ openai -culture -and -what-happens-next

Yates, J. (2020). Career development: An integrated analysis. In P. Robertson, P. McCash, & T. Hooley (Eds.), *The Oxford handbook of career development*. Oxford University Press.

Yates, J. (2022). *The career coaching handbook* (2nd ed.). Routledge.

Yeoman, R., Bailey, C., Madden, A., & Thompson, M. (2019). *The Oxford handbook of meaningful work*. Oxford University Press.

Yesilyaprak, B. (2012). The paradigm shift of vocational guidance and career counseling and its implications for Turkey: An evaluation from past to future. *Educational*

Sciences: Theory and Practice, *12*(1), 111–118. https://files.eric.ed.gov/fulltext/EJ978435.pdf

Yoder-Wise, P. S. (2021). From VUCA to VUCA 2.0: Surviving today to prosper tomorrow. *Nursing Education Perspectives*, *42*(1), 1–2. https://doi.org/10.1097/01.NEP.0000000000000774

You, J., Kim, S., Kim, K., Cho, A., & Chang, W. (2021). Conceptualizing meaningful work and its implications for HRD. *European Journal of Training and Development*, *45*(1), 36–52. https://doi.org/10.1108/EJTD-01-2020-0005

Zeng, Z. (2011). The myth of the glass ceiling: Evidence from a stock-flow analysis of authority attainment. *Social science research*, *40*(1), 312–325. https://doi.org/10.1016/j.ssresearch.2010.06.012

Zheng, L. (2019). How to show white men that diversity and inclusion efforts need them. *Harvard Business Review*. https://hbr.org/2019/10/how-to-show-white-men-that-diversity-and-inclusion-efforts-need-them

Zunker, V. G. (1994). Career counseling for individuals with disabilities. In V. G. Zunker (Ed.), *Career counseling: Applied concepts of life planning*. Brooks/Cole.

Index